Coaching Solutions

2nd Edition

Resources to accompany this book are available online at: www.continuumbooks.com/resources/9781855394407

Please visit the link and register with us to receive your password and to access these downloadable resources.

If you experience any problems accessing the resources, please contact Continuum at: info@continuumbooks.com

Also available from Network Continuum

Coaching Solutions Resource Book – Will Thomas
Success Comes in Cans – Kriss Akabussi with Tricia Hartley
Discover Your Hidden Talents – Bill Lucas
Using NLP to Enhance Behaviour and Learning – Terry Elston and Kate Spohrer

Available from Continuum

Coaching for Learning – Jacquie Turnbull
The Creative Teaching and Learning Toolkit – Brin Best and Will Thomas
The Creative Teaching and Learning Resource Book – Brin Best and Will Thomas
Everything You Need to Know About Teaching But Are Too Busy to Ask – Brin Best and Will Thomas

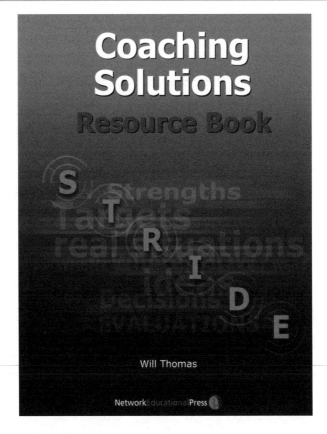

Coaching Solutions Resource Book – Will Thomas

Packed with practical tools, tips and techniques in over 80 resources for coaching in education and beyond, this is the perfect companion to *Coaching Solutions*.

The book provides practical ways to help individuals, teams and organizations secure peak performance through a coaching approach. Whether you are a new coach or an old hand, this book will make coaching more effective and more manageable.

Coaching Solutions

**Practical Ways to Improve
Performance in Education**

Will Thomas and Alistair Smith

network
continuum

Continuum International Publishing Group
Network Continuum
The Tower Building   80 Maiden Lane, Suite 704
11 York Road   New York, NY 10038
London, SE1 7NX

www.networkcontinuum.co.uk
www.continuumbooks.com

First edition published in 2004. Second edition 2009.

British Library Cataloguing-in-Publication Data
A catalogue record for this book is available from the British Library.

ISBN: 9781855394407 (paperback)

Library of Congress Cataloguing-in-Publication Data
A catalog record for this book is available from the Library of Congress

Typeset by Fakenham Photosetting Limited, Fakenham, Norfolk
Printed and bound in Great Britain by Bell & Bain Ltd, Glasgow

Contents

Foreword

Since its first edition in 2004, Coaching Solutions has been part of a revolution among enlightened leaders in education settings. We have witnessed, in many organisations, a focus on meaningful professional development, an ease with restoring trust and professionalism to teachers and a focus on the highest quality communication between colleagues and in classrooms. A rich collection of case studies and evidence have been amassing of the success of a coaching approach to leading, and learning in schools and colleges. This new edition highlights a range of this evidence and provides case studies of just some of the success stories. What Coaching Solutions continues to do in its new incarnation is exactly what it set out to do in 2002 when I first began writing it; the book provides access to the frameworks, knowledge and skills that make positive change happen.

Back in 2004, I set out to put coaching onto the educational map. This is certainly what has happened. I was controversial and exclusive about pressing coaching as *the* way forward, this was deliberate and calculated to encourage colleagues to notice it and to realize that true coaching really is a very different way of working to anything that has gone before. I see coaching as being a drawing out of learning from others, a personalized journey which is both highly effective in motivating people to take action and essential for learning to be transferable to other situations. The meanings of coaching and mentoring are, and are likely to remain, unsettled in academic circles. In Coaching Solutions I take a position on the meanings of these processes, which is simple but not simplistic, so that it can be communicated and acted upon.

Since 2002, I have coached hundreds of clients and trained thousands of people in schools, colleges, charities and businesses in coaching skills. Similarly I have worked with organizations to assist them to create an organizational coaching culture. Together, we have come to understand that there is a dynamic between the processes of coaching, counselling and mentoring which allows coaches and co-coaches to blend them to perfection in the service of those they support.

As I write this at the beginning of 2009, I sense that we are on the verge of an entirely new era in schools and colleges. There are very real problems to be solved in the country, in communities and on the planet as a whole. Education must respond to this. We have never been more connected in terms of technology and information and yet we have never been more capable of harming ourselves and our fellow human beings. We cannot afford to view education with a 1950s glow of classicism for classicism's sake. We need to re-engineer the trends and recognize the links between education and reality with an awakened immediacy. We need to promote community not egotism, emotional intelligence not impulse, social equality not celebrity, custodianship not consumerism and turn teachers and students back on to learning. This new era will see schools and colleges developing even higher levels of professional practice; it will embrace truly connected thinking in terms of how teachers and leaders in schools learn and continue to develop throughout their careers. It will enable all young people to discover the joy of learning and to know the genuine happiness that comes from using their learning to set themselves and others free.

It might be naive to say that what is contained in this book is the answer to these complex and wide-ranging issues. Yet I do believe passionately that the methodology within this text can build bridges and break down walls between people. I know from experience that it can open up positive, solutions-focused approaches to the real daily challenges faced in schools and in the home-lives of young people. I have seen how it can enable people to look beyond their own map of reality and acknowledge and appreciate other people's points of view, causing barriers to fall away. I witness daily how coaching releases people from the terrible nooses of duty and guilt they place around their own necks.

The new era of education will engage the new technology. This will be in the form of ICT and quantum leaps in our understanding of the brain and how it responds to language. It will also be in terms of the way we use age-old inter-personal communication technologies so as to reach young people and their parents in direct and honest ways, beyond class and privilege and through breaking down the false walls of hallowed academia. What you read about in this book is being put into practice across the country, and it is having profound impacts. It is having profound impacts not because it is new or complex, radical or renegade, but because it is the oldest technology on the planet, simple, honest, and down-to earth. Coaching is the art and science of pure communication, pure listening and pure empathy. It is about being connected, one human being to another, so that change can happen. Coaching is about each individual's search for a powerful essence within us. That powerful essence lives in our minds, and in our human spirit. That powerful essence springs from the deepest parts of us and ignites our purpose and our passion. That powerful essence is hope and all positive actions spring from hope.

Will Thomas
January 2009

Will can be contacted at:
www.willthomasblog.com
www.visionforlearning.co.uk

We are all connected

In 1967 Stanley Milgram, a Harvard professor with an interest in social networks, conducted an experiment to find the 'distance' between two people. The question he posed was 'How many acquaintances would it take to connect two randomly selected individuals?' To get started he chose two target people: one in Massachusetts and the other in Boston. They were not connected. He then picked two cities on the 'Great Plains' – Wichita and Omaha – and sent 160 letters to randomly chosen residents asking the person to send a postcard either to the target person directly – if they knew the person – or to someone whom they already knew who was more likely to know the target person. Forty-two replies made it back. One had gone direct, the largest number was 12. Most had surprisingly few intermediaries. Milgram worked out the median number as 5.5.

In 1991 John Guare wrote a play entitled *Six Degrees of Separation*. It is a play about interconnectedness. A mother tells her daughter,

> *Everybody on this planet is separated by only six other people. Six degrees of separation. Between us and everybody else on this planet. The president of the United States. A gondolier in Venice. … It's not just the big names. It's anyone. A native in a rain forest. A Tierra del Fuegan. An Eskimo. I am bound to everyone on this planet by a trail of six people. It's a profound thought. … How every person is a new door opening up into other worlds.*

Six degrees of separation suggests that despite the enormous population of the world at any one time we are all only six links apart – a network of six billion nodes holding us all together.

At the time of writing there are more documents on the world wide web than there are people on the planet, yet any document is, on average, only 19 clicks away from another. Research scientists are separated by four to six co-authorship links. Neurons in the brain by 14 synapses. All around us we see that the consequences of our everyday decisions affect others and ripple out beyond our immediate circle.

Now envisage a smaller and more distinct group, with direct communication between individuals – car drivers on any busy motorway around London. A network of decision making is communicated and the consequences are predictable patterns of traffic movement. Traffic density waves arise when each driver chooses his or her speed according to the speed of the surrounding vehicles. Each driver can react rapidly to the speed of adjacent cars – rapidly enough to match the occasional explosion of crowd behaviour. A knot of vehicles joining the motorway at a junction creates a local increase in traffic density and following vehicles have to slow to avoid collision. In heavy traffic, when the density of vehicles on the motorway is so great that they impede each other, that local increase in density creates a backwards wave that washes back through the traffic. It is observable from the air like waves rolling up onto a beach. It happens when the reactions of successive drivers are so quick that the change in speed propagates from one vehicle to the one travelling behind faster than the vehicles themselves are moving forwards.

This phenomenon comes about through the transmission of changes in speed from one driver to another. Occasionally there is a rear-end collision. But the very low frequency of such accidents (in relation to the number of cars using the motorway) testifies to the rapidity with which car drivers can respond to each other. Decisions you make affect all those round and many others besides. We are all interconnected.

We are often asked: 'Can you make someone learn?' The answer is no. Coercion, conformity and compulsion will get performers but not learners. For genuine learning, motivation comes when we set our own direction. But how?

How do we get to decisions that are likely to propel us forward when there does not seem an obvious route? What will the impact of such decisions be for ourselves and those around us? Direction can be determined by finding and asking the right question. Nelson Mandela, on a visit to London, observed

> *unsolicited advice is rarely listened to or respected, but solicited advice is treated with due care and attention, and creates bonds that are rarely broken or forgotten.*

If you have ever been stuck on a personal issue to the point where you begin to fixate on it and neglect others around you, the skills of the coach can help you. If you live with, look after or work alongside others who have got themselves locked into an unhelpful pattern of behaviour, congratulations; you are a social animal and the skills of the coach can help you. If you are a teacher, a trainer, a social worker, a doctor, a barrister or work in any profession that involves connecting meaningfully with others, the skills of the coach can help you.

If you have ever been stuck in a traffic jam and find yourself watching nervously in your mirror as someone surges towards you and stops, but not until the very last second, don't be too angry – you might just be connected.

Alistair Smith
May 2004

How to use this book

This book is a flexible guide to coaching in schools, colleges and universities. It sets out to make it easy for you to navigate around the text and to locate specific solutions to your coaching dilemmas and questions.

The book is divided into four sections, each composed of chapters, and includes the following elements:

- outcomes for the chapter – a summary of what you will know once you have completed the chapter
- preview questions – which stimulate your thinking about chapter content
- metaphors and stories
- core material
- case studies – which contain sample dialogues
- summary – learning points and questions to test and apply your knowledge
- review questions – to help you process your learning
- coaching masterclass – top coaching tips to make coaching effective.

This structure makes for a flexible approach to the use of the text. Here are some guidelines that you may wish to follow to help you get the most out of this book:

- Start at the beginning and work methodically through the book.
- Read the chapter outcomes first and then dip in.
- Read the chapter summaries first.
- Consider the chapter preview and review questions as a guide.
- Read the core text leaving out the stories and metaphors.
- Read the story/metaphor for a chapter and the outcome statements; allow some thinking time before reading the core material in the chapter.

Acknowledgements

Will Thomas

I am grateful to everyone I have trained and coached – your struggles, resourcefulness and successes have shaped this book.

I have so greatly appreciated throwing ideas around with Nick Austin, Sarah Mook, Simon Percival, Anne Copley, Jane Kerr, Nicky Anastasiou, Penny Clayton, Ian Berry, Tom Hill and Gavin Kewley. Thank you for being great coaches and good friends and for stretching my thinking in omni-directional ways.

Big thanks to Mel, my PA and general wonder woman, whose diligence and support are immense. To the Vision for Learning Associate coaches and trainers, thank you for your enthusiasm for pushing this great communication skill forward.

I would also like to thank the awesome teams working on coaching in West Sussex. The visionary and tenacious leader of the West Sussex Coaching Training Unit, Lesley Smith, and her dream-team, Mark Wilson, Chris Behagg, and formerly Mary Mugridge and Jen Weeks, with their skill and determination, have helped drive coaching forward in 40 schools. I would like to thank the schools in West Sussex directly for their tremendous work in making a difference to the lives of young people, through their work with coaching and other approaches to positive change.

In Warwickshire I would like to thank Chris Morris, Steve Pendleton, Liz Mynott and Elizabeth Furness who deserve special praise for their brilliant work in the LA and to Tim Over and his staff at The George Eliot School. Huge thanks also to Jean Ramsey for her wonderful enthusiasm and energy for coaching and for making such a difference at The Cooper School, and more widely in Oxfordshire and to Ben Baxter for supporting the development.

Thank you, all of you, for "putting it down on the ground" so successfully and for being the change you want to see in the world.

Coaching Solutions is for Mum, Dad, Sal and Richard for all their support, encouragement and belief. Dedicated to Robert Hunter on his 90th Birthday for his gifts of wit and wisdom.

Alistair Smith

I would like to thank Ani for all her encouragement and support in many ways.

> *It is through our connection with others that we give our gifts of enthusiasm and passion, and we receive back that energy from those same connections. In that exchange the world changes, just little bit, for the better. It's karmic, it's a personal choice and you reap what you sow*
>
> Will Thomas.

Orientation: putting coaching in context

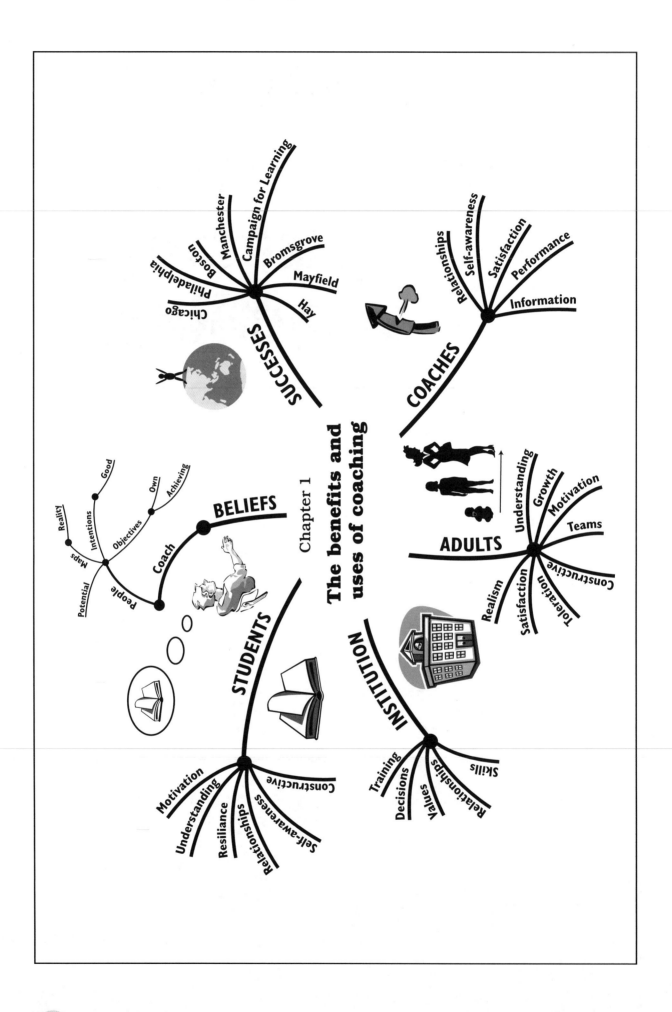

Chapter 1

The benefits and uses of coaching

IN THE ORIENTATION YOU WILL LEARN:

- the benefits and uses of the coaching process to students, staff and organizations
- where coaching has been successfully used to make positive changes
- that finding the right question can lead to the right answer

PREVIEW QUESTIONS:

- How will coaching benefit students?
- How will coaching benefit adults in schools?
- How will coaching benefit the whole institution?
- How do coaches themselves benefit from coaching?
- Where has coaching already enhanced performance?

Why you should be interested in coaching

People are all connected, separated some say by six degrees. The solutions to the issues we face are to be found when we identify the correct question to ask. Often the solutions lie close at hand and, more often than not, within ourselves, as does the motivation to make them happen.

Since the first edition of this text, there has been a whole raft of studies into the uses and effects of coaching in education. The CUREE report of 2005 identified a series of benefits that came from coaching in schools which included enhanced pupil outcomes, motivation and collaborative skills. For teachers they noted increased self confidence, willingness and capacity to learn and change alongside the development of a wider repertoire of teaching and learning strategies. The report also noted that learning to be a coach is one of the most effective ways to become an excellent teaching practitioner or leader. In 2006 a six-schools research project conducted by The National College for School Leadership found that coaching encouraged people to seek and take responsibility, reduce confrontation, enabled managers to become more productive and built organizational capacity through utilizing the full talents of staff, students and parents. Tangible evidence of the success of teacher coaching came from Newhall Green School in Manchester which, as part of a coaching pilot study, reported an average increase of 3 points in value-added score for students taught by teachers receiving regular coaching. In 2006, in the NCSL Research Publication *Time for Coaching*, Dr Neil Suggett, Headteacher, reported the findings of a study into the use of peer teacher coaching. He made six key findings public and these included: that there were 'positive impacts on the social and emotional atmosphere in school', a wide range of uses across pupils, parents and staff including self-coaching and team coaching. He found that coaching was effective across a range of approaches from a structured whole-school process to an intuitive leadership style. He concluded that 'coaching is an investment in time and money and that it produces gains for staff and pupils and builds organizational capacity'. In 2007, in the International Journal of Evidence-based Coaching and Mentoring, Paul Allan reported evidence that professional performance of the secondary teachers involved in his study had improved through them being coached. This was corroborated by third-party evidence as well as the evidence gathered within the study directly. Additionally in this study, Allan reports that participants had become more skilled and confident in their teaching and had found ways of working more effectively with colleagues, 'developing their professional relationships with others in a variety of productive ways'. A recent survey of headteachers by The National College for School Leadership suggests an enhanced understanding of coaching among heads questioned. The report cited that among the purposes that headteachers believed coaching can be put to were: addressing pupil behaviour, improving pupil performance, building teams, creating a success culture developing lesson planning, spreading good practice and supporting new headteachers.

Coaching is a process that helps others to enhance their performance and set their own direction. It is primarily about an attitude towards others. One researcher (Downey 2003) quotes four important beliefs a coach has about people. People:

- have huge potential
- have their own unique map of reality
- have good intentions
- are achieving their own objectives

The authors would also add to this a consideration: what if we all had the solutions to all of our problems within us – all of the time?

Holding onto core beliefs about people you coach is at the heart of what makes coaching so powerful as an agent for change. When you communicate confidence and trust in another person's ability to make choices, their performance goes up. It is this confidence that grows as coaching continues and allows people to take risks and enhance their capability. Neither the coach nor the person being coached know what is possible. There are no sure-fire predictors of potential. Maintaining a positive and open view is important.

We have our own maps of reality and we interpret the world around us in ways that are our own. On a minute-by-minute basis we decide where to focus our attention and how to interpret the evidence we find there. One person sees an incomplete task as failure, another recognizes the important successes they have made in reaching that point.

That people have good intentions is a core principle but one which should not be taken at face value. People need to operate in the best way possible for them, at that given time, in the circumstances they face and with the tools at their disposal. The coach helps the process along. A good coach helps others to find out what they want to succeed at, how they want to succeed and, indeed, what success means to them. In this sense coaching is about motivation and helping others find out what motivates them to achieve their goals.

In this book the authors promote what they believe is the kind of coaching that brings about real change. If you want people to progress, they need to change their behaviour. If you want sustainable positive changes in behaviour, then such changes must influence a person's beliefs. Non-directive coaching provides a unique approach to do this. The term 'coaching' in this book refers to a non-directive approach, a model that does not offer suggestions or advice, but instead promotes deep personal learning. The authors believe that for coaching to work it should build trust, operate within relationships that promote intuition, insight and resourceful thinking. When the coach is curious, really listens and is 'in the moment', a depth of learning occurs for those who are coached. Coaches who concoct solutions ahead of those they coach and then steer them towards those solutions ultimately fail. Those who shelve their agenda to rescue, and instead promote awareness, broker shifts in beliefs and behaviours that last. In this way the effects of the non-directive coach go far beyond the limited time individuals spend with them. When awareness increases, new sustainable futures are created.

The last aspect of the mindset of the coach is that people achieve their own objectives – perfectly, all of the time. At any one time in our lives we are working to an objective or objectives. The child who hits his friend and steals his chocolate is acting on a goal to acquire chocolate, or maybe to upset his friend. Despite this goal being one that we might not agree with as onlookers, it is nonetheless a goal and he is achieving it.

Similarly a teacher who has an overbearing way of maintaining discipline in the classroom and is reluctant to consider alternatives is still acting on a personal objective. This could be to survive with esteem and dignity intact, to feel able to impart information in an environment where it will be heard, to 'deliver' what the curriculum requires or any combination of these or others.

The question remains: 'What if people had the solutions to all their problems within them?' To be successful coaching requires optimism. Optimism is the foundation that underpins all the tools, techniques and tips you will read about here. A coach sticks with the belief that with the right environment the person whom they encourage will get there in the end. So many solutions that we receive from others fall short of the mark in some way or another. A good coach does not judge, does not correct, does not fix a broken personality and does not impose their own will. This is the most difficult and ultimately the most rewarding part of the role.

What are the benefits of coaching?

In a school, college or university coaching can help students, adults and the institution itself to improve performance.

Ten ways to benefit students

1 Improve decision making.

2 Improve motivation and understanding of what motivates.

3 Enhance understanding of the way students think and learn.

4 Provide greater understanding of what holds them back and moves them forward in achieving success.

5 Increase resilience and improve stress tolerance.

6 Improve relationships with peers and adults.

7 Create greater readiness to accept and act upon feedback.

8 Develop a solutions-focused approach to change.

9 Increase self-awareness.

10 Provide a tool for constructively dealing with unhelpful behaviour.

Ten ways to benefit adults and those who work with others

1 Enhance personal effectiveness (working smarter not harder).

2 Improve academic performance of students.

3 Encourage reflectivity and professional growth.

4 Improve understanding of how to motivate others.

5 Create more effective teams.

6 Develop techniques for constructively challenging unhelpful behaviours.

7 Improve tolerance of adults and young people.

8 Enhance energy and job satisfaction.

9 Open creative thinking pathways.

10 Enhance awareness of the setting of realistic goals for adults and others.

Ten ways to benefit institutions

1 Improve performance of students, teachers and support workers.

2 Enhance development of values, vision development and planning.

3 Improve interpersonal relationships and enhance teamwork.

4 Enhance the collective skill bank among staff.

5 Provide a constructive way to challenge negativity and limiting beliefs.

6 Create a cross-institution approach to giving and receiving feedback that will support formative assessment.

7 Provide a means for understanding and challenging unhelpful behaviours.

8 Develop more creative and innovative problem solving.

9 Embed decision making throughout the organization.

10 Provide added value to formal training.

Coaching is supportive and challenging. Its principles enable change to be effected by individuals without confrontation. The simple skills and processes are easy to learn and in most cases we all have these skills developed to varying degrees. It is a process that builds independence and demands excellence. Above all it is a means of getting what you need from others in a way that also suits them. Invariably coaches benefit from the process of helping others to enhance their performance.

Five ways to benefit coaches

1 Enhance relationships with colleagues, parents and students.

2 Improve performances of those who contribute to the coach's success.

3 Increase self-awareness.

4 Create a great sense of professional and personal satisfaction.

5 Help keep in touch with areas of learning that may not directly impact on their role but are important aspects of their organization.

Who has found coaching successful?

Humans are complex. Two humans together are the sum of their own individual complexities and the complexity of their relationship. Add 60 other adults to this who are equally complex and 900 children (who don't yet know they are complex!) and you have what we call a school. How complex! Some schools have used coaching as a means of helping adults and children talk to each other in a simple, purposeful way.

The 'Coaching at Work Survey' (2000) conducted by the Campaign for Learning found that 80 per cent of managers believed that coaching had helped their organization and that a growth in the use of the techniques was evident, with 74 per cent of small organizations now using coaching compared to 41 per cent in 1996. The survey concluded that: 'managers were extremely positive about the benefits of coaching and agree that it helps motivate employees, enhances team morale, generates responsibility on the part of the learner and helps retain staff'. Additionally, it drew out from its research that 'managers also believe that coaching is a workplace technique that should be available to all employees regardless of seniority' and suggested that this technique can be embraced by all organizations regardless of size.

The 'Report on Executive Coaching' compiled by the Hay Group showed that 100 per cent of respondents felt that coaching had improved their effectiveness. Some 86 per cent had observed positive leadership behaviour changes and 71 per cent acknowledged the value of coaching. Despite relatively few organizations currently measuring links between coaching and improved performance, 40 per cent reported a measurable link.

At South Bromsgrove Community High School, Year 9 students were invited to take part in a confidence-building programme that consisted of an initial morning training session to introduce them to the concept of self-development and to help them recognize their strengths. This was followed by six coaching sessions at approximately one-week intervals with a trained coach. Each session focused on an area of personal development that the students chose for themselves. Throughout the programme students made excellent progress. Pre- and post-coaching assessments showed improvements in self-confidence, communication skills and clarity of direction. Many of the students focused their sessions on defining their future career plans and linking this to their goals in and out of school.

When we give up our right to choose we give up our right to succeed.

Phil McTague, former headteacher at South Bromsgrove Community High School, commented more generally about coaching in school: 'It is critical in a climate of targets that a non-judgemental strategy that is analytical and reflective is used. This generates positive self-improvement. Coaching can make this happen … but it is often an invisible earning!'

Review questionnaires completed by teachers and students showed that the coaching work had had a positive impact on the confidence of many students in classroom-learning scenarios and one-to-one work. This was with both adults and their peers. Students reported a greater sense of direction and focus and a deeper understanding of their own strengths and self-management. They were able to rationalize information more effectively and make decisions that were more in line with their future goals.

Manchester Consulting Incorporated carried out a study with one hundred senior leadership personnel from 1996 to 2000. The research concluded that there was an estimated return on the amount invested in the coaching of 5.7 times. It is very early days in the field of educational coaching to be making such specific measures of impact, but nonetheless there are many schools and colleges around the world buying into the coaching ethos and reporting significant changes both quantitatively and qualitatively. Oakley College in Gran Canaria and Kings College in Madrid have both invested in training staff as performance coaches and can see the benefits that developing a solutions-focused approach can bring to a school.

A report in *Education World* magazine (2003) outlined the success of a coaching programme rolled out across every school in Boston, Massachusetts, USA. Here a whole-school change coach worked with schools to implement structures of coaching within the schools. The coach worked with senior staff, teachers and students. At Ludwig van Beethoven Elementary School, the principal is quoted as saying that 'the coaching has really encouraged kids to be independent readers and writers. The model works very well when implemented properly'. He goes on to credit the coaching programme as 'energizing and empowering the school'.

C.W. Henry Elementary School, West Mount Airy, Philadelphia, USA, has used coaching to help teachers to 'move beyond labeling children with real or assumed deficits and explore student behavioural problems from the point of view of the students'. The school reports that the programme has also helped teachers deal more effectively with parents (Bambino, 2002).

Where coaching has been fully embedded in Chicago schools there have been up to 70 per cent improvements in student scores on basic skill tests (Rock 2002).

Lesley Chandler, consultant to the National School Improvement Network, reports her experiences as an education coach in *National School Improvement Network News* (Autumn 2002). She works with headteachers using non-directive coaching techniques to help them enhance their performance. She explains how she finds that 'the individual is in a better position [after coaching] to make conscious choices about behaviours, decide when to use the most valuable more frequently and spot where ineffective habits bite into day-to-day practice and relationships'.

Adding coaching to training has been shown to have great benefits in embedding the learning from formal training courses. Olivero and colleagues in *Public Personnel Management* (1997) quote the results of the effects of productivity on a public agency following coaching. The study conducted over a three-month period showed an 88 per cent improvement in the productivity of those workers who were coached following their formal training course. This compared to just a 22.4 per cent increase in productivity for those employees who received training alone.

'doing it turns knowing it into energy '

The Mayfield School, Portsmouth, has had a successful history of training teachers from a variety of atypical backgrounds and creating excellent practitioners of them. Borne out of a crisis in teacher recruitment, they developed an excellent teacher-training programme spearheaded by Ian Cox and Mike Harbour. Their approach to coaching in the school had extended beyond the early days of supporting unqualified teachers to operating across the school. They used trios of teachers: each trio consisted of a trained coach, a newly qualified or unqualified teacher and another member of staff. The school created opportunities for regular liaison in these trios, with the trained coaches eliciting discussion and goal-setting with follow-up. One of the trained coaches in the programme explained how coaching had freed her from the burden that she felt, to be the provider of solutions for those she worked with. It released that perceived need to solve for others and created the ethos of self-solution. The very positive effect of this on the school is evident from the comments of many of the coaches in the school.

One of the important aspects to this institutional approach is the inclusion of all the staff, regardless of experience, in a process of structured reflection. While the agenda for reflection remained with the individuals, the structure in terms of grouping and time-resourcing was created by the school. Consequently the main barriers to coaching taking place are removed and the reflection process can occur with minimum disruption.

A Manchester classroom teacher used performance-enhancing coaching techniques to prepare students for the GCSE and A-level exams. Working with the whole group, he devised a visualization and affirmation programme to assist them with managing their stress levels in the lead up to the exams. He also worked with individuals on goal-setting, using coaching techniques to enhance their motivation for classroom learning and revision.

The authors have come across so many stories of success using coaching approaches. One unforgettable example is of a boy called Tom who was dyslexic and failing in school. Using non-directive coaching techniques over a three-month period, he made tremendous improvements in confidence. He made key decisions about his future and what he wanted to do beyond school. His dream was to go to college to train as a gamekeeper. For this he needed his science grade to be a D. He was, at the time, scraping an F grade. During the three months of coaching he worked on career goals, motivations for the future, confidence in the classroom, attitudes and approaches to difficult situations and exam fear/fear of failure. Tom went into his exams feeling confident and successful. The day his results came, as he looked at his science result, upon which his future at that point hung, his face was a mixture of smiles and tears. He hadn't achieved the D grade he needed, but instead scored a C. Against all the predictions, he had overcome his limitations and out-performed the expectations of many around him.

One local authority has embraced the benefits of coaching and set about supporting 40 schools to use coaching to develop teacher performance and enhance classroom practice. Led by Lesley Smith, the Coaching Support Unit has enabled schools to structure coaching in a whole variety of ways. The team consisting of Lesley, Mark Wilson and Chris Behagg and formerly Jen Weeks, have enabled the schools to develop the skills of lead practitioners in coaching, and to build appropriate structures to support the growth of coaching conversations. Warwickshire Local Authority are similarly engaged in developing coaching approaches to developing classroom practice in their schools. For further information about these projects you can turn to Chapter 11 for their case studies.

Other schools are now setting themselves the goal of becoming a 'Coaching School' and are putting in place training and structures to enable children and adults to benefit from the skills and techniques that help them to think and behave in resourceful ways.

Summary

In this chapter we have explored the benefits of coaching for adults, students and whole institutions. A range of educational and commercial organizations have experienced the benefits of these processes through:

▶ recognizing that helping processes can make a difference to performance of staff, students and the organization as a whole

▶ investing time to enable coaching

▶ investing resources (including training) to enable coaching

▶ using specific coaching approaches to help others

▶ thinking creatively about how such help can be delivered and where it might benefit the community

▶ recognizing that coaches benefit from coaching others as they coach them.

Questions

1 What are the benefits of coaching for students, teachers and institutions?

2 What are the biggest challenges facing you in your institution right now?

3 What are the biggest challenges facing you professionally in your current role?

4 Given what you currently know about coaching, how might it help you with the issues you raise in the questions above?

5 What ideas or issues currently hold you back from meeting your challenges?

6 What benefits might coaching bring to your organization?

Masterclass

▶ Be visionary in all that you do – what would your coaching school be like?

▶ Model for others the best practice you have in coaching daily.

▶ Communicate succinctly what coaching is to everyone who is willing to listen.

▶ Dispel the myths about coaching – it is not therapy.

▶ Desire the benefits that coaching will bring your school, your department, your colleagues, your students and their parents.

▶ Commit personally to lifelong learning, not just of content and skills, but of personal growth and development, behaviour and action.

▶ Begin listening more than you speak and notice how others respond to you and to one another.

What is coaching?

Chapter 2 Defining coaching

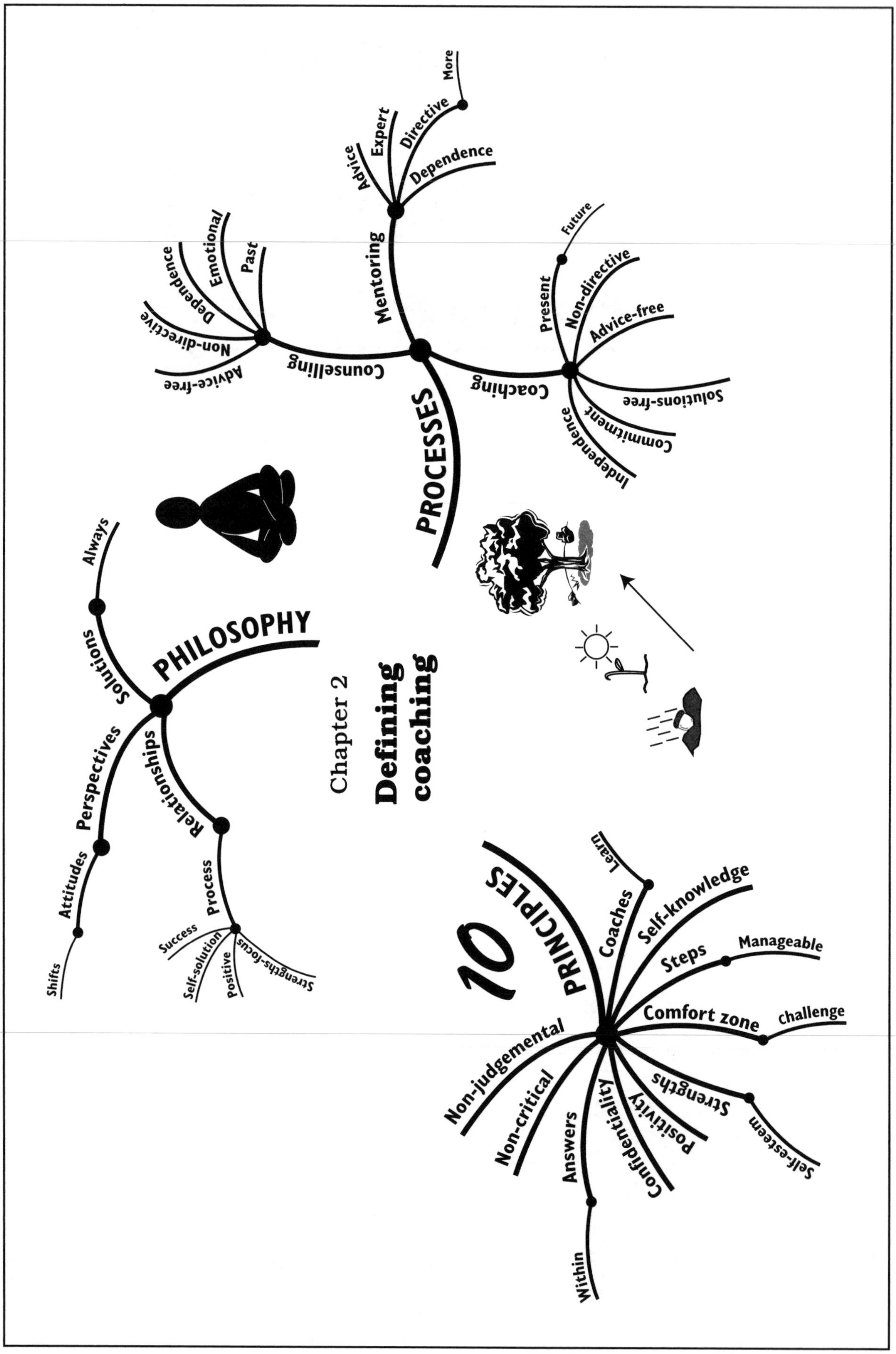
Chapter 2
Defining coaching
PHILOSOPHY
Solutions
Always
Perspectives
Attitudes
Shifts
Relationships
Process
Success
Self-solution
Positive
Strengths-focus
PROCESSES
Counselling
Advice-free
Non-directive
Dependence
Emotional
Past
Mentoring
Advice
Expert
Directive
More
Dependence
Coaching
Present
Future
Non-directive
Advice-free
Solutions-free
Commitment
Independence
10 PRINCIPLES
Coaches
Learn
Self-knowledge
Steps
Manageable
Comfort zone
challenge
Strengths
Self-esteem
Positivity
Confidentiality
Answers
Within
Non-critical
Non-judgemental

Chapter 2

Defining coaching

IN THIS CHAPTER YOU WILL LEARN:

- what coaching is
- what coaching is not
- the nine principles of coaching
- how coaching differs from counselling and mentoring

PREVIEW QUESTIONS:

- What is coaching?
- How does coaching differ from mentoring?
- How does coaching differ from counselling?
- What are the nine principles of coaching?
- What is the essence of coaching?

Shift perceptions, change the behaviour

Tim Vigors was a young RAF pilot who was part of the Battle of Britain in the summer of 1940. He was one of a number of young men who kept a diary of his experiences. He was stationed at Hornchurch with 222 Squadron. Vigors shot down an enemy plane on 9 September before he himself was hit. He crash-landed, unhurt, in an allotment in Dartford. Surrounded by greenhouses, cabbages and old men leaning on forks, he climbed out, recovered his parachute and was given some tea and whisky by the locals. As he was unable to make it back to Hornchurch, he arranged to stay with his aunt who had a flat in London. He then remembered to call the squadron – his voice was met with relief. But that night he had a taste of what Londoners were going through.

'Sirens were wailing. Searchlights were lighting the sky over to the East and the thuds of exploding anti-aircraft shells blended ominously with the screech of the sirens. The drone of bombers could be heard above the racket and then the bombs started to rain down.'

Early the next morning, parachute slung over his shoulder, he set off for Fenchurch Street to catch a train to his base, passing through streets which the night before had suffered the damage. He had to catch a bus and asked two policemen for directions to the bus stop. They offered to show him the way.

'We walked through the arch onto the road and there was a queue of about a hundred people lined up by the bus stop. As we approached a number of people started looking at us curiously. "There's a bloody Hun!" said one of the locals.'

The crowd surged forward and Vigors realized what was happening. 'The blue-grey colour of my uniform was not dissimilar to that worn by pilots of the Luftwaffe … My head was covered by a crop of light blond hair. My parachute, helmet and flying boots made me look like somebody who had just got out of an aircraft. With a policeman on each side of me, they had taken me for a captured German.'

The three backed against a wall while the policemen yelled that the pilot was one of their own, but nobody was listening. 'Now there were about forty around us and those at the back of the crowd were pushing forward on the leaders. I was suddenly scared. These people who had seen their homes going up in flames meant business. "Hell," I thought to myself. "What a way for a fighter pilot to get killed: lynched by his own people." But then those at the front of the mob realized their mistake. 'The ferocious hatred in their eyes turned to horror. "He's RAF," they yelled and started to try and push back the crowd behind them … then the reaction set in. I was quickly hoisted on to the shoulders of a few of the front division and carried through the crowd with everybody cheering and trying to clap me on the back.'

What is coaching?

Within seconds the perception of the group of Londoners confronting Vigors is changed and, consequently, their behaviour reversed. Shift the perception and you change the behaviour. The rapidity with which this can occur is impressive. In any group, meanings are mediated by the way the group interacts. Do not doubt the significance of this for an organization such as a school. Until perceptions are shared and surfaced, group thinking shapes behaviours. A core benefit of coaching is that it drills through group thinking.

What exactly is coaching?

Coaching philosophy holds that there are always solutions to overcome barriers, and shifts in attitudes will be there that will prevent even the most persistent limits to progress from knocking you off course.

As we will discover throughout this book, although coaching is about techniques, it is primarily about attitude. It is about challenging the popular culture that says 'Things are terrible and we can only expect worse' and replacing it with a mindset that says 'Anything is possible if what we believe in is worth it and we will find a way to achieve it.'

The attitudes and techniques included in this book are specifically designed for use in schools, colleges and universities.

Introducing coaching

The terms 'coaching', 'mentoring' and 'counselling' are often used interchangeably. Let us look at what coaching is and what it is not.

For most of us the first time we come across the term 'coach' is in relation to sport – the tennis coach who rallies small, dehydrated children during summer school into producing perfect serves, or the golf pro who tweaks our swing. Each coach examines our approach and advises us on ways to improve our technique. But how does this idea of coaching fit with the current use of the word? Perhaps we should to go back to the origin of the word 'coach' in order to consider the current definition.

A coach is a vehicle for the conveyance of an important person to their chosen destination.

Now if we change the words 'a coach' to 'coaching' in this definition, we have some idea of the education and commerce meaning of the term. Coaching is a way of helping another person to reach their destinations. 'Destinations' means the goals that a person wants to achieve or needs to achieve within the institutional setting.

Those destinations may be exam grades, understanding how to overcome fear, improving relationships with friends or colleagues, achieving a promotion, improving student behaviour, managing a team more effectively, or building teams. It may be that the destination is the improvement of teaching practice or leadership.

Coaching will usually involve helping another to decide just what that destination is in the first place. But there is an important distinction: coaching is not about giving advice. In fact coaches never advise. They facilitate the learning of others. Once you have coaching skills, you will be able to use them in just about any situation where another person or organization wishes to progress. Coaching is context free.

If you consult the coaching texts, you will find a range of definitions:

 *Coaching is the art of facilitating the performance, learning and development of another.*

(Myles Downey, 2003)

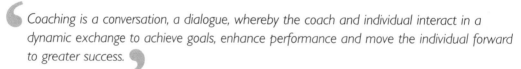 *Coaching is a conversation, a dialogue, whereby the coach and individual interact in a dynamic exchange to achieve goals, enhance performance and move the individual forward to greater success.*

(Zeus and Skiffington, 2001)

Another consideration is:

The process of coaching is non-directive, allowing the person you are coaching to explore their own issues in a positive, supportive relationship with their coach. This may be set against an agreed back-drop within an organizational coaching scenario.

Working with the definitions above and with experience of working as a coach in the education field, the definition of non-directive education coaching that shall be used in this book is:

 *A strengths-focused approach to facilitating the learning of others*

Will Thomas 2008

The coaching process can be used successfully in a group and also in a one-to-one situation, and therefore this definition may refer to a group as well as a single person.

Nine principles of coaching

In order to provide opportunities for others to learn about their own performance, limitations and solutions, it is essential to create a climate for learning that encourages and supports risk-taking. Everyone gets maximum benefit from coaching in a climate where it is safe to disclose information and share ideas that they have never divulged before. To ensure that this trust is built, the following is essential to coaching excellence:

1 Be non-judgemental and non-critical.

2 Build rapport and respect another person's model of the world.

3 Believe that people can find their next steps.

4 Build and maintain agreements about how we will work together.

5 Be positive and believe that there are always solutions to issues.

6 Enable others to access resourceful states through strength recognition.

7 Challenge individuals to move beyond their comfort zone.

8 Break down big goals into manageable steps.

9 Act to increase choice and balance.

The Nine principles explained:

1 Be non-judgemental and non-critical: this principle exists to encourage unconditional positive regard for those being coached. It also serves as a reminder to coaches to 'be mindful' of their own judgements. The non-judgmental element of the principle refers to thoughts and the non-critical element refers to how we communicate those thoughts.

2 Build rapport and respect another person's model of the world: drawn from Alfred Korzybski's concept of the map not being the territory, this principle is core to working with people of diverse experiences, cultures and social conditioning which may differ from our own. We would contend that it is only through respecting difference that we can grow the necessary trust for people to freely explore their thoughts and feelings about change. If rapport is a mutual feeling of trust, then respect is the way to win that trust. Rapport or rather a lack of it, we would suggest, is at the heart of why relationships are not working. Similarly where rapport exists trust co-exists. This is empowering for the coach, as rapport is something that can be built through high-quality listening, reflecting back the words of others and clarifying your understanding of their issues. This principle also embraces the importance of being open to learning from those you coach. Being willing to learn from others communicates great respect and guards against stagnation and arrogance.

3 Believe that people can find their own next steps: this principle exists to challenge any belief the coach has that (s)he knows best, and it is designed to empower those being coached. An early challenge that novice coaches often have is to switch off their internal problem-solving system. This can lead to coaches thinking ahead in a conversation and developing questions that steer coachees towards the coach's preferred solution. Not only is this practice against the spirit of coaching, it is potentially disempowering and controlling. It also pre-supposes that the coach utterly understands the model of the world from which the coachee is operating.

Holding the belief that people can find their own next steps also guards against us rescuing other people. Rescuing others can feel worthy for the Good Samaritan, but can maintain a coachee in the realms of helplessness and dependency.

4 Build and maintain agreements about how we will work together: high-quality communication, honesty and trust are all built from knowing the boundaries of a relationship and a process. Setting the parameters of your coaching conversations is key to building the trust you need to operate together. Similarly it is key to being able to restore trust if one or other party breaks the code you have defined or if unexpected events occur and boundaries need to be redefined. On our Vision for Learning Coaching programmes we explore a variety of approaches to building agreements. One of the simplest and most effective approaches is to write down a list of what will motivate you both in your coaching relationship and what will de-motivate you both.

5 Be positive and believe there are always solutions to issues: if the coach doubts that a solution can be found, it tends to be communicated to the coachee. Our inner beliefs and intentions can so easily leak out through our actions, our body language and our choice of words. A coach struggling with this area will need to work on their own self talk and use simple techniques to turn negative internal dialogue that interferes with their ability to support others into more empowering words. The case for coaches to have supervision – having someone who coaches you – is strong, particularly where issues that you meet in your coaches trigger unresourceful thought patterns in you.

6 Enable others to access resourceful states through strengths recognition: building people's awareness and connection with their strengths is a crucial approach to building their capacity to make changes. In coaching we spend time pointing out and questioning people to enable them to tap into the memories of their past successes. This is much more than just a memory, however; it is used to lift people into a resourceful emotional state. This positive 'state' becomes a powerful ally in helping people to tackle actions which have unhelpful emotions attached to them, e.g. feelings of guilt or fear. Coaches can also use these strengths to pull people from negative states into positive states during coaching conversations in order to create progress with a problem.

7 Challenge individuals to move beyond their comfort zone: people can become locked in habitual patterns which destine them to repeat their own history. Encouraging them to think differently and act differently is (obviously) the key to change. In coaching the use of open-style questions to provoke alternative thought patterns and enable them to consider alternatives is important. Coaches must be willing to be provoking in their choice of questions and to challenge assumptions which coachees voice. This takes courage, but is at the centre of the service to the people you support. Challenge should always be offered in the context of having a positive rapport with individuals.

8 Break down big goals into manageable steps: Einstein is paraphrased as having once said that things should be as simple as possible, but no simpler. People often complicate situations and processes. The successful coach assists them to break down complexity through asking questions that demand specific thinking and that create steps eg What specifically will you do? When will you do it exactly? What will you do first? Next? Then? Finally?

9   Act to increase choice and balance: Always seek to increase the choices a person has available to them. Moving people from a position of no choice or an imperative releases and empowers them. It similarly enables them to make balanced choices that are right by their own moral code. Being in line with your values in the decisions you make brings a strong sense of purposefulness in actions you take. The coach should seek to support others to act with authenticity. This means exploring a range of options, of pushing and pulling, of being creative, analytical and evaluative. It also means testing options against fitness for task and against the impact a course of action will have upon themselves and others.

How is coaching different from other helping processes?

Coaching differs from other helping relationships such as mentoring and guidance in that it does not offer advice nor do coaches suggest that they are experts. Coaching sits along a continuum of helping processes, as represented in Figure 2.1 below. Directive processes have advice and instruction at their heart; non-directive processes do not involve advising or telling, but instead rely on questioning and reflecting back what people say in order to assist them to make their own choices.

```
                                              NON-DIRECTIVE

                                    COUNSELLING

                          COACHING

                MENTORING

          GUIDANCE

     TELLING

DIRECTIVE
```

Figure 2.1 The helping continuum

Counselling tends to work through looking at the past, whereas coaching works essentially by encouraging individuals to look at the present and the future. Coaching is very definitely not counselling, and if coaches find that a person has deep-seated emotional traumas from the past, it is not for the coach to deal with these but to refer the person on to a suitably qualified therapist.

Working with the coach, people learn to recognize their strengths. Knowing your strengths and having a coach recognize and reinforce these makes it easier for people to examine aspects of their work or behaviour that are not productive or could be improved. In other words, the better you feel about yourself, the easier it is to look at those parts of you and your work that could be improved.

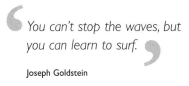

You can't stop the waves, but you can learn to surf.

Joseph Goldstein

The terms 'mentoring' and 'coaching' are sometimes used interchangeably. At the simplest level, coaching is a process and relationship within which the person being coached decides what the course of action will be and devises their own solution. In mentoring, the mentor may provide advice and have specific knowledge about the area of support they are providing. Arguably one of the dangers of mentoring advice is that there can be a difference in status between the mentor and the person they are mentoring. This can lead the mentee to feel that they must take the advice even if they feel unsure about it. Coaching seeks to enable people to take their own decisions and to seek their own advice and guidance as necessary.

There will no doubt be those who disagree with the authors on this point but, in simplistic terms, mentoring may involve the mentor providing solutions, and non-directive coaching involves people finding them for themselves. Coaching accesses a deep level of self-motivation and learning for the person who is being coached. It helps people to order their thoughts and move themselves in achievable steps to the next level of performance.

The following comparisons are an attempt to simplify a complex relationship between coaching, counselling and mentoring. The lines between the processes are fuzzy and it is in the interests of clarity, in defining non-directive coaching in this book, that we make some generalizations here.

Coaching

- Generic helping skill
- Non-directive
- Advice is not given
- Solutions focused
- Belief that individuals hold the answers
- Based in present and future
- Strengths focused
- Commitment to specific actions
- Promotes high degree of independence
- Uses the skills of questioning, reflecting and clarifying

Counselling

- Looks backwards and at the present
- Non-directive
- Advice is not given
- Not usually solutions focused
- Belief that individuals hold the answers
- Operates at emotional level often
- May promote a degree of dependence
- Dependent on style of counselling, may use skills of questioning, reflecting, and clarifying

Mentoring

- Mentor has expert knowledge/experience
- Specific advice given
- May be solutions focused or explorative
- Mentor has the 'real' answers
- Usually directive at some level
- May/may not result in specific actions
- Can promote dependence upon mentor
- Uses the skills of questioning, reflecting and clarifying

As we have already explained, a coach focuses an individual in the present and the future, assisting the individual to stay positive and resourceful. Grounded in the present, coaches encourage people to look for resources they have in their present state. While the coach may invite individuals to reach back into the positive past, they do not take them into the negative past (see Figure 2.2). Coaches see little value in taking individuals into their past, unless it is to use a positive experience as a springboard to achieve a goal. If individuals should stray into this negative territory, the coach uses specific techniques (discussed in Chapter 7) to restore a more resourceful state of mind.

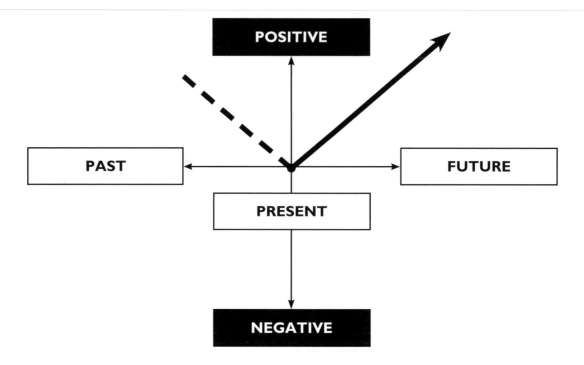

Figure 2.2 Coaching timeline

Mentoring is very useful where factual information needs to be imparted to others or where watching a mentor work appears to be the best approach for the new learner. A disadvantage is that it can produce clones of the mentor and, in some models of mentoring, can disempower the learner. The power differences in this relationship need careful management and there can be a tendency for learners to become reliant on the mentor for solutions. Of course, one person's solution may not suit another, and it may not yield long-term changes in behaviour.

Counselling is appropriate where a person is suffering from deep-seated emotional traumas. It is a highly skilled process that requires proper training and is usually a long-term undertaking. Coaches should not involve themselves in this kind of relationship unless they are qualified counsellors. Coaching will inevitably influence emotions for some people, and counselling skills are part of the coach's toolkit. These counselling skills can be used to help people acknowledge and deal with emotions in relation to the issues they bring. There is a world of difference between counselling and counselling skills, and coaches must be ready to recognize the boundaries of their capability and refer people to qualified professionals as necessary. It may be entirely appropriate for a coach to continue coaching an individual while they are having professional therapeutic support. This can work well when there is an agreement with the counsellor and the person being coached.

The Triangle of Support

In the early days of introducing coaching into schools and colleges, some students of the craft saw the process of coaching as being exclusive, that no solutions could ever be offered. Coaching is in fact part of a dynamic relationship between which can be seen as one of three corners of a triangle of support. To withhold great ideas and tried and tested approaches on the part of the coach would be churlish. The true dynamic of coaching is knowing when to draw out ideas from others and when to offer them. Judging this dynamic is an "ego-less" process, one that puts asides one's own self esteem needs and concentrates on what is right for the individual in front of you.

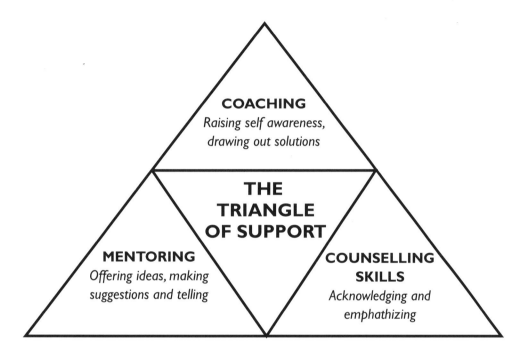

Fig 2.3 The Triangle of Support – © Will Thomas 2008

This triangle of support places coaching at the top of the graphic, giving it status as the core empowerment process. There is, however, a unique blending process in practice that occurs as there will be times when the other processes of mentoring and counselling skills are required. For example, in the context of idea generation (see Chapter 6, The STRIDE model) and in the spirit of coaching principle number nine (act to increase choice and balance, p. 21) you may judge it as appropriate to offer further ideas to your coachee. These should always be offered as genuine options and this carefully reinforced with your language, e.g. 'How would you feel about some other options being added in here? It's just another idea ... what about ...?'. There may be times when to coach in the first instance is inappropriate, particularly where someone is operating from a position where they are choosing not to take control of a situation and demanding you fix the problem. In some cases, in the interest of building rapport it can be helpful to offer a few ideas, and then move into a coaching style of support.

Similarly, counselling skills come into play at certain times, in a support relationship. For example, in emotionally charged situations, often before a coachee is able to move towards positive solutions, they will need to feel understood and that the person listening empathizes with their plight. We sometimes refer to this as "hearing their pain". Unless a person in this sort of situation knows you appreciate their plight, they will be unwilling to let go of that 'pain' and move on. On the receiving end of this, if you have ever been in a situation where you were deeply troubled by something and a well-meaning and highly positive individual intervenes before you felt heard, you might well have wanted to attack that person verbally or either physically! The 'counselling skills' corner of the triangle is there to emotionally support the coachee and to help build rapport. We would argue that you can only move a person forward as fast as you have the rapport to do so. While coaching is primarily designed to help people go from 'good to great', it has immense applications to working with people in deeply troubled states of mind; however, it must be used in this way in the context of the triangle to enable people to be acknowledged and to increase choices. Coaching, we believe, is about being in the service of another, and in this sense a coaching conversation will be a mixture of coaching (mainly) but also the other processes of mentoring and counselling, blended as a way of provoking independence in the coachee. Counselling skills are not the same as counselling. We must always remember that unless we are qualified counsellors, there will be boundaries to our practice in the counselling skills corner of the triangle. In essence, if we find ourselves week after week operating in the counselling skills corner, it may be that the person we are working with needs skilled counselling support, and it is then our duty as coach to help that person towards that kind of support.

Coaching remains, in our view, the most effective way of achieving independent thinking in others. Mentoring and counselling skills may also be required to prepare people for the coaching process. This blended support may occur in distinct stages over time or seamlessly within one conversation. The blending process is both an art and a science and comes with practice, experimentation and training.

Summary

Coaching:

▶ *is a process that enables people to come up with solutions that suit them personally*

▶ *encourages individuals to work out the steps to success that suit their own circumstances*

▶ *promotes independent thinking and encourages people to take responsibility for finding their own solutions*

▶ *creates the climate for individuals to examine their own strengths and to use them to achieve their goals*

▶ *avoids the pitfalls of advice, which may not always suit the capabilities and circumstances of the person receiving that advice*

▶ *is not a panacea, but it is one more essential tool in your toolbox to promote self-motivation and enable others to make change happen*

▶ *engenders choice and individualized learning and it is this that intrinsically motivates others to be the best that they can be*

▶ *Coaching, counselling skills and mentoring can be seen to exist within The Triangle of Support. The processes can be blended in practice to provide a unique cocktail of support to meet the needs of the individual.*

Questions

1   How would you define coaching?

2   A colleague asks you to explain the difference between coaching, mentoring and counselling. What would you say?

3   Consider the nine principles. For each one consider your current approach to helping people. Score each statement from one to ten, where one means 'emerging approach', that is, needs development, and ten means 'highly developed'.

4   Using the scores from 3 above, consider what strengths you have that have enabled you to develop your highest scoring areas.

5   How can you use your strengths to develop an area that you would like to improve? What is your first step? Where do you go next?

Masterclass

▶ *Notice when others are using coaching, counselling or mentoring methods in everyday conversations.*

▶ *In each case, notice the impact of the help on the recipient.*

▶ *Notice when you are using these different helping skills.*

▶ *Consider the relationship between the nine principles of coaching – how do they interact with one another?*

▶ *Develop the ability to listen and wait.*

▶ *When you feel the strong urge to jump in with a solution – don't! See what happens.*

▶ *Be aware of how others react when they are told how to do something, compared to being asked questions that help them come to their own conclusions.*

▶ *In classrooms – elicit more, instruct less.*

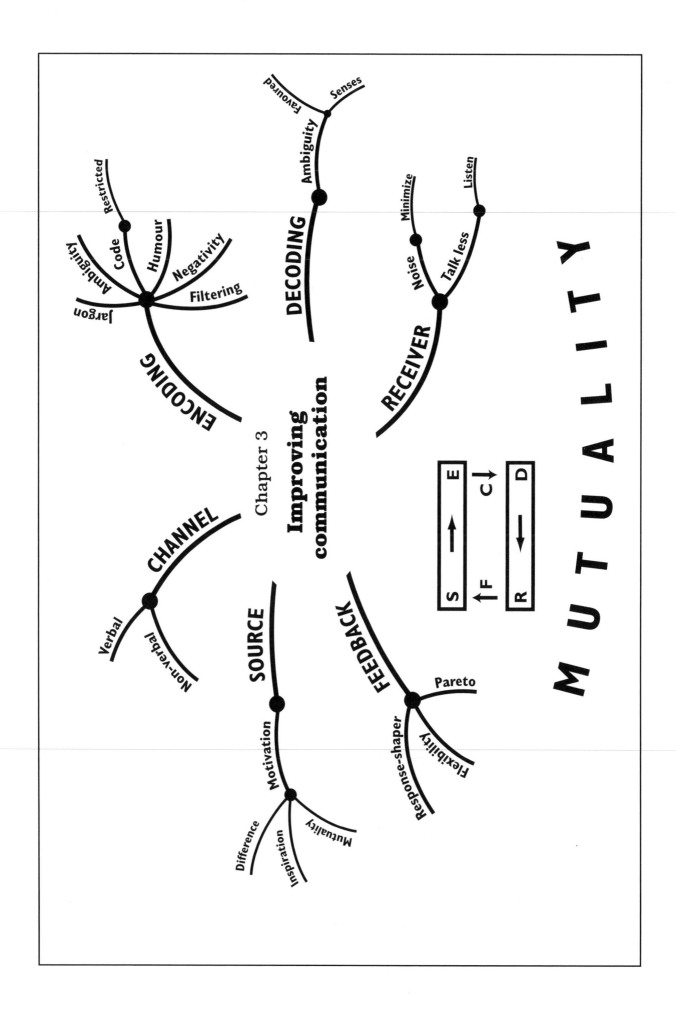

Chapter 3

Improving communication

IN THIS CHAPTER YOU WILL LEARN:

- a communication model and how it can be used
- the process of giving and receiving messages
- the importance of mutuality to coaching
- three ways to develop mutuality
- how to keep language clean

PREVIEW QUESTIONS:

- When any communication between humans takes place, what is most important?
- When you give an instruction to different colleagues, do you change the emphasis? If so, why?
- Are your messages always understood in the way you intended? What do you do if not?
- What is the role of the coach in clear communication?

Far-off seeing

Our two families lived side by side. We must have been among the first in the street to get television. I never saw the neighbour's: my mother wouldn't let me go round to their house. Our television was large, highly polished and so heavy it took two men to carry it in. It took a while to heat up and even longer to cool down. My dad used to say not to sit too close to it when it was on or you might get radiation burns. He'd been in the army so he knew about such things. There wasn't much to see on the television, only two channels, both in black and white. It often broke down in the middle of a programme – half way through *I Love Lucy* – and my dad would bang the mahogany surround knowingly. If that didn't work, there was a complex and more sustained ritual involving the exchange of valves.

The valves were stored in a Christmas lights box under the stairs – little candle-shaped goblets of *glass*, with intricacies of wire hidden inside. There was a special oven glove worn for the trialling of valves. Replacements were placed in order on a tea towel laid out in a special way on the fireside rug. If successful, valve exchange meant you could catch the denouement of 'ILL' before making a cup of tea. If unsuccessful, valve exchange was followed by statements like 'It must be the tube' or 'Needs to cool down for a bit'. It was a man thing with its own ordered thinking, bits and bobs of technology and a special code. The tube 'going' was akin to a national disaster. This necessitated a visit to the radiogram shop in the morning. All plans for the *Black and White Minstrel Show* on Saturday night would be put on hold. Then one day the neighbours got a new aerial.

The aerial went on the chimney pot and had to be pointed in the right direction to pick up a signal. This involved their whole family – dad on the roof holding on to the pot and twisting the aerial in the general direction of Edinburgh to the south to catch the signal, son holding the ladder, daughter beside son at the foot of the ladder conveying messages, mother indoors watching the picture. Information went from the pot to the foot of the ladder and indoors. Then a response came from indoors to the foot of the ladder and up to the pot again. As my mother hung out the washing she was witnessing the true pioneers of the new media at work next door: technological frontiersmen.

'At it?' from the pot.

'At it?' from the ladder.

'No – at no it!' from inside.

Adjustments would be made to the aerial. As dad swayed in the wind, the son, who was in the bottom set at the junior secondary, hung on to the ladder with grim determination.

'At it now?' from the pot.

'At it now?' from the ladder.

'No – at still no it!' from inside.

Swearing followed by further adjustments. The son's face pressed tight against the ladder.

'Now – at it?' from the pot.

'Now – at it?' from the ladder. A pause.

'Aye – at it!' from inside.

Smiles all round. The technology mastered. The airwaves tamed. The son lets go the ladder to lift his arms in triumph, flush with success.

Improving communication

Television is a word derived from the Greek. Translated literally it means 'far-off seeing'. Any communication system can be seen to involve the sending of messages from a source to a receiver through a channel or channels. The process involves encoding and decoding messages. The success of the system is also shaped by feedback and interference or what is known as 'noise'.

Televisions and ladders are used here to represent the complexity of any communication system involving two or more humans. Giving and receiving clear, unambiguous messages is complicated as soon as any human becomes involved. 'Send reinforcements we are going to advance' soon becomes 'Send three and fourpence we're going to a dance' if the system allows distortion. Understanding human interaction can benefit from an appreciation of communication models such as the very basic one provided in Figure 3.1.

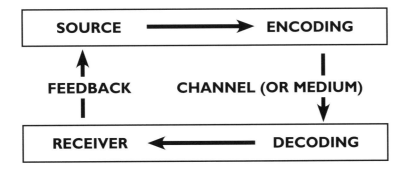

Figure 3.1 A basic communication model

The source of the information is, in this case, up on the ladder. The encoding is in language, the channel of communication is voice, decoding is through language. The receiver acts on the communication, encodes a response – 'At no it' – which constitutes the feedback to the source. Simple at face value – but, of course, throughout the system there is noise. 'Noise' means anything that threatens to distort the message. The wind makes the question be misheard and so decoded incorrectly. The instructions are misunderstood. The mother dislikes the idea of television, so deliberately gives incorrect information. Very quickly the quality of the communication is impaired. As soon as a human is involved, predictability of response can no longer be guaranteed.

Transferring the model into a coaching context provides a useful means of appreciating the complexity of human interaction. Outlined below are some observations that will help you keep the communication system 'clean'.

A basic communications model: source

As the source of a communication, the coach needs to embody the 'mutuality principle'. Coaching is not coercion, cheerleading or counselling. To be successful it requires mutuality of respect for each other and for the process itself.

Mutuality is partly a consequence of being able to establish and maintain rapport in the relationship. Rapport is about getting along with each other, identifying commonality and building from there. Dale Carnegie wrote about this very topic in the 1930s in his book *How to Win Friends and Influence People*, but it need not be about 'winning' anything. There is a basic humanity in trying to locate common cause. To do so requires three things: respect for the complexity of human motivation, an appreciation that others think differently and a willingness to suspend the need to interpret intent.

Complexity of human motivation

Let us assume that humans operate in their own interests and with the best resources available at the time. That is not to say we are all operating in the same way and with the same resources. For some, their interests are to be 'well-off' – this could be financial, professional or spiritual – or to be healthy or, equally, to be 'unhealthy'. For others, their interests may be 'served' by constant rowing with a partner or having a 'sick' child or spending more than they can afford.

If we take this starting point then we do not sit in judgement. We approach mutuality. The complexity of human motivation requires respect.

Tanni Grey Thompson is an Olympic athlete who has won medals at the paralympics in four different events. She gives motivational talks and uses a photograph of herself as a young girl in the Brownies to illustrate a point about motivation. A group of about ten young girls are in a school playground skipping. Some girls are frozen by the camera in mid-air as they skip. Tanni is there too, smiling broadly. Her skipping rope is caught in mid-air, half-way between her wheelchair and the ground.

Others think differently

In his book *The Essential Difference*, Simon Baron-Cohen uses his research into the causes and consequences of autism to describe the 'essential' difference between male and female thinking. He suggests a continuum of maleness and femaleness characterized by a high concern for systems and structures at one extreme, and a high concern for relationships and empathizing at the other. A fascinating book, but one like any other that offers a 'grand theory' to inform, delight and surprise rather than provide a blueprint. If you wanted a reminder of how dramatic the difference in the way we think can be, read Mark Haddon's book *The Curious Incident of the Dog in the Night Time* (2004). It tells a story from the point of view of a 15-year-old boy with Asperger's Syndrome. In the book the boy describes how he thinks:

> *My memory is like a film. That is why I am really good at remembering things, like the conversations that I have written down in this book, and what people were wearing, and what they smelled like, because my memory has a smelltrack which is like a sound track.*

And later,

> *Other people have pictures in their heads too. But they are different because the pictures in my head are all pictures of things which really happened. But other people have pictures in their heads of things which aren't real and didn't happen. (p. 96)*

Coaching is not about correcting unproductive thought patterns. You cannot change the way someone else thinks. You can invite them to choose alternative strategies, but otherwise it's about using what is there. What is there can delight and surprise. It is about enabling others to see the choices available to them.

Suspend the need to interpret intent

At the core of mutuality is a curiosity about others and also a readiness to resist sitting in judgement. A person's past is not broken and it is not your job to fix it! Coaching is not mind reading. A habitual need to interpret leads you into a developmental dead-end.

Simon Weston is a Falklands veteran who was very badly burned when his ship, *Sir Galahad,* was bombed during the conflict. Weston endured years of painful surgery and eventually recovered, although his treatment continues to this day. A down-to-earth Welshman from a valleys community, he has turned his personal adversity to his advantage and the advantage of others. His charity, Weston Spirit, works with hundreds of young unemployed people to help them find direction in their lives. He, too, gives inspirational talks. His facial features are well known, often seen on the covers of books and magazines. He tells the story of how he and his wife went out to eat in a restaurant in Cardiff shortly after they had just met. They had almost finished their own meal when a middle-aged couple who had been sitting nearby throughout the evening approached. Weston braced himself for the by now customary request for an autograph or, at the very least, a few kind words. The woman spoke: 'We'd just like to say, we think it's awful – you coming out looking like that. It's spoiled our meal. You should have more respect. I'm going to have nightmares tonight.' She then turned on her heel and left.

The 'source' in any coaching communication operates in ways to secure mutuality. Part of this is care in how communications are encoded.

A basic communications model: encoding

In simple communications models, encoding entails making messages accessible to sender and receiver. This typically occurs through spoken language, but there is also the possibility of codified gestures, looks, silences and other non-verbals that sit alongside talk. Meanings are also encoded via the context in which messages are exchanged. The same topic discussed in a bar and in a boardroom carries a different gravitas. In coaching it is worth asking: 'How is my message being received?' 'What can I do to make it easier to receive?'

It is more than stating the obvious to remind you to take care in how you express yourself in language. Avoid the following clarity traps.

Ambiguity

When asking a question or giving an instruction – do just that. Strip out any possible misinterpretation by the receiver by avoiding ambiguity – unless, of course, you are choosing to be ambiguous, but that's a different topic! Ambiguity has been one of the cornerstones of poor communication in classrooms for several generations:

'Can we take our coats off now please?'

'What am I thinking?'

'Someone's being naughty'.

'Let's behave, shall we?'

Negativity

A question or instruction with a negative focus – 'Don't do that!' – can have the effect of the receiver querying, 'Why not?' or 'What might it be like if I did?'

Filtering

Filtering involves manipulating the meaning so that it appears better to the receiver. Filtering increases in likelihood as the status disparity between sender and receiver widens – it is hard to give your manager bad news! Filtering also increases in likelihood as the consequences for the sender become more stressful – it is hard to live with the consequences of bad news!

'I don't think the results were so bad, at least not when you compare them to …'
(get real – they were awful, so let's get on with doing something about them)

'No, he's not upset at all …'
(in truth, he's at this very minute in a cupboard bawling his eyes out)

'Shall we ignore that for the moment?'
(hard to when the blood is dripping onto the carpet)

For a coach, filtering can be a useful tool to create resourcefulness before examining potentially difficult feedback. It is important, however, to acknowledge in the first instance the perceptions of those you coach and to address the realities based on the frames of reference being used; for example, national standards, internal targets and so on.

Restricted code

Teachers do 'good' restricted code! Words and phrases that have little meaning outside of classrooms proliferate:

'Woe-betide anyone who …'

'Have you seen the error of your ways?'

'Just what do you think you are doing?'

Jargon

Education is full of TLAs (three-letter acronyms) and terms which are susceptible to misinterpretation. Jargon is a good way of separating insiders from outsiders or, in other words, restricting the accessibility of your message. A close cousin of jargon in the coaching world is the cliché. Avoid clichés like the plague! Here are some favourites:

'Let's take a rain check.'

'Thank you for sharing that with us.'

'Correct me if I'm wrong.'

Humour

The sender encodes the message as a joke, the receiver – with a very different sense of humour – does not find it funny, misses the point and breakdown occurs. For a coach who is attempting to build mutuality through rapport, humour is high risk. Tory Member of Parliament Anne Winterton told a joke at a private party relating to cockle pickers in Morecambe Bay. No doubt her intent included building a sense of rapport with her audience. This was ill-advised in the context of the tragic deaths of 20 of these young people the month before. She was asked to resign from the party and, some time after, did so.

A basic communications model: channel

The channel is the mechanism of delivery of any communication. In our example, the sender encodes the message in language and then communicates that message through the channel of the spoken word.

Non-verbal communication

This used to be called body language, plain and simple. Crucially important for the coach, building mutuality through rapport is about sensitivity to non-verbal signals – yours and theirs. Here are some observations for non-verbal communication in formal coaching sessions:

- *Orientation* – position yourself, without obstructions such as desks and tables, so that you are free to move closer to the person you coach, if necessary.

- *Posture* – relaxed without being sloppy, attentive without being stiff.

- *Mirroring* – to build rapport, mirror and match the physical gestures of the other person. Do so without parodying. Be subtle in this.

- *Open and closed gestures* – if someone leans back and folds their arms as you are talking to them, it is a clear signal of a shift in their thinking.

- *Mirroring body language* – this encourages the person with whom you are talking to relax and be at ease. You can do this through open and closed gestures: folded arms is a closing gesture, open palms is generally interpreted as inviting of trust.

- *Facial expression* – 'the eyes have it!' The slightest emotional response is leaked through the tiny movements of the eyes and the mouth.

It has been suggested that we can talk at about 150 words per minute (wpm) in a Western European language, listen at over 1,000 wpm and process at 400–500 wpm. The more complex the non-verbal dance taking place as we speak, the more these rough numbers are likely to reduce. This is in part why the request to the very young child, 'Look at me when I'm talking to you' increases the brain power needed to listen and decode complex verbal and non-verbal messages simultaneously. Simple open and unambiguous gestures are needed.

Some people believe that alternative channels of communication in these days of 1.59 billion UK text messages sent monthly are making us quicker and more efficient at decoding. More efficient does not mean more effective and the opportunities for misunderstanding in text, picture and sound text, email, tele- and video-conferencing, and discussion forums abound.

A basic communications model: decoding

The sender encodes and the receiver of the message decodes. Decoding is our way of unravelling the meanings in any message. It sounds simple, but it is far from being so.

There are cultural differences that surround the simplest of human gestures. The easiest text on this is Desmond Morris's book *Peoplewatching*, called *Manwatching* in its original edition. He has whole sections on gestures and the differences in meaning across the world. Take the simple gesture of forming a circle with the tips of thumb and forefinger. In the UK it means OK; in France it only means OK if you are smiling at the time, otherwise it has the opposite meaning; in Japan it has a completely different meaning – money. The more complex the sender's message, the more hazardous the decoding.

Favoured listening occurs when we want to hear something in the message that accords with our viewpoint at that time. Coaches need to remove their ego from the system and avoid favoured listening.

One way of understanding ego in communications is to use the model of parent, adult and child relationships developed in Transactional Analysis (TA). In TA the 'transactions' are communications between two parties. The roles that the sender and receiver assume shape the way the messages are given and received, and thus influence the overall pattern of relationships. Ideally transactions should occur in adult-to-adult mode. All too often there is an imbalance in the transaction that leads to forms of manipulation. For example, a sender in parent mode may adopt a means of communicating the message that is an attempt to assert control, create dependency or even nurture. Typically, the sort of behaviour a parent may exhibit. A sender in child mode may adopt a means of communicating the message in an attempt to gain sympathy or concern or even admiration. Typically, 'attention seeking' is part of the repertoire of childhood. Now imagine two mature persons are attempting to communicate but do so in either of these modes. What then occurs is highly egocentric and difficult to decode.

In what roles do you communicate?

Parent	Parent
Adult	Adult
Child	Child

A simple question such as 'Why did you do that?' carries a whole new set of meaning. It could, for example, carry the sting of adult rebuke or, alternatively, be a child-like and plaintive cry for sympathy. TA teaches us how to understand the roles adopted and read the scripts that lie behind these roles. A coach needs to work towards an adult–adult communication.

Humans are phenomenal information processing machines. Data from the world about us comes in through the senses and is then assimilated and made sense of. Over time humans develop sensory acuity. We become good at noting the data and develop a 'shorthand' for quick interpretation. We become adept at associating sights, sounds, feelings, smells and tastes with experiences, events and behaviours. This process is highly subjective. At Wimbledon, for the tennis player the smell of freshly cut grass means something different to the groundsman who has to cut it or to the fan who hopes to go and watch what happens there. A coach benefits from knowing about sensory acuity and its quick interpretation because it can help improve the quality of communication. If I know that I am using the same or a similar 'shorthand' to you when we are in dialogue, I can be more confident in the clarity of our communication. Given health, we are all adept at constructing visual representations, rehearsing sounds and experiencing physical sensations.

Crudely put, the language we choose to use reflects the shorthand way we make sense of what happens around us. I may choose to express myself in colourful, pictorial language with lots of vivid images. I use words such as 'picture', 'look', 'see', 'show', 'look' and 'image' in everyday conversation and I am good at remembering the look of things. Ask me for directions and I will point out the landmarks along the way.

Or perhaps for me sounds evoke experiences. Someone says the word 'Wimbledon' and I'm there: I can hear the television theme tune, players' voices, the sound of the ball hit cleanly off the face of the racket. I use words such as 'hear', 'sound', 'say', 'talk', 'ring', 'listen' and 'tune' in everyday conversation and I am good at remembering the sound of things. Ask me for directions and I'll talk you though the route.

Or maybe there's nothing like doing it. Say the word 'Wimbledon' and I can feel myself touching the top of the net, or squeezing the grip or adjusting the height of my throw. The word evokes the feeling. I use words such as 'feel', 'touch', 'move', 'grip', 'run' and 'walk' in everyday conversation and I am good at remembering the 'feel' of things. Ask me for directions and I'll want to take you there or draw you a map.

If you are a grass-seed salesman, then paint vivid word pictures of bright-green lawns for your visual customers, talk up the benefits for your auditory customers and let your kinesthetic customers run their fingers through the seed. If you are a coach, pick up on the sorts of language being used get an insight into patterns of thought. Adapt your language.

A basic communications model: receiver

A good coach works hard to advantage the receiver of the message. The first message is talk less. Understanding and respecting human difference, a desire to develop mutuality, remove ego and achieve clarity of meaning drives this.

Noise

Noise is the 'technical' term for any phenomenon that disrupts the communication process. In our television example it could be that the television signal is disrupted because of a weather change. Noise disrupts the to-and-fro of communication. In a coaching context respect for the mutuality of the process means that the coach avoids potential disruptions by finding the right physical space and the right time. As they say on the property programmes – location, location, location. Research in the 1980s suggested that in the typical American office as much as 40 per cent of white collar workers' time was taken up with listening. If we listen at 25 per cent efficiency, how much of the communication is lost? So, find a room where you will not be interrupted, turn off the phones and clear away the clutter.

Simple things matter, such as:

- Get to know and use a person's name.
- Mirror and match their verbal and non-verbal communication.
- Give time for processing questions.
- Avoid tipping your receiver into a 'role' – maintain an adult-to-adult transaction.
- Monitor the feedback you get closely.

A basic communications model: feedback

In our communications model, feedback is what happens after the message has been sent and assimilated by the receiver. The feedback a coach gets shapes the coaching response. Interpreting feedback provokes tension between the professional objective role of the coach and the human need to interpret intent.

Clichés about the importance of feedback abound. Feedback is 'The breakfast of champions', 'Without feedback we do not grow' and 'There is no failure only feedback'. Feedback has become an industry in itself. We call it the Customer Satisfaction industry. One of the saws of the CS industry is that a satisfied customer tells one other person, a dissatisfied customer tells eight other persons. Satisfaction surveys are important to the future of the business.

In schools, student response approaches – 'ask the customers' – are gaining new life. Students can evaluate their teachers electronically and online. The success or failure of such ventures depends entirely on how the information is used. It is the same in the coaching role. The coach adjusts their response based on the feedback and does so with flexibility. To be flexible requires mutuality and a range of alternative tools such as those provided by this book.

For schools, finding the ideal coaching situation has to be worked at. This does not mean that you cannot gain advantage from being flexible. Adopt the 'one-minute manager' approach. Ian Goswell is assistant headteacher and Learning and Teaching coach at Brookway High School and Sports College, Manchester. His role includes coaching colleagues through their teaching issues. He points out that sometimes this happens 'on the run' and, having had a formal session, he prompts their thinking through short, 'in the corridor' sessions that require him to ask maybe one or two succinct questions. Coaching in a hurry will be discussed later in the book. Alistair uses a focus solution rule that he asks teachers and schools to apply: 'Don't come to me with a problem unless you come with two solutions at the same time.' Try it across your school!

In his book *The One Minute Manager* (1981), Ken Blanchard talks about the direct approach of the successful manager: 'tell me what is happening in exact observable terms, now tell me what you want to see happening … if you can't tell me what you want to see happening you don't have a problem yet. You're just complaining.' One-minute goal setting applies the pareto principle of 80 to 20 where 80 per cent of your really important outcomes will come from 20 per cent of your goals – so focus on the goals that will give the best return.

Summary

▶ *Communication would be a relatively simple process if no other human was involved.*

▶ *Knowing the stages of the communication model helps the coach remain focused on the professional role and the 'customer'.*

▶ *Acting to avoid 'noise' – the interference in the communication system – is the role of the coach.*

▶ *Building rapport, asking open curious questions and leaving space for processing thoughts is actually what enables individuals to find solutions.*

▶ *A good coach enables those whom they work with to be delighted and surprised by their own resources – essentially they work with what is already there.*

▶ *Words correctly and cleanly communicated carry great power, open up pathways of thinking and enable others to really think.*

Questions

1 Now that you have read this chapter, how well are you communicating?

2 What aspect of your communication process could you work on to improve?

3 When do you seek feedback from those you communicate with about how effectively you communicate?

4 When you coach others how do **you** build rapport?

5 How much of the time you spend listening to others is actually spent listening? How much time do you spend thinking about the next question or the solution that you think is best? What might the impact be on the person you are coaching?

Masterclass

▶ *Become familiar with the communication model and look for evidence of it in action.*

▶ *Suspend ego, judgement and status while you coach.*

▶ *Focus on the other person and do not filter their message via your own expectations.*

▶ *Monitor your coaching language for negativity, ambiguity, jargon and codes.*

▶ *Avoid jokes!*

▶ *Become familiar with your own body language and be aware of what you **do** as well as **say** in the coaching role.*

▶ *Remain in adult mode throughout.*

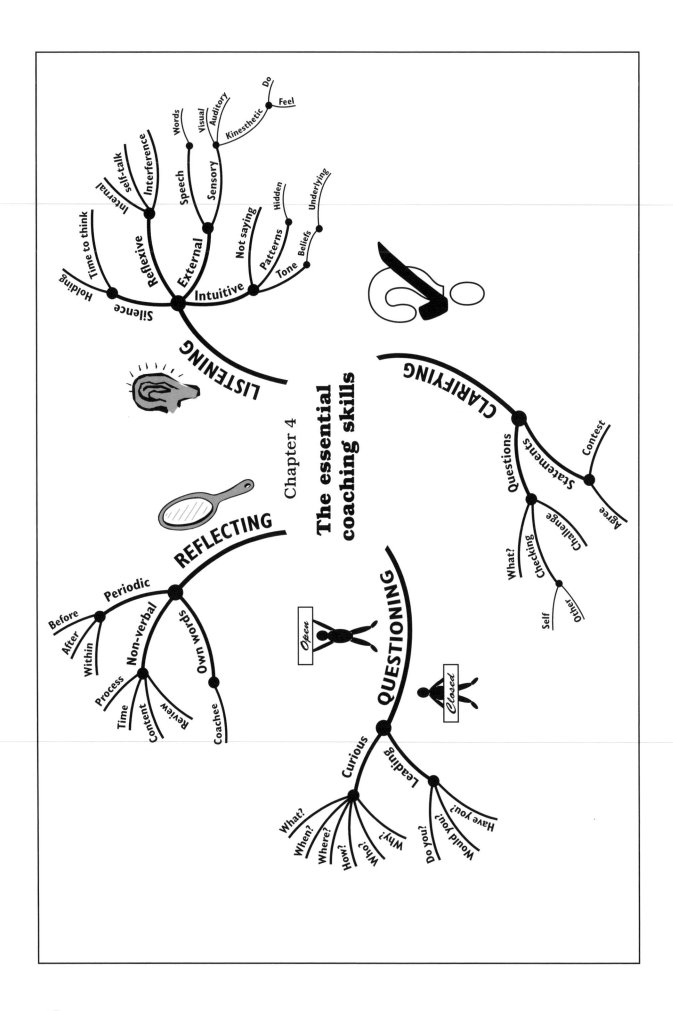

The essential coaching skills

Chapter 4

LISTENING

Silence
- Holding
- Time to think

Reflexive
- Internal
  - self-talk
- Interference

External
- Speech
- Sensory
  - Words
  - Visual
  - Auditory
  - Kinesthetic
    - Do
    - Feel

Intuitive
- Not saying
- Patterns
  - Hidden
  - Tone
  - Beliefs
    - Underlying

REFLECTING

Periodic
- Before
- After
- Within

Non-verbal
- Process
  - Time
- Review
  - Content
  - Coachee

Own words

CLARIFYING

Statements
- Contest
- Agree

Questions
- What?
- Challenge
- Checking
  - Self
  - Other

QUESTIONING

Open

Closed

Curious
- What?
- When?
- Where?
- How?
- Who?
- Why?

Leading
- Do you?
- Would you?
- Have you?

Chapter 4

The essential coaching skills

IN THIS CHAPTER YOU WILL LEARN:

- the four core skills of coaching
- about the four facets of listening
- how you already have these skills and can enhance them
- the essentials of good questioning

PREVIEW QUESTIONS:

- What are the essential skills of the coach?
- What does it mean to listen?
- What part does silence play in coaching?
- How is intuition involved?
- What does a coaching session sound like?
- What kinds of questions should I use?
- How do carefully phrased and placed questions unlock potential?

Painting by numbers

Miss Overn took us for Bible classes. She was a Sunday school teacher and a formidable character. She wore glasses with their own eyebrows attached and they were on a chain around her neck. Dull, heavy, brown tights covered her legs.

The day she put her briefcase down on the floor in some cat poo we all sniggered; but she didn't. We did Bibles on Sundays, in silence. If we were good and listened, she let us colour pictures that she drew for us of disciples and donkeys. She asked questions that made you feel uncomfortable, such as 'Are you stupid boy?', and questions that had only one answer, such as 'Do you think Jesus was a good person?', 'Don't you think the Bible is interesting children?', 'Have you any idea what Jesus was thinking?'

She was very good at special questions too. These told you exactly what you should think, such as 'Would green be a better colour for this bit of the picture dear?' 'Would God like you to put your finger there?' Sometimes questions had answers that only Miss Overn knew, such as 'Do you know who Isaac's brother is?' Come to think of it I often did know the answer to these special questions – it was 'no'. When she asked the questions we would guess and guess. She would tell us 'Nearly', 'Nearly', 'Not quite dear' and sometimes in sharp tones 'You need to think child, think!' We thought she was scary and we thought she was very clever to know all the answers to so many questions.

When I look back on it now, I think of Sunday school as a kind of painting by numbers. Miss Overn knew which colours went where. She knew the numbers that told her where they went, but she never showed them to us. I sometimes think that she wanted us to think just like her. I am very pleased that I learned to think differently as I would not like to be like Miss Overn. I don't think I learned very much in Sunday school, except that I didn't much like it ... how clever Miss Overn was about Bibles ... oh, and that Jesus and God didn't much want me to think for myself.

The essential coaching skills

Will's experience of Bible class may strike a chord, not so much for the experience itself, but for the way adults ask questions of children and sometimes of each other. Our first experience of being asked questions plays its part in beginning to frame the way we ourselves use questions. The answer you receive depends upon the question you ask. But to receive the correct answer requires you to ask the correct question: for every one correct answer there are many hundreds of correct questions. Coaching is in part about using the correct questions in the correct manner.

The story of Miss Overn may represent an old concept of teachers and certainly a characterization that many of us can identify with. Fortunately the situation in the UK has now moved to a more accessible and human model of interaction in classrooms.

There are four core skills in coaching practice:

- listening
- reflecting
- clarifying
- questioning.

Let us take each skill in turn and examine how it can be used to bring out the best in your colleagues, students and institution.

Listening

 To really listen is to offer another person a moment of unconditional and total presence

How often are we frustrated by our partner, colleague or child when they are clearly not listening? The tell-tale signs of missing eye contact, lack of response, interruptions, suggested solutions and so the list goes on. Being listened to can be a rare occurrence. When someone is really listening to you, there is a feeling of being special, of being understood. In coaching it is this focus, this empathy and active attention to the person you are coaching, that is the coach's most important skill. We actually create a space to think.

Conversations in everyday life can be characterized by one-upmanship, talking over another's sentence end and the finishing of another's sentence by the 'listener'. The misinterpretation of what someone has said because of the interference of the listener's own personal expectations or experiences is all too common.

The decisions we make when listening have an impact on the shared experience of the coach and the coached. How we respond to what we hear, see and feel when we listen is the impact. We may do nothing, but this still affects the person we are coaching. We may choose to reflect back what has been said or clarify whether we have understood it accurately. We may also respond with a question. Coaching is as much about knowing when to interrupt as it is about knowing when to listen. Silence is actually processing time.

There are four types of listening:

- reflexive listening
- external listening
- intuitive listening
- holding silence.

Reflexive listening

This is what the coaches hear in their own minds about themselves. A constant chatter goes on inside your head; some of this is in response to what you are listening to from outside and some from your own daily self-talk.

We say a great deal to ourselves internally, so it is important when we are listening to others to be aware of what is potentially interfering with our listening from within. Issues and ideas that you hear from others often trigger internal dialogue. That is fine – you would not be human if it did not happen. What does matter is what you do next with this information. All too often in conversation we allow our own interpretations and experiences to come to the surface and we bring them into the conversation. Remember that when you are coaching, you are helping someone else to be successful and your own issues have no place there. So be aware of your reflexive listening and prevent it from getting in the way of what the person being coached is saying.

There is a cardinal rule in non-directive coaching which is that we do not step ahead of the person we are coaching and plan the route to a solution for them. If we think ahead and plan a solution we formulate questions that steer rather than promote learning. An individual will pick this up and realize that they are in fact being directed. This closes down the freedom to think and will derail the coaching process. The key challenge for many trainee coaches to learn is that we must silence our inner agenda in order to solve the problem ahead of the individual we coach. When we allow ourselves to be curious, to ask innocent questions and to be with people not ahead of them, we support them to learn about their situation fully. When we problem-bust for them in our minds, our questioning becomes directive – it closes thinking rather than opens it. We become quickly frustrated that individuals are not moving in the direction that we want them to. It leads us to communicate solutions and frustrations in verbal and non-verbal ways. Coaching is a process of helping that goes deeper than problem-busting. It is about us understanding our beliefs and adjusting our behaviours to meet our best performances. Only the person being coached can fully appreciate this level of complexity, and if we think we know the answer for someone else, we are most probably just kidding ourselves.

If you want to derail the kind of deep learning that we are encouraging in this book, then solve problems in your head for people while they speak and be several steps ahead of what you think they are thinking. They will realize very quickly that you are not listening to them, you do not trust them to make their own decisions and you do not value their opinion. You will impact negatively on their self-esteem and confidence and they will end up half-heartedly trying your solution. On the other hand, be with them, be curious about everything they say, pick up on the words and metaphors they use and explore them together using open questions, and you will leave them feeling truly respected, valued and trusted. Above all they will find genuinely useful ways to improve their performance and develop thinking pathways that allow them to be more independent. In the authors' experience people will be highly motivated, completely sure about their path and totally committed to the goals they set. Clear your coaching mind to clear the coaching space, be in the moment and never ahead and you will create the space for real learning to happen.

Below are two dialogues that illustrate the impact of reflexive listening on coach and individual.

Case study: reflexive listening

A teacher coach and a Newly Qualified Teacher (NQT) are meeting to discuss the NQT's week. They are mid-session when the NQT raises an issue about a student's behaviour.

Part A: allowing the interference of internal dialogue

NQT	I'm having some behaviour problems with Carla in my Year 10 set.
Teacher coach	(*teacher's own internal dialogue kicks in*) Oh god not her, I have loads of hassle with her too. She just won't sit still and she's always disturbing my lesson.
NQT	(*shoulders drop and facial expression becomes more serious*) I just don't know what to do.
Teacher coach	(*again internal dialogue operates*) I've tried just about everything and am at the end of my tether as well! I'm not sure I can help here.
NQT	So even you find her impossible? And you've been teaching for much longer than me.
Teacher coach	Oh yes, she's really difficult – pretty much unmanageable in my opinion.
NQT	So there isn't much point trying then? What should I do?
Teacher coach	I don't know. But I'm sure we'll think of something.

Here the sharing of internal talk sets up a feeling of shared hopelessness about the situation. This is something that can occur in conversations between people who share the same issues, and where coaches allow themselves to be strongly associated with the problem.

Part B: an alternative approach where reflexive listening is used to decide what to do about internal dialogue triggered by the coaching situation.

NQT	I'm having some behaviour problems with Carla in my Year 10 set.
Teacher coach	*(hears self-talk about her own problems with this student and decides to ignore them because they may be unproductive thoughts in helping the NQT)* Tell me about her behaviour.
NQT	Well, she's a great kid, one of the most switched on in that group, but she will cause a scene. The trouble is when I tell her to spit her chewing gum out in class she gets really angry and it disrupts the whole class.
Teacher coach	*(remembers a similar incident in her own classroom with Carla and how she dealt with it – chooses to say nothing about it)* How would you like things to be?
NQT	I'd like Carla to behave appropriately in lessons.
Teacher coach	OK, what's happening right now?
NQT	Well, she comes in with chewing gum in her mouth, I yell at her and she goes ballistic – my lesson is ruined.
Teacher coach	What makes her mad?
NQT	*(long pause)* I think … *(smiles)* … it's me yelling at her.
Teacher coach	What are you thinking right now?
NQT	That I'm going about this the wrong way. If I react differently to the chewing gum, she'll react differently to me.

In the next five minutes, the NQT had come up with a strategy to deal with Carla with a lower level intervention. The result was a greatly improved relationship between her and Carla over the following months.

External listening

This is what the coach hears from the person they are coaching – the words they say and how they say them. A person's preferred way of experiencing the world (visual, auditory or kinesthetic) is picked up along with all the other information they are telling you. This gives valuable clues as to how the coach responds. Matching the sensory nature of the language another person uses helps them to believe you are listening.

Intuitive listening

This is what the coach feels intuitively about the person they are coaching – what the person being coached is not saying. At the intuitive level, we are listening for areas in the conversation that are avoided and for patterns that may emerge as we listen. We can then draw the person's attention to these patterns.

Case study: *intuitive listening*

At a senior team meeting headteacher Lucy asked a colleague how he felt about the proposed cashless cafeteria system. His reply was 'I think it's a good … idea.' Lucy picked up on the emphasis on his last word. She was about to move on to seek Anne's opinion, but sensed that there was more that he wanted to say. Pausing, she encouraged him, 'I sense a "but", David.' 'Yes there's a big "but" …' and he went on to outline his concerns.

Listening to, recognizing and acting on tonal clues from individuals can be an important way of getting at what people really think. Too often we ignore these and ride over the beliefs that hold back the thinker from committing to action.

Holding silence

Typically we do not allow others sufficient time to think. The deeper thinking processes that access beliefs and bring about changes in perspective and action are often arrested by the interruption of a well-meaning colleague. The most potent coaching interactions are those where the coach remains silent for long periods, but the person being coached is allowed to think very deeply. Building courage to say what a person really thinks is part of the process of making changes. Courage can be arrested by the premature intervention of a coach.

Case study: *holding silence*

Steven, a Year 9 boy, was often getting into trouble in class. He was rude to teachers and drew attention to himself when open learning activities were set. He had been referred to the head of year, Tony, by a number of members of staff.

During the course of the discussion that took place between Steven and Tony, it became apparent that Steven lacked direction and purpose in school. Tony asked him questions about school and what he thought of it. Immediately, negative comments came from Steven. Tony then asked him what he wanted to do with his future. Steven replied quickly, 'I suppose I'll work at the brush factory like my dad and mum – it's close and they get decent money.'

Tony sensed the downbeat tone in Steven's voice. 'Steven, what do you really want to do with your life?' Steven paused and the head of year watched his facial expressions as he considered the question. Time seemed to pass slowly for Tony and he felt like jumping in with another question. But he waited. After about a minute, and just as Tony was about to interject, he noticed Steven sit up proudly and say, 'What I really want to do is join the army, as an officer.' Tony asked him, 'How will you get there?' Steven then proceeded to discuss the steps he might need to take, beginning with finding some information about how he might join. The transformation in Steven's attitude was immediately apparent. As he left Tony's room, he turned to him and said, 'You know, Sir, I've wanted to join the army for so long, but my dad always said it's a dead end, so I've kept quiet about it. This is the first time I've said anything to anyone about it – thanks, Sir.'

Over the coming months, with further support, Steven transformed his attitude in class and around school. He joined the army cadets. His grades gradually inched up as he became more focused on what he really wanted to achieve, and teachers commented on the much more positive attitude he had towards his learning. Had Tony interjected and disrupted Steven's thought processes in that crucial minute, it might have been months before he found the courage and the opportunity to articulate his wishes.

Silence is important in coaching. You will note that silence is recorded in both the exemplar dialogue from those being coached and the secondary source dialogue included here. This simple expression of a pause in the coaching flow is euphemistic. Silence is powerful because it is essentially not empty space but in fact processing-time. Processing time is the time we take to receive new information, decide how it fits with our model of the world, formulate an opinion and then surface the response in words before saying it. It can, in reality, take considerable time. In your work as a coach, trainer and teacher provide processing time when you want people to think deeply about an idea. Give them permission to be silent; for example, 'Take what time you need to think about this.' When coaches succumb to the temptation to fill the silence, they seriously interrupt the flow of thinking and prevent often important realizations from taking place. Interruptions stop learning.

Myles Downey (2003) recognizes that silence is often only an external factor. It is usually the case that when someone is silent, they are in fact engaging with an internal dialogue. He notes that 'novice coaches are often afraid of silences in their coaching and will jump in with more speech or questions'. He recognizes the importance of silence in processing ideas.

He also recognizes 'another kind of silence that occurs when the individual does not know what he is supposed to be doing'. This is the time to move the session on. Eye focus in the middle distance can show that individuals are in thinking mode. Often the breathing can become quick and shallow when someone is uncomfortable with the silence rather than using it. They may hum or use impotent phrases like 'well, anyway' or sounds that help fill the space – 'mmm' or 'eh'.

Some recent research on eye contact and young children conducted by Dr Gwyneth Doherty-Sneddon at the University of Stirling suggested that 'gaze aversion' was part of how a young person minimized distractions while listening to instructions. For many youngsters the phrase 'Look at me when I'm talking to you' gets in the way of their ability to absorb mental load. As a concentration technique, looking away after being asked a question was shown to be particularly successful with very young children.

In using silence in coaching it is important to make people aware at the outset that it is OK to take time to think things through – silence is OK.

One person took to saying 'I don't know' after every question he was asked when being coached. The coach's initial reaction was to ask another question. Very soon the coach became concerned that she was not succeeding as a coach. She changed tack and the next time he said 'I don't know', she waited. Then when he said 'I don't know' again after a few seconds, the coach responded, 'OK, Ali, I want you to take all the time you need to think about this question and, if it helps, write down some ideas. Just let me know when you have had enough time.' Three or four minutes later he said, 'All right, I'm ready.' 'What have you got?' asked the coach. 'I have six ideas,' he replied. And he had and they were really good ones!

Chandler (2002) explains that the support in coaching comes from 'high quality non-judgemental listening'. In this sense the coach is using their own silence throughout the process of coaching. Against this backdrop, one might say that while there may be audible silence in coaching, it is very rare for there to be intellectual and emotional silence. Great coaches recognize this and allow people space to process this information. Curiously, many coaches report that at the end of a coaching session, when they ask what an individual has learned today, the person being coached will often come out with things that were not articulated during the session. This interesting phenomenon is called 'delayed disclosure'. It is worth mentioning that for every delayed disclosure that we hear, there may be others we do not hear. It is this knowledge that properly conducted coaching processes trigger changes in thinking that are not immediately articulated that sustains the coach powerfully when individuals appear to make little progress within a session and adds to the interest that coaches have in the process.

Reflecting

One of the difficulties people have in making decisions is that they think in so many different directions they lose track of the most important ideas. Coaches can help a person to track their thinking by periodically reflecting back what they have said. It is important when doing this that the coach uses the words that the person used as closely as possible. Typical reflections could go like this: 'I notice you are saying that you are still getting up at 8 a.m. You have said in the past that you wished to rise at 7 a.m to give yourself time to get ready for school.'

Asking how the reflection sounds is important. Checking that what you have said accurately reflects what others have meant can also help to clarify your understanding. It can also help them to new insights into their own understanding.

Case study: reflecting

In a discussion between a governor and deputy headteacher, the governor uses the skill of reflection to help the deputy head stay on track with her thinking.

'What I really want us to do is provide the students with a powerful student council that will give them the opportunity to express their opinions and tell us what their needs are,' said the deputy.

'I hear you say that you want students to have a council so that they can express what they are thinking and tell you what their needs are. Yet earlier in this conversation you said you were tired of hearing about the petty issues about toilets and school rules from members of Year 11,' reflected the governor.

The deputy paused. 'There's a bit of conflict here isn't there!' she said smiling.

'What are you noticing?' replied the governor.

'That I'm ignoring many of the things that students find important, that affect their everyday lives. If I want to have a truly effective student council, I have to be open to all their concerns and be prepared to listen and act. That would make the council really effective.'

Clarifying

Typically the coach will clarify by asking a question: 'So are you saying that you feel unable to get up earlier because you need eight hours sleep?' This gives the person you are coaching the opportunity to agree or contest your understanding of what they have said. Clarification checks that what you understand about what has been said is what the other person actually meant. As with reflecting, clarification often has as much impact on the understanding of the person being coached as on the coach. It is the only time in coaching that we would use closed questions.

Questioning

After listening, questioning is perhaps the next most important skill of the coach. The correctly formulated question can have the effect of opening up new channels of thinking and removing blocks to progress.

With the exception of some clarifying questions, all other questions in the coach's toolkit are open ones. They begin with 'what', 'when', 'who', 'how' and 'where'. They encourage extended responses based on deep thinking.

As you coach, try to rediscover that child-like curiosity you had when you were very young. Take nothing for granted and maintain focus on open questions, utilize the essential tool of curiosity to help those you coach to overcome limiting beliefs and enhance their performance. Whitworth et al. (1998) say that 'coaching is about naturally drawing attention to what the individual is curious about'. They outline the difference between coaching questions that are 'curious' and those that are 'fact-finding' or 'information-gathering'. Curious questions provide insight and encourage individuals to resolve challenging thoughts and move forward.

Curious versus leading

Curious questions help coaches to encourage deeper understanding in others. The following table summarizes the formulation and impact of curious and leading questions.

| Open/curious questions | Open questions beginning: What, why, when how, who, where | These questions are open ended and can stimulate deep personal insight. |
| Closed/leading questions | Leading questions begin: Is it …, Don't you think …, Would you agree … | These questions are closed and close down avenues of personal reflection. |

Although we have identified 'why' questions as curious and open, they have some limitations. In the first instance the 'why' question can narrow the field of thought. It can suggest, like a closed question, that there is a specific right answer to the question. Additionally, 'why' questions can be invasive. They can evoke a defensive response and this can affect the rapport between the coach and the individual. An alternative is the use of 'what' in place of 'why'. For example, a coach might ask 'Why did you do that?' and may get a defensive response that avoids the key issue. If instead one asks 'What did you aim for when you responded in that way?' followed by 'What was the outcome of your response', the question can be easier to answer truthfully.

Zeus and Skiffington (2003) concur, urging 'caution against the use of the "why" questions'. It is generally agreed that why questions can generate defensiveness in an individual and 'can lead to a never-ending cycle of inference and speculation'. Asking 'why' can also 'deteriorate into an intellectual competition between the coach and client'. They note that 'the sensitivity, warmth and curiosity displayed by the coach can offset many of these potential hazards'. In other words using 'why' is a judgement call and depends on the relationship you have with the person you are coaching.

The closed questions, at best, carry the coach's beliefs or opinions and, at worst, can be coercive and directional. This can create tensions when you are being coached in deciding the direction to move forward. Here the coach is not the 'empty vessel' or impartial listener that they ought to be.

The following dialogue represents a coaching conversation between a teacher and a student. It illustrates the use of open questioning to enable the student to think through a challenge and resolve it for himself. You may like to consider how the responses of the teacher compare to your own in a similar situation.

Case study: open questions

A Year 10 student, Jon, came to his form teacher appearing depressed.

Teacher   Hi, Jon, how are you?

Jon   I'm fine.

Teacher   I'm noticing that you look a bit sad. How are you really?

Jon   Not so good, actually. I'm feeling a bit low.

Teacher   Tell me about it.

Jon   Well, all my friends seem to have stopped liking me.

Teacher   What leads you to say that?

Jon	Well, over the last six months they seem to avoid me and they don't hang around with me at school or call for me at home. They don't like me.
Teacher	What would you like?
Jon	To have my friends back. I miss having a laugh.
Teacher	What are your strengths, Jon?
Jon	Well ... er ... I'm getting really good marks in all my subjects – I'm up to C and D in everything now and I'm doing really well in the footy team.
Teacher	Excellent, tell me about that.
Jon	Well, I've just got the hang of things in school over the last six months and I seem to be doing really well at sport.
Teacher	What other strengths do you have?
Jon	I'm confident, yes ... confident.
Teacher	Yes you are. That comes across. So you're strong academically, obviously clever and very confident. How can you use these strengths to help you with the problems you're having with your friends?
Jon	That's where I'm stuck. I just don't know why they're behaving like this. Even my best friend Phil has blocked me out.
Teacher	OK, you really want your friends back, but you don't know why they've blocked you out. Jon, if you secretly knew what the problem was, what might it be?
Jon	(*very long silence*) I ... I do know what it is.
Teacher	(*silence*)
Jon	I ... I've kind of been getting a bit cocky since my grades have gone up and I've been saying stuff to my friends.
Teacher	(*silence, warm supportive smile*)
Jon	I've been a bit too full of myself and I think they got fed up with the put-downs from me all the time.
Teacher	OK, Jon, where do you go from here?
Jon	That's the scary bit – I feel a bit if an idiot. I suppose I have to talk to them. That's scary.
Teacher	How will you use your strengths to help you?
Jon	Well, I know I can be confident, so I suppose I just have to go for it.
Teacher	What would make this easier?
Jon	(*pauses*) If I spoke to Phil first and then each person individually, so all four knew.
Teacher	What will you say?
Jon	That I've been an idiot and I'm sorry.
Teacher	How will you feel saying that?
Jon	Nervous and stupid. I can't be an idiot with grades like I've got can I?
Teacher	What will you say?
Jon	(*pauses*) I suppose if I hold off on saying I've been stupid, but ask them why they've blocked me out.
Teacher	How will you react to what they say?

Jon	Well, if I want my friends back, I'll say I'm sorry.
Teacher	What will sorry mean?
Jon	Mmm … It'll have to mean that I'm going to be different with them in future.
Teacher	How will you be different?
Jon	(*pause*) I need to think about that quite hard.
Teacher	(notices the time and needs to wrap up the conversation) OK, so what have you decided to do?
Jon	I'm going to think about how to behave better to my friends.
Teacher	When will you do that?
Jon	Today and tomorrow.
Teacher	What else?
Jon	I'm going to call Phil and ask if we can meet up. I'm going to ask him why he's blocked me out and see what he says.
Teacher	When will you do that?
Jon	In a couple of day's time, on Thursday evening – he's at home then.
Teacher	That's great, Jon. How would you feel about coming to see me again once you've done this?
Jon	Yes, that'll be really helpful. I'll find you as soon as I've spoken to Phil. Thanks, I feel so much better.

The outcome of this coaching conversation was that Jon spoke to Phil. Phil was initially hostile but Jon had decided that he should let him speak his mind. He then apologized. Phil accepted his apology and agreed to speak to the other three friends. Jon was re-integrated into the group and his responses to his friends became more sensitive. He continued to enjoy improved performances in academic and sporting terms.

In this example conversation, notice how Jon is able to examine his own weakness while still remaining positive and forward-focused. He is able to answer questions honestly and plan his next step, using in a sense the very characteristic that had created his difficulty – his confidence – to resolve his issue. His teacher says very little. She asks a small number of short questions and reflects what he has said. She draws attention to his strengths and challenges his self-deprecation at one point.

In Chapter 7 you will find further explanation of the nature of questioning in coaching. You may wish to come back to the dialogue above and re-read it once you have a further insight into the STRIDE coaching model and the range of questions available to coaches. In Chapter 7 we identify the eight core open question types and provide a bank of questions that you can use with the STRIDE coaching model outlined in Chapter 6.

With practice, coaches learn how to listen on four levels, to clarify and reflect, and to use the right question at the right time to motivate and support those they coach. This may seem daunting but with increased awareness and practice you will further develop your capability. After all, these approaches are not new, they are just finely honed versions of the communication skills you already possess.

Summary

Miss Overn, with her closed questioning and painting by hidden numbers, missed so many opportunities to inspire and develop Will and his friends in the Sunday school. Her insistence on closed questioning, her critical tone and content, ensured an insecurity that mitigated against learning. In non-directive coaching, coaches use the following techniques:

▶ *The four key skills of listening, reflecting, questioning and clarifying*

▶ *Active listening on four levels: reflexive, external, intuitive and holding silence*

▶ *Reflecting back what others have said using their own words*

▶ *A range of specialized question types – these are explored further in Chapter 7*

▶ *Open questions – although these are used almost exclusively, a coach may clarify by using closed questions.*

Questions

1   *What coaching skills are displayed in the last case study?*

2   *What types of questions are being used in the last case study? What is the impact of each question?*

3   *What has struck you most about the coaching skills section of the book? How will you enhance your communication in future?*

4   *You are asked to help a colleague who has some problems with time management and is often overdue with deadlines. How would you approach this? List the questions you might use to support them towards change.*

5   *Which questions are best for generating options when we are coaching?*

6   *Can you recall a situation when you took someone else's advice and it turned out to be unsuitable for you, though it had worked for them? What was the outcome?*

Masterclass

▶ *Allow processing-time.*

▶ *Look for signs within a silence as to whether it is productive or whether the individual is unclear what to do. In the latter situation move the coaching on.*

▶ *As you converse with others in the next few days, notice the reflexive listening that goes on in your own mind.*

▶ *Help people to feel further at ease with you by adding the phrase 'Take the time that you need' to the end of a question, then repeat the question again.*

▶ *A great way to get someone to sum up what they have learned with you is to say 'Could you crystallize what you have learned for me?'*

▶ *Short open questions are often most powerful. They have the least direction and so allow individuals to think more freely. Try: Where are you? What's next? What do you want? What could you do? What do you need?*

▶ *Notice how often people around you use closed questions. Practise turning their closed questions around in your head into open questions.*

▶ *Spend time with others where you ask nothing but open questions.*

▶ *Practise being silent with others after you have asked a question. Notice the self-talk that goes on in your head when you begin to feel uncomfortable. With people you know well, practise leaving the silence longer than feels comfortable and notice what benefits arise.*

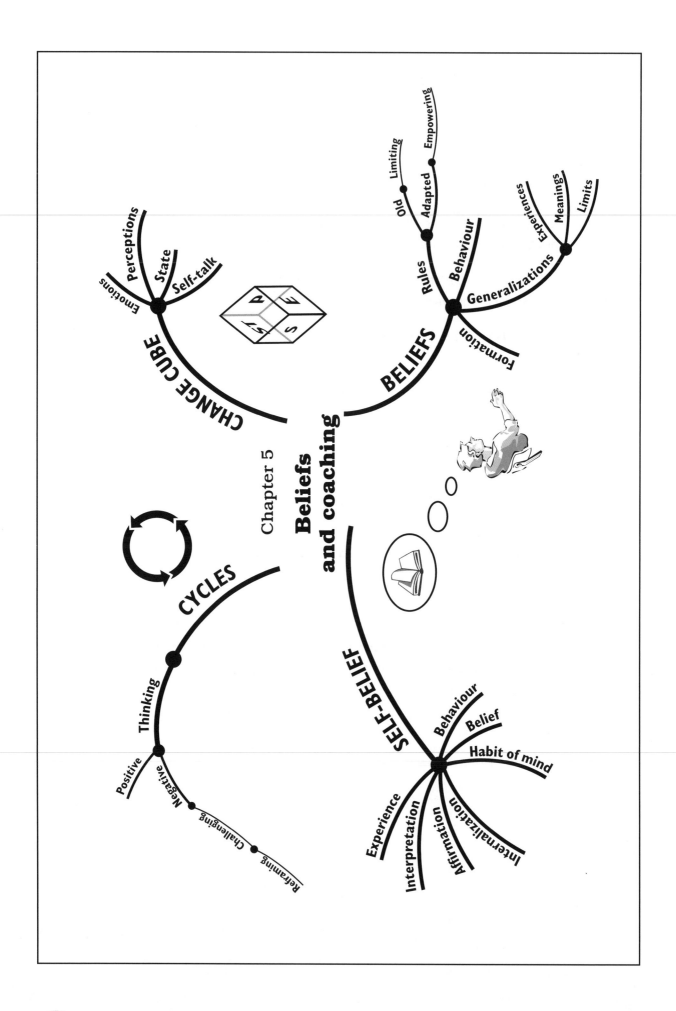

CHANGE CUBE
- Emotions
- Perceptions
- State
- Self-talk

BELIEFS
- Rules
- Behaviour
  - Old
  - Limiting
  - Adapted
  - Empowering
- Generalizations
  - Experiences
  - Meanings
  - Limits
- Formation

CYCLES
- Thinking
  - Positive
  - Negative
    - Challenging
    - Reframing

SELF-BELIEF
- Behaviour
- Belief
- Habit of mind
- Internalization
- Affirmation
- Interpretation
- Experience

Chapter 5

Beliefs and coaching

Chapter 5

Beliefs and coaching

IN THIS CHAPTER YOU WILL LEARN:

- what beliefs are
- how beliefs form
- why the beliefs that formed yesterday are so important to us today
- how presuppositions in our language tell others what we believe about them
- how we can alter beliefs using the Change Cube approach

PREVIEW QUESTIONS:

- In what ways do beliefs form?
- How do experiences from our past affect the decisions we make today?
- Why can we seldom be really sure about the beliefs that underlie what people say?
- How do you identify and challenge the beliefs of individuals in your organization in pursuit of improved performance?
- What beliefs are you taking into your work and how are they helping you? How are they holding you back?

Take a look inside and let them go …

It was a balmy summer's evening, around dusk, as Jack walked slowly along a dusty winding track on his long journey. Lifting his left foot only partially off the ground to reduce the risk of the dangling sole falling from his shoe, he day-dreamed. As he rounded a sharp bend, his thoughts somewhere else, he stumbled suddenly, falling forwards. As he recovered himself, he looked around and realized he had fallen on an old man lying by the road side. 'I'm so sorry old man,' said Jack dusting the old man and himself down. The old man stood up and introduced himself. Jack reciprocated and offered to carry his knapsack. The knapsack looked so heavy. The old man declined and they walked together for several miles.

As dark set in the old man asked to sit down.

'I'm tired,' he said. 'I've been carrying this bag so far.'

'I would be happy to carry it for you,' said Jack.

But the old man declined once again. After a rest, they carried on along the road by the light of a lamp, chatting as they went. A few more miles down the road and the old man said 'I'm so weary, my pack is heavy, and I must stop to sleep.' Jack felt tired too and they both fell asleep under an old oak beside the road.

The next morning Jack awoke before the old man, who was snoring loudly. There in front of him was the knapsack. Jack was fascinated to know what was inside — it must be so valuable for the old man to decline letting him carry it.

He wrestled with his conscience for a while before checking the old man and then gently slid the knapsack towards him. He was struck by its lightness. He undid the drawstrings and was surprised to find that the knapsack contained nothing but straw and a few seeds, a seashell and a piece of paper. As Jack stared in surprise, the old man awoke and smiled.

'Interesting eh Jack?' Startled, Jack looked up.

'I wasn't stealing anything,' he said.

'I know you weren't Jack,' replied the old man.

'Why is this so heavy old man, the contents are so small?' asked Jack.

'It's heavy because those things are my thoughts, bad and old, been and gone, things from the past, but I carry them with me wherever I go,' said the old man.

Jack looked thoughtful and paused a long time before he replied, 'Maybe it's time to let them go.'

'Maybe it is time,' said the old man and smiled.

The old man stood up and lifted the knapsack, he walked over the track to a stream on the other side and slowly, carefully emptied the contents into the water, watching them float away.

The two of them walked all morning that day, a spring in their steps. The old man relieved and happy.

We carry so many burdens in our knapsacks for such a long time. Take a look inside and let them go …

Developing solutions – the Change Cube

This chapter explores the impact of beliefs on behaviour. To consistently change an individual's behaviour, it is necessary for them to challenge and modify their belief system. In coaching we work to a very simple model of changing beliefs and behaviour that is summarized in the Change Cube shown in Figure 5.1.

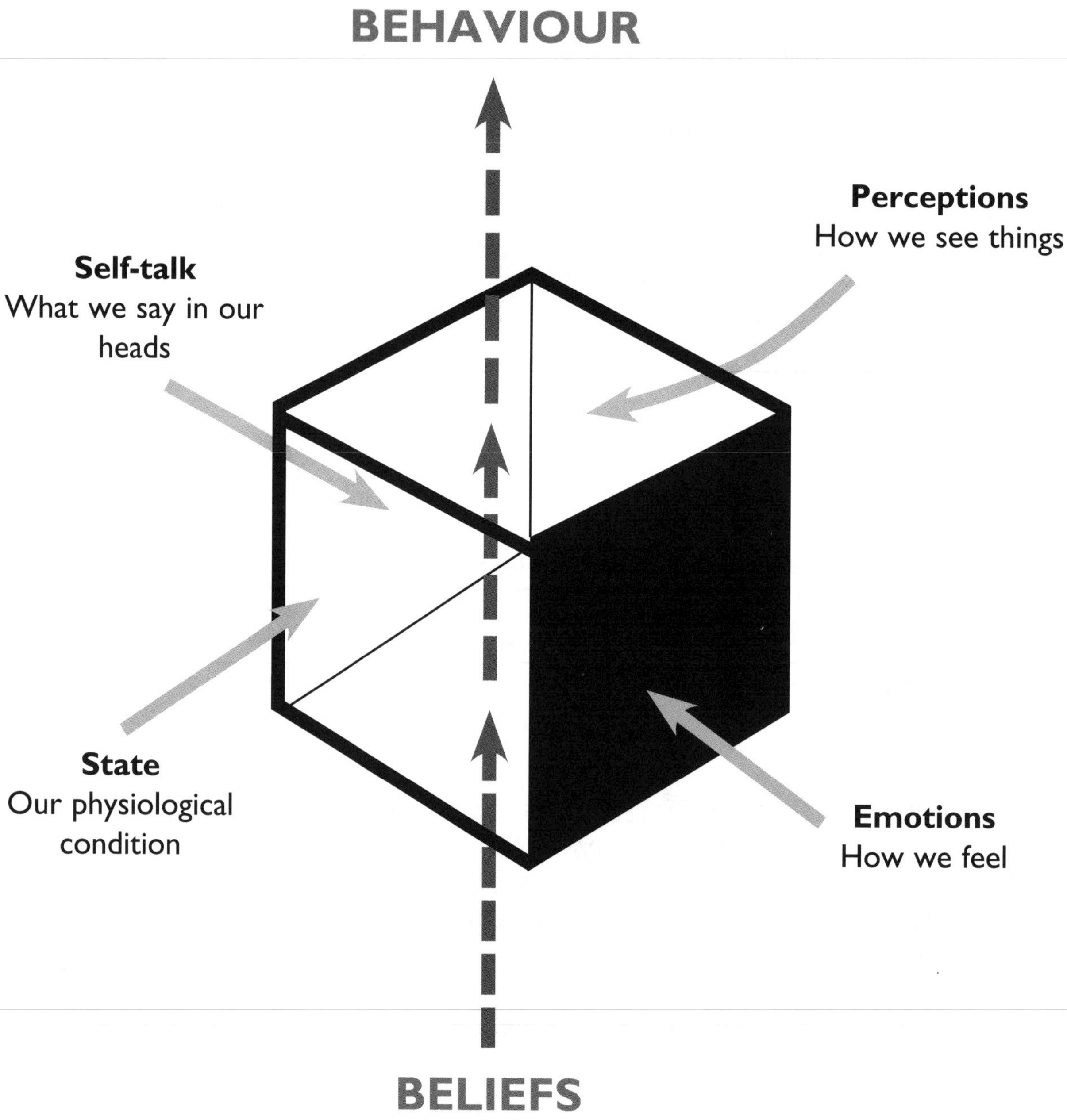

BEHAVIOUR

Perceptions
How we see things

Self-talk
What we say in our heads

State
Our physiological condition

Emotions
How we feel

BELIEFS

Figure 5.1 The Change Cube – © G. Kewley and W. Thomas 2004

In this Change Cube beliefs are shown as the base or foundation of the box. The lid is shown as the behaviour and the sides of the box represent the factors that, when changed, will affect the behaviour and the beliefs interchangeably. In other words, change the beliefs and you change the behaviour: change the behaviour and you change the beliefs. The routes to altering beliefs and behaviour are through:

- changing self-talk (what we say to ourselves in our heads)
- changing physiological state (physical position, hydration, nutrition, and so on)
- changing perception (the pictures we see of a situation or problem and how we view that problem)
- changing emotions (what we feel about the situation or problem and the physical sensations associated with it).

When coaches help individuals and groups to modify their self-talk, perceptions, physiological state, or feelings, they directly affect the beliefs and therefore the behaviour of the individual. Throughout the remainder of this book the techniques outlined provide various approaches to modifying these factors of personal experience. The Change Cube in its own right represents a useful model for identifying and shifting limitations on performance.

Before discussing the range of techniques available to coaches to broker change, the nature of beliefs will first be explored. Put forward here is a simple model of belief development that is in no way an attempt to embody the wide and varied research into the field, but is a basic navigational tool to help the reader understand where the authors start from.

The nature of beliefs

Beliefs are ideas we no longer question. They are the thought programmes running in the background of our minds, moving between our conscious and unconscious. Each belief summarizes an experience from our past, a generalization in a given situation, a way of achieving something or avoiding it. Each belief provides a shorthand instruction for how to behave.

Some of these beliefs are great at bringing us closer to what we need, and others, out-moded and out-dated, create anxiety and discomfort for ourselves and others. Some of these beliefs cause us to react inappropriately and this can hold us back from our best performances. Understanding our belief systems can enable us to filter out and shift the beliefs that hold us back and utilize those that propel us forward more effectively.

According to Dilts (1990) beliefs come in three main forms:

- as generalizations about a relationship between experiences
- as generalizations about meanings
- as generalizations about limits.

In each case the common denominator is the generalization. We construct internal rules about relationships, meanings and limits as a result of our habitual interpretation of experiences and in order to ease the process of decision making.

- 'Bad behaviour in schools is caused by caffeinated drinks' represents a generalization between relationships: cause and effect.
- 'I am a bad teacher' is a generalization about meanings.
- 'I can learn to juggle two balls but I can't learn to juggle three' is a generalization about perceived limits.

We make sense of the complex world around us by creating simple rules for past experiences that we sometimes use to interpret new experiences. Had we to rationalize and logically process each new decision in our lives, we might run into immense pressures for time. Beliefs become shortcuts to decision making and as generalizations help us to react quickly without making prolonged logical decisions.

So generalizing helps us act more efficiently, allowing thought processing to be reduced and making many decisions we take to be made quickly. Or does it? A good proportion of our beliefs, on the whole, serve us well in making decisions. However, there are some beliefs that we hold that make generalizations that do not fully fit the situation or that are not based on truly logical foundations. These kinds of beliefs can hold us back and are referred to as limiting beliefs.

Limiting beliefs can be about a number of things. For example:

- personality (confidence, eccentricity, sense of humour)
- image (size, weight, skin tone, shape)
- intelligence (our IQ, that of others, common sense, artistic ability)
- other people (friends, enemies, bosses, parents, children)
- groups of people (with beards, company directors, double-glazing salespeople, the old)
- institutions (police force, schools, Inland Revenue, role-playing games clubs)
- opportunity (my weight held me back, if only I had tried harder at school, others had a better start in life than me)
- performance (I can achieve a B grade, my class can't learn, others always succeed and I fail).

What would you add to this list?

The psychology of self-efficacy or self-belief is well developed and complex.

Experience:	you have an experience which impacts on your conscious awareness.
Interpretation:	you attempt to make sense of this experience.
Affirmation:	you test this sense-making with and through influences and influencers in your immediate world.
Internalization:	you begin to adapt your thinking as a consequence.
Habit of mind:	your thinking hardens and becomes a habitual form of response.
Belief:	you generate patterns of belief to support this mode of thinking.
Behaviour:	future responses are shaped by such beliefs.

The first example that follows is of a five-year-old boy experiencing school. Without denying the complexity of influencing factors, let us take the possibility of this pattern of experience and response as illustrative of what we mean.

Experience:	the boy is expected to sit still and listen for long periods of time.
Interpretation:	the boy attempts to make sense of his unhappiness at having to do this.
Affirmation:	influencers at home and elsewhere signify their own frustrations at having a similar experience.
Internalization:	the boy begins to 'understand' why he does not enjoy school.
Habit of mind:	the boy begins to 'believe' that he never will enjoy school and starts to invest in this belief.
Belief:	the boy 'believes' he is predestined – like his parents before him – to dislike, and therefore fail at, school and behaves accordingly.
Behaviour:	the boy's future responses are shaped by the prophetic quality of his belief.

The second example is from a teacher who has convinced herself that some children are victims of circumstance and, as such, are beyond learning productively while at any school.

Experience:	over a period of years this teacher has been verbally abused while teaching her classes.
Interpretation:	this teacher understands that children's behaviour has got worse and that teaching has become more challenging as a consequence.
Affirmation:	this teacher sees colleagues around her who share a similar experience.
Internalization:	this teacher begins to 'understand' that some children, and therefore some classes, are beyond control,
Habit of mind:	gradually this teacher begins to 'believe' that the issue of control is the shaping factor in her success as a teacher,
Belief:	this teacher invests in the 'belief' that children's changed behaviour over the years is outside her control, therefore there is nothing she can do to avoid verbal abuse.
Behaviour:	in the future this teacher will do what she can to avoid teaching.

The third example is from a teacher who has convinced herself that some children are victims of circumstance and, as such, need even more support to learn productively while at any school.

Experience:	over a period of years this teacher has been verbally abused while teaching her classes.
Interpretation:	this teacher understands that children's behaviour has got worse and that teaching has become more challenging as a consequence.
Affirmation:	this teacher sees colleagues around her who share a similar experience.
Internalization:	this teacher begins to 'understand' that some children, and therefore some classes, need a wider variety of teaching methods if they are to be helped.
Habit of mind:	gradually this teacher begins to 'believe' that the issue of control is the shaping factor in her success as a teacher.

Belief: this teacher invests in the 'belief' that children's changed behaviour over the years is within her control, therefore to avoid verbal abuse she must be even more skilled in her use of a variety of teaching techniques.

Behaviour: in the future this teacher will do what she can to develop her teaching.

Beliefs emerge through an inter-play of conscious direction to the data that surround us and unconsciously through the affirmation of response. We can allow beliefs to harden and then direct our everyday thoughts, responses and behaviours. In other words we can allow them to become rules by which we live. Often (though by no means always) beliefs develop their own attend para-language that we hear in our heads.

Ten common self-talk phrases that expose limiting beliefs

1 I'm no good at maths. (I am not mathematically intelligent.)

2 My son always looks unhappy. (I have made him unhappy.)

3 Other people get all the opportunities, I always lose out. (I am unlucky.)

4 My parents were mean to me and I'm always going to be scarred by the experience. (I am a disadvantaged person.)

5 I'm always the last person to know any gossip that's going around. (I'm less popular than other people.)

6 I'm fat and stupid. (I am worthless.)

7 Everyone around me has nice clothes – I always look untidy. (I'm unattractive.)

8 I can't cry about things that are happening to me. (I am insensitive.)

9 This school is useless. (This school does not meet my needs.)

10 The headteacher is failing. (I don't like her, because she is more successful than me.)

Of course the same statement can have a range of different beliefs underpinning it. For example, 'My son always looks unhappy' can have a range of beliefs attached to it, such as:

I was unhappy as a child so I have passed it on.

My parents argued and fell out all the time.

It's just how we are as a family.

We don't talk about it as it makes things worse.

It means we have a harder time making and keeping friends.

I am useless at making and keeping friends.

I don't want to talk about this as it opens up a can of worms.

Things are as they are meant to be.

Having no friends makes me unhappy.

Some beliefs are quite simple and logical, others are immensely complex and have flawed logic in them. No doubt you will be able to add further statements to the list. The point is that beliefs are personal and while we often find people who experience similar limiting self-talk, the belief and the origin related to that talk can vary widely. Beliefs are as varied as the experiences of the individuals who formed them. What is even more intriguing is that beliefs are seldom singular entities. They will often be combined together to form complex overlaps that we call belief systems.

The first belief on the common self-talk phrases list above might be multi-layered. For example, say that the child in question feared their father because of unpredictable behaviour, a belief about authority figures and unpredictability might develop as a rule. Then the father tells the boy to walk to the shop 300 metres away, but he has never set foot out of the house alone before, there is a fear about this trip around the unknown or fear of strangers and so on. On top of this is the feeling of pressure in dealing with money to buy a paper when the child is already in a state of high anxiety. The shopkeeper is busy and when the boy takes a long time to count his money he makes a remark in a sharp tone. The boy links that to counting, numbers and money and is humiliated by the experience in the shop. It might sound far-fetched but this is how complex beliefs systems can begin to develop. The boy's rules are then:

Money is humiliating.

Money and numbers are the same.

Money numbers and authority figures are unpredictable and make me feel anxious.

Numbers and authority figures make me anxious.

Teachers and numbers make me anxious and I can't do numbers when I am anxious.

I can't do maths.

These rules may not make complete sense to you or I, but that is the point about limiting beliefs, they often do not make sense because they are generalizations and miss out vital details and logical steps. Our memories are not perfect and our cognitive abilities as youngsters are still developing, so we delete, select and distort important details.

A coach working alongside an individual can work with the self-talk to help the individual overcome the limiting belief and adjust it or replace it with a new more appropriate idea. One very successful technique is the 'Specific Challenge'. When limiting self-talk is exposed by someone, challenge the statement with 'What exactly is it that …?' Follow the example below.

Case study: challenging

Child (or adult)	I can't do maths.
Coach	What exactly is it about maths that you can't do?
Child	Well, I get so nervous about subtracting.
Coach	What specifically is it about subtracting that gets you so nervous?
Child	It reminds me of counting money, getting change.' (*here's the belief association*)
Coach	So, if subtracting didn't remind you of money, what could you do then?

Child	I could feel relaxed and have a go.
Coach	So what could your first step be?
Child	I could relax before I do the maths.
Coach	OK, how could you relax?
Child	Well, thinking about being outdoors helps me relax.
Coach	OK, so before you do your sums, you could think about being outdoors. What could you think of when you think about being outdoors?
Child	Walking about in the fresh air.
Coach	Right, so what else could help you relax before your maths?
Child	I could take some deep breaths – I've seen others do that and it makes them calm.
Coach	Is there anything else?
Child	No.
Coach	So what will you do to relax before doing your sums?
Child	I'm going to think of being outside in the garden and take some deep breaths.
Coach	How many deep breaths do you need to take?
Child	Five breaths … yes, five.
Coach	OK, how would you feel about doing that now?
Child	(*smiles*) Yes, OK.
Coach	How do you feel now?
Child	Really good.
Coach	OK, just before you do your subtraction, what do you experience?
Child	(*thinks at length before speaking*) I hear a voice.
Coach	Tell me about the voice.
Child	It says you can't count backwards.
Coach	So it says you can't backwards. What else does it say?
Child	It says you can't count backwards when there's a teacher around.
Coach	When can you count backwards?
Child	When I'm playing games with my friends.
Coach	And what do you say to yourself when you count backwards with your friends?
Child	I don't say anything, I just do it.
Coach	How is that different to being with your teacher?
Child	My teacher scares me.
Coach	How does scary feel?
Child	It feels tense and nervous and uptight.
Coach	How would you like to feel in class?
Child	Happy and relaxed – like I am with my friends.

Coach	So what could you do to feel relaxed in class?
Child	Well, I could think of my friends and how good they make me feel and do my breathing, can't I!
Coach	That sounds great. So what are you doing now when you are with your teacher doing subtraction?
Child	I'm relaxing with my friends in class and breathing five times to feel relaxed.
Coach	What else are you doing?
Child	I'm telling the voice in my head to shut up.

The above dialogue is a real situation and the child concerned used the strategy she devised to great effect. The coach had some idea of the belief system that was operating for the girl, but did not get the full picture from the conversation. This is very often the case with coaching and the questioning really followed the girl's thoughts. As previously explained, excellent coaches intuitively follow their curiosity. In the session above it is unlikely that the coach helped the girl to fully understand her belief, but he enabled her to take the next step towards overcoming the limitation. She found that thinking about relaxing situations enabled her to relax and telling the voice in her head to be quiet enabled her to try the sums. Before telling the self-talk to be quiet she would not even begin. Without beginning, there was little hope of any success.

Extreme limiting beliefs can paralyse an individual's ability to act rationally. Phobias are powerful beliefs with (usually) high levels of generalization. In other words, significant details are omitted or not understood by the phobic individual. This allows some experiences to become so threatening that a powerful adrenal reaction is stimulated and a person overreacts to a situation as judged by those around them.

To his surprise, Will worked with two unconnected people within a four-week period with a phobia of puppets. Their fears were so strong that they were distracted away from the learning process they were engaged in and enjoying, and both felt an intense urge to leave the room.

One lady had a vivid memory of a time when she had been very scared at a birthday party as a small child. She explained that they had had a firework display and one of the fireworks had failed to ignite. Her father, wearing a glove puppet for fun, had gone back to the rocket when it suddenly exploded into the air almost hitting him. Her mother had been extremely distressed by this and her father had attempted to calm both his wife and his daughter by making light of the incident using the puppet's 'voice'. She assumed that the distress caused by the firework upsetting her mother had somehow been incorporated traumatically with the puppet. In the mind of a young child, a simple rule had been made on that day: puppets and fireworks are dangerous. This is the belief that she carried with her throughout her life.

Beliefs do not always have words associated with them, sometimes there is no internal dialogue obvious to the belief-holder. In working with these kinds of belief, some of the advanced techniques included in Chapter 9 are helpful. The authors have often found that when people are asked to give a voice to their actions or to a moment just before they act, they use an 'if and then' statement. For example, '*If* I touch cats, *then* I will get bitten/scratched.'

We use the model that assumptions can grow from experiences where our mind has made patterns and created rules based on these experiences. Since many of these rules are made when we are very young, the rules may comprise incomplete logic or inappropriate associations between ideas, events or objects. When we are very young we have relatively few experiences to draw on and negative experiences in particular may not be balanced with positive ones as beliefs form. Similarly we may lack the language to articulate internally or externally what has been learned. Beliefs that favour negative outcomes can be attached to very generalized situations such as taking risks or experiencing new learning and this can have serious consequences for motivation and learning. If these generalizations act at an identity level, they have very powerful effects.

Flexibility in examining and adjusting our beliefs or personal rules is of great benefit. Having a fundamental belief that it is helpful to re-examine our core beliefs and values helps us to adjust beliefs to meet changing needs over time. This can actually reduce perceptions of stress and make personal change challenging and exciting. Coaching encourages people to re-examine beliefs.

When we are flexible in evaluating our beliefs in the light of new experience, we can make more sophisticated rules. We stroke cats that purr and brush against us and move away from cats that hiss and arch their backs. Beliefs that form around deeply traumatic experiences often remain fixed and inflexible and can lead to responses in adulthood that cause distress and that are no longer appropriate to the degree of independence and choice we have as adults. The coaching relationship and process helps people to evaluate these beliefs.

Some of the beliefs that we uncover when we coach are supportive of a person meeting their goals. There are also beliefs that hold them back and prevent them from succeeding. These beliefs become apparent to the coach often through what is said or sounds that the person being coached makes when asked a question. It is a coach's role to raise the individual's awareness of their beliefs and to challenge those beliefs that seem to hold back the individual from succeeding.

Limiting beliefs can harden into limiting attitudes. One of the simplest ways to look at the impact of limiting attitudes is to consider the resourceful and limiting thinking cycles as shown in Figures 5.2 and 5.3.

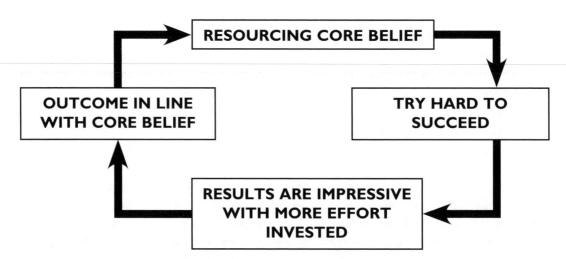

Figure 5.2 Resourceful thinking cycle

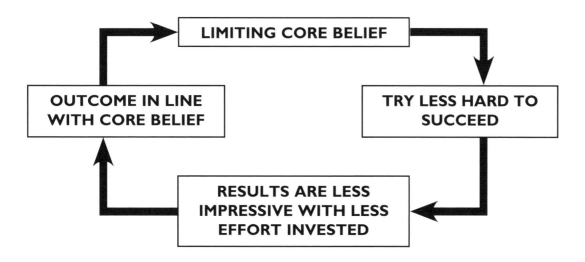

Figure 5.3 Limiting thinking cycle

The cycles show that how we think about a situation affects what we perceive and how much effort we put into making our actions successful. These cycles work for individuals, teams and institutions. In his book *Learned Optimism* (1991), Martin Seligman refers to optimism and pessimism as attitudes for success and failure. He suggests that optimism can be learned.

Challenging limiting thinking cycles

People who exhibit limiting thinking are in some discomfort. They feel that circumstances outside their control are making their lives difficult and that there is a permanence about this. In challenging their thinking cycle we must adopt sensitive and careful approaches. Essentially, upon recognizing the limiting thinking cycle the coach will help the person being coached to change their perception of the situation. This is done through a variety of techniques that will be referred to as 'reframing'. While reframing can be a complex process, the aim will be to keep it simple.

Reframing

As previously stated, negative self-talk can stem from limiting beliefs. Many limiting beliefs when vocalized are statements that have an 'all or nothing' quality about them and are heard a great deal in schools from adults as well as children.

Truisms, or Universal Quantifiers, (Martin 2001) can lead to distortions of reality as in the following examples:

- 'It's not what you know, it's who you know' – meaning that unless you already know the right people, you will not be successful.
- 'She never smiles' – meaning that at no point in her life has she smiled.
- 'I'm working so hard and just don't make any progress' – meaning I haven't made any progress at all.

One generalization people make regularly is to think of the world around them in 'all or nothing' or categoric terms:

- I am kind or I am unkind.

- I am wise or I am foolish.

- She is intelligent or she is stupid.

Instead of viewing these thoughts on continuums, we think we must be one or the other. For example, there might be a continuum between kind and unkind. We can argue that at some points in our lives we might act unkindly and at others we act in a kindly way. We are not one or the other all the time. Maintaining people in a resourceful state of mind to enable forward progress often means challenging their belief that they are one thing or another. For example, working in a continuum mind-set where the continuum exists around kindness might look like this:

Kind	**Unkind**

The person we are coaching has a negative mind-set because they are saying that they have acted unkindly towards someone and therefore they are unkind. They see themselves like this:

Kind **He's not here**	**Unkind** **He's here**

What the coach can do is to ask a question that will reframe this mindset so that the individual can think of ways in which they are kind and preferably place themselves along a continuum. The coach might respond:

Coach	So I think you're saying that you are an unkind person.
Individual	Yes I am.
Coach	How are you kind?
	Or
	How can you contradict that statement?
	Or
	How could appearing unkind actually mean you being kind?

So how do we respond to statements people make about limiting beliefs? There are a range of approaches here and you will find others later in the book.

Belief-related statement	Challenge
• I can't do this, it's too hard. (I am not up to the job here.)	• So you haven't been able to do this in the past. It has been too hard. What could make it easy now? • Pretend for a moment that you have already done this. As you look back at your achievement what is the first step that you took?
• I'm no good at maths.	• What is it exactly that you find challenging? • When have you been good at maths? • When did you decide this and why?
• I'm not the kind of person to enjoy things.	• When do you enjoy things? • What kind of things do you enjoy?
• Other people get all the opportunities, I always lose out.	• How do you manage to choose not to take those opportunities?
• My parents were mean to me and I'm always going to be scarred by the experience.	• It seems to you that your parents were mean to you. How might you be a better person for this experience? How can you use what you have learned to your advantage? • How, now that you think about it, are you actually better off for the treatment you feel you had as a child?
• I'm always the last person to know any gossip that's going around.	• What is it about knowing the gossip that helps you?
• I feel fat and stupid.	• In what ways are you slim and intelligent? • How might you contradict what you have just said?
• Everyone around me has nice clothes – I always look untidy.	• When *do* you have nice clothes?
• I'm always getting picked-on, it makes me unhappy.	• Tell me about what makes *you* happy.

The above are just a few examples of ways in which one can challenge negative thinking cycles.

For a fuller set of tools for challenging unresourceful beliefs, see Chapter 1 and read up on Meta Model 1, in *The Coaching Solutions Resource Book*, the practical companion volume to this text.

Summary

In this chapter we have discovered that:

▶ *beliefs are rules that we make for ourselves*

▶ *beliefs are often simplified and generalized*

▶ *beliefs can hold us back and propel us forward*

▶ *beliefs may be simple rules or complex ones with multiple levels*

▶ *our beliefs show themselves to us through our self-talk, our feelings, what we see around us and how we behave*

▶ *our beliefs can be re-evaluated through careful questioning.*

Additionally:

▶ *A coach's role is to challenge limiting beliefs.*

▶ *We have begun to learn how this can be done using language patterns.*

▶ *We can help others to shift their limiting beliefs and develop more useful ones through encouraging them to evaluate what they hear, see, feel and do.*

▶ *Working with self-talk, feelings, internal and external visual representations can help others to make meaningful progress and enhance their performance.*

▶ *Gently challenging the words of others who are locked into negative thinking cycles helps them notice how they are resourceful and can think in ways that enable them to solve problems and improve performance.*

▶ *The Change Cube Model shows how if we change our perceptions, our self-talk, our physiological state or our feelings towards a situation, we can influence our beliefs and our behaviours.*

Questions

1 What are beliefs?

2 What effect have your beliefs had on your career?

3 What kinds of limiting and liberating beliefs do you have about:

▷ Your work?

▷ Your leisure time?

▷ Your role as a parent?

▷ Your role as a son or daughter?

▷ Your role as a leader of people?

▷ Your ability to influence others?

▷ Make a list of limiting and liberating beliefs in each area – which beliefs do you operate from most of the time?

4 A parent comes up to you at parents' evening and explains that she wants her daughter to be given an easy time in your subject because she is no good at it and this is 'Hardly surprising because, I was useless at it too.' How would you address this?

5 How would you use the positive beliefs cycle to help your Year 9 pupils prepare for their SATs exams?

6 What do you believe are your strengths? What beliefs do you have that enhance your performance?

Masterclass

▶ *To find out more about your beliefs, try this:*

▶ *Make lists of five things you learned from:*

    ▶ *a parent*

    ▶ *your teacher*

    ▶ *your peers.*

▶ *Make a list of ten things you:*

    ▶ *must do*

    ▶ *should do*

    ▶ *could do*

    ▶ *always do*

    ▶ *never do.*

▶ *Then try out the SPECIFIC CHALLENGE technique on your above lists.*

▶ *Listen out for phrases like 'I can't', 'I won't be able to', 'It's impossible', 'It's bad … (time of year, year group, idea)' as signs of underlying limiting beliefs. Challenge these kinds of assertions with open questions that request more detail: 'How specifically is it a bad?' or 'How exactly is this impossible?'*

▶ *Use the Change Cube Model as a way to analyse the responses of the people you coach. Encourage them to identify the perceptions, the self-talk, the physiological factors and the feelings and consider these as foci for questioning where limitations are apparent.*

How do you coach?

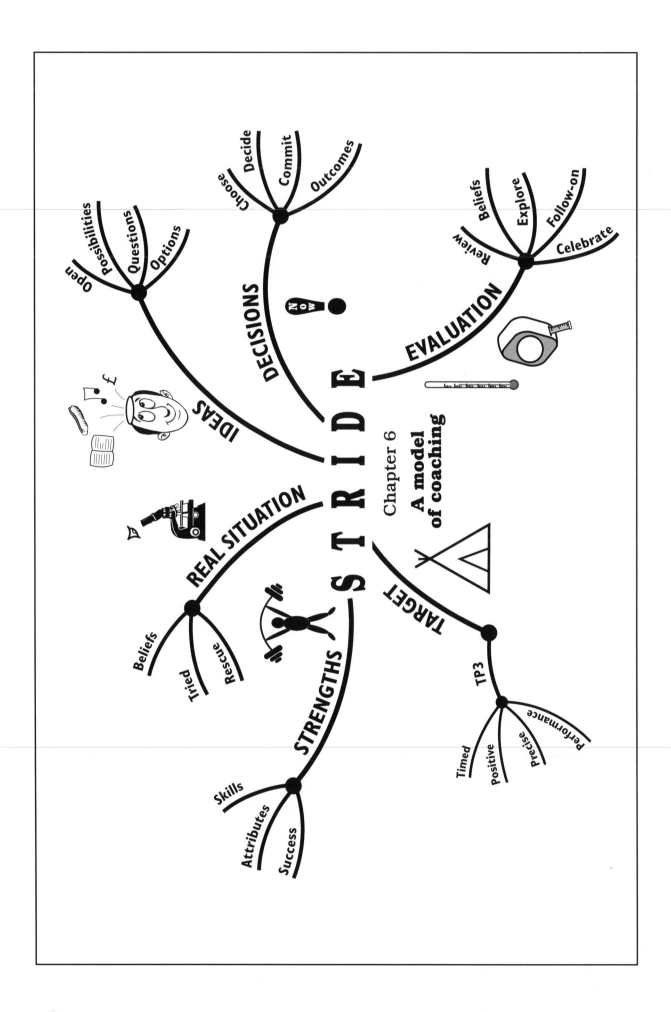

Chapter 6

A model of coaching

IN THIS CHAPTER YOU WILL LEARN:

- about the structuring of a coaching session
- about the time scales involved in coaching others
- about the **STRIDE Model**
- how to gauge the commitment of those you coach
- how to coach effectively even when time is short

PREVIEW QUESTIONS:

- How can you structure a coaching session?
- How do you achieve and check commitment in those you coach?
- What do you do when your people get stuck?
- How do you encourage your people out of negative frames of mind?
- What do I do if I do not have 30 minutes for an extended session with someone?
- How can busy teachers embed coaching when the pressures on time are so great?

The wise men and the elephant

Six wise men of India
An elephant did find
And carefully they felt its shape
(For all of them were blind).

The first he felt towards the tusk,
'It does to me appear,
This marvel of an elephant
Is very like a spear'.

The second sensed the creature's side
Extended flat and tall,
'Ahah!' he cried and did conclude,
'This animal's a wall'.

The third had reached towards a leg
And said, 'It's clear to me
What we should all have instead
This creature's like a tree'.

The fourth had come upon the trunk
Which he did seize and shake,
Quoth he, 'This so-called elephant
Is really just a snake'.

The fifth had felt the creature's ear
And fingers o'er it ran,
'I have the answer, never fear,
The creature's like a fan!'

The sixth had come upon the tail
As blindly he did grope,
'Let my conviction now prevail
This creature's like a rope'.

And so these men of missing sight
Each argued loud and long
Though each was partly in the right
They all were in the wrong.

Rudyard Kipling

A model of coaching

The one constant factor in schools and colleges over the last decade has been change! Maintaining a motivated workforce in the light of continual shifts in priority and approach has become a high priority. So why is it that change after change is accompanied by such prescriptive approaches to achieving goals? To really motivate individuals towards change is to give them greater autonomy over what they do and how they do it. Every person, like those exploring the elephant, will have a different take on the same situation. Consequently, developing solutions that will drive themselves to completion is largely about tailoring them to the values and skills of those who action them. Whether the targets come from the top down or are generated by individuals, the choice about how people work towards achieving them can be highly motivating. The greater the choice in defining the target and the approach to achieving it, the higher the level of motivation to succeed.

This chapter explores a simple structure that enables you to smooth the pathway for others to resolve their own problems and enhance their performance. The STRIDE model is a framework to enable individuals and teams to consider the steps to make lasting changes. It is also a tool to enable people to consider the elephant from the perspective of others.

The acronym STRIDE represents a flexible and rigorous coaching structure as represented in Figure 6.1.

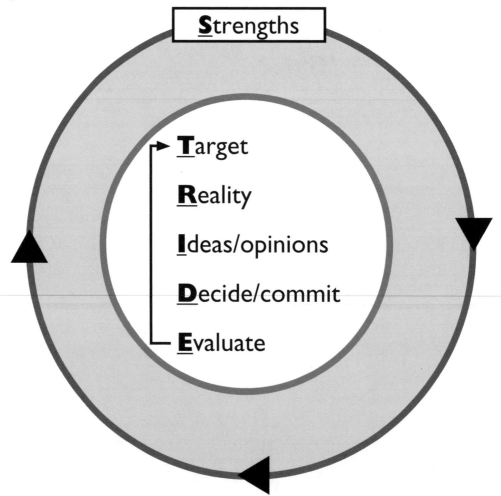

Strengths

Target

Reality

Ideas/opinions

Decide/commit

Evaluate

Figure 6.1 The STRIDE model – © Will Thomas 2002

Coaching solutions using the STRIDE model

STRIDE is a simple model for structuring change in others. It orders the process by which others define goals, overcome limiting beliefs and take manageable steps towards those goals. Before moving on to the STRIDE model you may like to remind yourself of the principles of coaching referred to in Chapter 2. The nine principles of coaching represent the vital foundation to this model. Without the appropriate attitudes and state of mind of the coach this model will not be effective. It should be borne in mind that while this model contains all of the key elements to successful perception shift in coaching, it is NOT necessarily a linear model. So for example it may be that the reality is discussed first and then in order to draw the person out of a negative reality towards a solution, a positive future target is developed and from this ideas are generated. It may similarly be the case that a person cannot focus on the future owing to their feeling so unresourceful, and so time spent reflecting on their strengths will put them in a better state of mind to consider ideas. The STRIDE model should be seen more as a check list and may be approached intuitively according to what is presented by your coachee. This approach also tends to ensure that coaching remains flowing, natural and conversational.

The STRIDE model

Strengths
Paying attention to strengths and maintaining people in a resourceful mindset.

Target
Identifying the target to be achieved and exploring motivation to achieve it.

Reality
Exploring the current situation in relation to the target and identifying limiting beliefs.

Ideas
Seeking ideas that might succeed in achieving the desired target and overcoming limiting beliefs.

Decision
Selecting the most appropriate option from the ideas generated.

Evaluation

There are two parts to the evaluation phase:

1 *Evaluating the solution now:* exploring commitment to agree decisions.

2 *Evaluating later:* agreeing a time to follow up on the actions taken following the decision.

The STRIDE model explained

Strengths

A huge body of research recognizes the importance of developing and maintaining high levels of self-esteem in people throughout change management. Since coaching is fundamentally about change, it follows that high levels of self-esteem are essential to the process. When we receive feedback from others, we can respond in a variety of ways. This may depend on a whole range of factors, but one significant factor is the way in which that feedback is delivered. What makes the difference between feedback and criticism is often about the way the information is delivered.

Look at the two contrasting situations in the case study below.

Case study: strengths 1

Teacher	Jenny, I've marked your homework and want to talk to you about it.
Pupil	OK.
Teacher	You really need to think more carefully about your presentation, it isn't good enough for someone of your age. At least I can read it, I suppose. This section on Hinduism hasn't been thought through and frankly you haven't understood the question. It was about comparing and contrasting. Do you know what that means?
Pupil	(*no response, stares at the floor*)
Teacher	Haven't you read your textbook on this topic?

This is an interesting dialogue (or monologue!) that Will witnessed in a classroom a few years ago. The teacher approaches with a stern face and that primes Jenny for some criticism even before he has opened his mouth. She may even have stopped listening to him straightaway before he actually gave her any feedback. He begins with a chunk of criticism, which is about a less important aspect of the work, the presentation. He then launches into a criticism of her understanding of the material, followed by a further criticism of her ability to understand the question. The Jenny makes no response but stares down at the floor, gripping her pencil in pulsing movements, which is a classic pose for someone who is emotionally upset. The use of closed questioning adds nothing to the interaction, since Jenny is only able to respond with 'yes' or 'no'.

What other feedback would you give about this teacher's approach?

Case study: strengths 2 (alternative)

Teacher	(*smiling*) Hello Jenny, I enjoyed reading your homework.
Pupil	Thank you sir. (*smiling*)
Teacher	I particularly liked the way you defined Hinduism. It shows that you have a clear understanding of its main points and how it differs from other religions.

Pupil	(*nods, smiles and furrows brow*)
Teacher	You made some clear contrasts between Hinduism and other religions. I liked the points you made when you compared Christianity with Hinduism.
Pupil	I thought a lot about that part.
Teacher	So well done. Now how do you think you could you make this piece even better?
Pupil	I found this difficult, because I'm not really sure … (pauses) I'm not really sure what it means sir … the word 'comparison' … in this situation.
Teacher	What does comparison mean for you away from school?
Pupil	Well, looking for things that are the same. But how can things be the same when the religions are so very different?
Teacher	You've just come up with an interesting question for yourself. How do you think things can be the same when the religions are so very different?
Pupil	(*long pause*) Ahh, right … so I have another question for myself – what do people get from religion? Now that's really interesting because it's a bit deeper down than the customs and practices isn't it?
Teacher	Those are interesting thoughts. You've come up with some really interesting questions for yourself here. One of your many strengths is just that, Jenny, you're great at asking the right questions of yourself. Well done. Just recap the questions you'll go away and think about.

In case study 2 the teacher has a productive conversation, where he begins to coach the student while paying attention to her strengths. By using open questions he enables her to demonstrate strengths that he can then draw on. There is rapport developing here and her emotional bank account is filling up well. For her teacher to make reference to the presentation is now a safe next step because the two individuals are in rapport. This student is clearly able and it is interesting to consider how far the influence of the teacher extends in each interaction and what the nature of the continuation is.

Throughout case study 2, the teacher is exploring the student's strengths. He has noticed first the best parts of what she has done, rather than focusing on those bits of the work that need development. This is a useful mindset for us when we are responding to work. He has carefully used some language that presupposes that what Jenny has produced is good when he says 'Now how could you make this piece even better?'

When we notice and draw attention to another person's strengths, they feel good about themselves and they feel safer about working with you. There is less risk attached to exploring the weaker area of their performance and they are actually quite willing to accept constructive feedback and, importantly, much more likely to act upon it. What is tremendous about this teacher's final line is that his interaction does not stop there. Jenny clarifies the questions that she will ask herself (and they are her own questions) and she goes away highly motivated by her own successes and the recognition of her teacher to move towards further success. In case study 1, the teacher has succeeded in placing the student into a less resourceful state of mind, and this has diminished the returns significantly. There is little positive forward progress in this example.

In formal and informal coaching situations, recognizing strengths is vital to build and maintain rapport and trust between coaches and individuals.

Rescue techniques

An important reason for paying attention to strengths when coaching is that they can rescue both you and the person you coach should that person become trapped in a negative thinking cycle. Remembering that coaching is about maintaining people in a positive, present and forward focused mindset, there are times when people become strongly associated with bad experiences and we need to help them find a way out. There are a number of helpful ways to achieve this.

Consider the following situation, which is followed by some strategies.

Case study: rescue techniques

KS Co-ordinator	Hi Jon. When can we talk about the planning for next term?
Colleague	Not now. I'm absolutely snowed under.
KS Co-ordinator	When would be convenient?
Colleague	I just don't know. I've so much stuff to complete for yesterday and it's all getting on top of me.
KS Co-ordinator	What do you need?
Colleague	A way out right now. It all seems impossible.
KS Co-ordinator	What kind of way out?
Colleague	One that let's me dump some of this stuff I have to do so I can concentrate on one thing at a time.
KS Co-ordinator	So you want to concentrate on one thing at a time.
Colleague	Yes, that's exactly it.
KS Co-ordinator	How many things are you currently doing at the same time?
Colleague	Well, I'm doing umpteen things at once and getting nothing done!
KS Co-ordinator	Jon, I've known you for a while and I know you have a host of strengths that get you through. What strengths can you draw on right now to help you?

Colleague	(*stops, looks up and thinks, puts down large pile of books he is carrying, pauses*) Well, Gill, I think I'm able to see the big picture and that's what makes me effective. And the thing is, I haven't been using that strength for a little while now! I actually need to look at all the things I think I have to do 'by yesterday' (*slight emphasis, almost self-deprecating towards his earlier words*) and prioritize them. After all I can only do one thing at a time! Thanks, Gill, I'm going to do that straight after school today … thanks.
KS Co-ordinator	You're welcome, Jon. Let me know how you get on.

The KS Co-ordinator uses a powerful rescue question: what strengths do you have that you can draw on to help you? Almost straight away there is a pause. Jon, who has been reacting rather than thinking until this point, stops. He then moves very quickly from talking about his burdens to focusing on his strengths, and then to almost mocking himself and recognizing that he has already provided himself with the answer to his problem. He needs to stop and think. While the question in itself focuses the recipient onto his strengths, it also has a subtle effect in terms of shifting the emotional and physical state of mind. Because it is an unusual question to ask, it has a surprise effect and focuses Jon away from his troubles. Other interesting techniques for doing this will be examined later in the ideas section of this chapter.

Paying attention to individuals' strengths leads to:

- enhanced rapport
- greater trust between coach and individual
- enhanced self-esteem, confidence and willingness to take risks
- greater willingness to accept and take on board feedback
- enhanced recognition of these strengths and greater readiness to use them in future challenges
- coaches having a knowledge of the individual's strengths for challenging times when negative mindsets are present
- people recognizing their own strengths, so that they can respond quickly to rescue questions and remain resourceful
- people building an inventory of genuine personal strengths to help them deal with challenges they face when their coach is not present.

Focusing on strengths leads to enhanced performance. Throughout the STRIDE model we pay attention to strengths, noting them in the individual's conversation and selectively making the individual aware of them through reflecting them back. They are our biggest assets when individuals find themselves in unresourceful frames of mind. Encouraging children and adults to keep a record of the strengths they discover is a powerful way of developing self-esteem and resourcefulness beyond the initial intervention of the coach. Of course, every great coach needs to know what their own strengths are – what are yours? How do you feel about recording your strengths?

Target

Defining the target is crucial to the success of the coaching session. Careful construction of the target with the individual ensures that there is a benchmark to align with and adjust as necessary throughout the coaching process. Wherever possible it is helpful to write down the target in precise terms, so that both coach and individual have a clear idea of what they are heading for. Defining the target should explore the negotiable as well as the non-negotiable aspects of the target.

A range of areas that might be worked upon include:

- pupil who wants to improve their freehand drawing technique
- learning support assistant who wants to develop better rapport with a student they work with on a one-to-one basis
- primary school teacher who wants to improve their marking effectiveness
- secondary head of maths who needs to enhance their department's value-added scores
- assistant headteacher who wants to be more effective in project management for a forthcoming whole school change
- headteacher who wants to enhance their presence and confidence in whole school assemblies
- parent who wishes to manage their son's challenging behaviour at home more effectively.

With any of the situations above the first move for the coach is to help the individual explore what they want to achieve in detail.

Using the TP³ model to define good quality targets

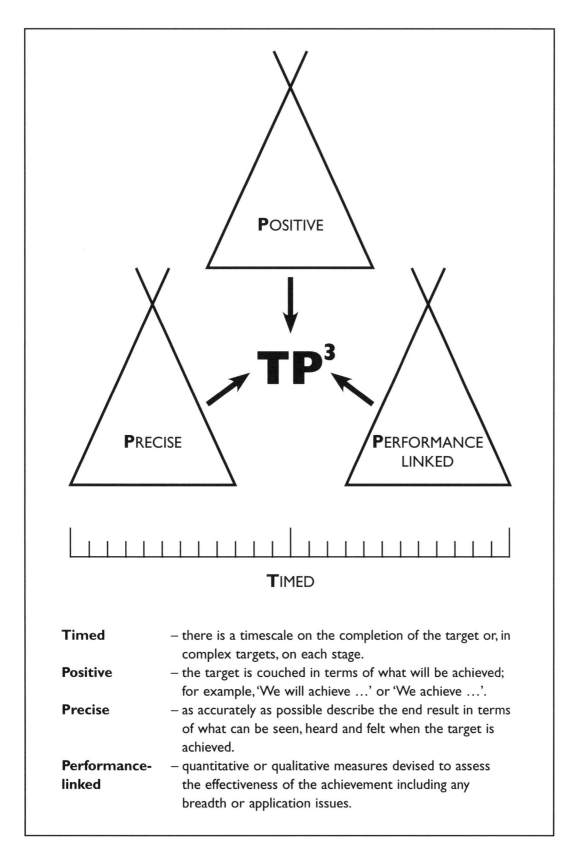

Timed	– there is a timescale on the completion of the target or, in complex targets, on each stage.
Positive	– the target is couched in terms of what will be achieved; for example, 'We will achieve …' or 'We achieve …'.
Precise	– as accurately as possible describe the end result in terms of what can be seen, heard and felt when the target is achieved.
Performance-linked	– quantitative or qualitative measures devised to assess the effectiveness of the achievement including any breadth or application issues.

Figure 6.2 The TP³ target-setting model – © Will Thomas 2003

Below is an example of using the TP³ model.

Case study: target-setting

Coach	Gerry, what do you want to achieve?
Headteacher	To stop all the complaints about how badly we deal with parental concerns in school.
Coach	So you want to stop all of the complaints about how badly you deal with parental concerns in school?
Headteacher	Yes.
Coach	What do you want to put in place of the complaints?
Headteacher	I want parents to feel all right about coming school to talk to us and to feel that their complaints are dealt with quickly.
Coach	So you want to ensure that parents feel all right about coming into school to talk to us and to feel that concerns are dealt with quickly? So what will you see, hear and feel when parents have that feeling?
Headteacher	(*pause*) I'll see the foyer with parents coming in to see us.
Coach	What do you notice about them?
Headteacher	They look content and relaxed … happy faces … happy to be in school.
Coach	What are they saying right now?
Headteacher	(*closes his eyes*) They are chatting about being supported, and looking forward to seeing their child's teachers. They are saying how great the school is at handling their concerns.
Coach	You are in that foyer with them, seeing and hearing all of this. How do you feel right now?
Headteacher	(*eyes still closed and smiling*) Brilliant. This is exactly how I want it to be.
Coach	Standing in this scene now, what you are experiencing?
Headteacher	I see contented, happy parents saying great things about the school and feeling that we really support our parents … and get things resolved quickly.
Coach	How quickly?
Headteacher	Within ten minutes they've spoken to the receptionist and have contact with an appropriate member of staff within that day.
Coach	Coming back to today, noticing the colours in the room and the sounds around you … how fully do you feel back into Wednesday (*voice lowers, tone softens*), today?

Headteacher	Yes, I'm here with this. Ten out of ten.
Coach	Thinking of that future, what target will you set and when will you achieve it?
Headteacher	We'll have happy, contented parents who know their concerns will be dealt with effectively.
Coach	So you have happy, contented parents, who know their concerns are dealt with effectively and within the day of contact. What can you measure to know you have this?
Headteacher	Yes, good question. I'm not sure we can measure happiness, or, for that matter, even ensure that parents are happy! Perhaps that's unrealistic, but we can deal effectively with enquiries within one day of their initial contact.
Coach	When will you have this?
Headteacher	By the start of the new school year, which is two terms away.
Coach	So let me recap the target. Your target is: to deal with parental concerns effectively and within the day of contact by an appropriate member of staff. What will tell you that you have this?
Headteacher	Well, me standing there listening and following up the experience they have I suppose. But I can't be there all the time.
Coach	Who can?
Headteacher	The receptionist, and she could have some questionnaires that would capture the comments.
Coach	How would that work out?
Headteacher	It would work for some parents, but others have difficulties with reading and writing, so it might even drive them away! But I could get the teacher dealing with their enquiry to ask them a few simple questions about how we dealt with them and that would work … that would definitely work.
Coach	So you are dealing with parental concerns effectively within one day of the initial contact. You know this is the case because you ask them some simple questions when their enquiry is dealt with. You have this outcome in two terms.
Headteacher	Yes, that's excellent. Spot on!
Coach	On a scale of one to ten, where one is not committed and ten is totally committed, how committed are you to this target?
Headteacher	I'm a ten on that one, definitely!
Coach	Brilliant, now let's look at the current situation …

The coaching session has helped the headteacher to do a number of things:

1   Within the first few sentences the coach encourages the headteacher to state what he wants. In this case, the outcome is to stop something happening. The coach enables the individual to say what he wants in place of the outcome he wishes to avoid. This focuses the individual on a positive outcome very quickly.

2   The coach encourages the headteacher to place himself in the future at a time when the desired outcome is achieved. This allows the individual to get really associated with the excitement and enjoyment of the finished target. It also provides a valuable anchor point for looking back towards the present (that is, while still in the imagined future) and seeing how they achieved the imagined future.

3   The coach begins to probe the headteacher further by checking out the performance-linked aspects of the target when he asks the question 'How quickly?'

4   The coach also probes to find the timescale of the target, which is discovered to be two terms. Later in the STRIDE model the individual will explore how realistic the precision and the timescales are, but for the time being this 'futurescape' for their target is an ideal starting point.

5   Notice how the coach reflects back the target, yet changes the verb tense to move the target from 'We will have' (future) to 'We have' (present). This is subtle yet very important because it presupposes that the target is already achieved. This helps the individual to believe that their target is achievable.

6   The coach also encourages the headteacher to consider the realism of the target, 'What can you do to know you have this?' The headteacher is invited to question the goal of happy contented parents – which may not be within the control of the headteacher!

7   Checking commitment is another useful tool in coaching. The Coaching Academy (2002) cites that individuals who score less than seven on these kinds of commitment checks usually do not achieve their target. It is always important where the individual scores less than ten to ask, 'What is the remainder about?' – for example, a score of eight out of ten leaves a remainder of two, so ask what the other two is about. This can give vital information about limiting beliefs or other limiting factors, which you can explore further in the reality section of the model.

An important final step for coach and individual is to write down the target so that it can be referred back to throughout the remainder of the session and in later sessions. It is not unusual to come back to targets and adjust them throughout the coaching session, as happened in the illustration above. Coaching is an exploration and, consequently, new learning emerges throughout. This new learning informs us and from this we adjust our sights.

It is vital to take time to explore targets thoroughly. The target shown above, despite TP[3] refinement, is still a big target and further coaching is likely to break it down into a series of sub-goals. Considering the dialogue overleaf, what could the coach do to add further precision to the goal?

Encouraging people to set targets is a crucial part of achieving success. In institutional settings, targets may well be imposed and may have little or no element of negotiability in them. It is important for coaches to establish how individuals feel about imposed targets and this should be explored within the target section of the model.

Low scores on the 1–10 scale often reveal an imposed target. The emotions surrounding imposed targets can be mixed and the coach can help individuals to deal with these by asking questions that explore the flexibilities of the target, the person or the body that has set them. Additionally, where there appears to be no flexibility in the target itself, exploring the choices and options around how the individual can go about achieving the target is crucial. Even the most draconian of management teams that imposes targets without discussion or debate will have latitude for the way tasks are carried out or the way in which the individual thinks about the target. It is this exploration of the choices and freedoms that enables the individual to gain greater ownership of both the target and the process by which they achieve the target. It may also be the case that the coach will end up exploring a wish in the individual to challenge a target if it is imposed.

As coaches we are following the agenda of the individual to a great degree in the interests of achieving the targets set. To some readers this may seem strange, considering that institutions have goals and invest in coaching support, yet the whole premise for coaching is that the individual follows their own agenda. Only the individual can truly know the stairs they must climb between where they are and their goal, and coaching is respectful of this and the personal ownership of the process they go through.

Reality

Following the establishment of the target, the coach has already noted some of the skills and attributes that the individual possesses and is keyed in to looking for the individual's strengths. This becomes very important as we explore the reality. Potentially, in this section of the model we are exploring what is not working and what has been tried but has not worked, and we begin to unearth the limiting belief or beliefs that hold back the individual.

Within the exploration of the reality, the coach again uses open questions to help the individual to understand the situation more fully. Let us continue the coaching session that we began earlier in the target section.

Case study: the reality

Coach	(*from the target setting*) Brilliant, now let's explore the current situation. Tell me about it.
Headteacher	(*deep breath*) I constantly feel as if we're not doing a good job with meeting parents' needs in school. I never feel we deal with concerns quickly or effectively. I feel we're failing here.
Coach	Tell me about a time when you have met parents' expectations.
Headteacher	(*long pause*) Mmm ... Well we had a letter only last week from a parent who was delighted with the way we dealt with a bullying incident involving her child.
Coach	How did that feel?

Headteacher	Well, it was wonderful. It added some weight to the work we've already been doing to improve our effectiveness in dealing with parents' concerns at the school.
Coach	So you're already working on some approaches to improve in this area?
Headteacher	Oh yes, quite a bit.
Coach	Tell me about other successes in this area.
Headteacher	Over the last term we've had a number of written and verbal responses that have been very positive about dealing with bullying, absence follow-up and academic concerns that parents have had.
Coach	So how do you feel about this?
Headteacher	Well, naturally, we feel … I feel great about this. It's excellent news.
Coach	Just a moment ago you had said that you had felt you weren't doing a good job with meeting parents needs in school. How realistic was that feeling?
Headteacher	(*laughs*) Not at all! We've done a lot of work on this area and had some great feedback from parents on this. I suppose when you're busy and you've got your head down, you don't always notice the progress.
Coach	What are the benefits of noticing the progress?
Headteacher	I actually feel good, more motivated about the work we're currently doing. It's working … on the whole.
Coach	What have you done so far to improve things?
Headteacher	We've had a parents' consultation evening where they were able to put across their views and concerns – we've discovered a great deal from this. We've improved our newsletter and now post it direct to parents to ensure it reaches them. We include specific issues which can reduce the need for parents to come into school.
Coach	That sounds excellent. So it's working on the whole. So what is there left to do?
Headteacher	Yes, good question. Well I think it's the time element really. To be really honest with you, I sometimes just get to the point where I feel I can't spare the time for all the concerns that come into school. I just get swamped. I don't feel that parents get the instant response that they need from me.
Coach	So you feel that parents need an instant response and you don't have the time to provide it. Let's just check back to your target. You said you want a situation where you have parents who know their concerns are dealt with effectively and within the day of

contact. You know this is the case because you ask them some simple questions when their enquiry is dealt with. You will have this outcome in two terms. Where are you with this now?

Headteacher Mmm ... I think there's something else coming through now. We've had quite a few bits of feedback that say that we are really meeting parents' needs. We've also had one or two instances where some feedback has come in from parents that have said I responded too slowly. It's going to be useful to get some feedback from parents when they come in, but in many ways we get this anyway. There's something else here that's becoming important, and it's about time. I just don't have enough time to deal with all the contacts that we get from parents; I pride myself on keeping a handle on everything that happens in the school, but I just don't have enough time. Sometimes I tear my hair out trying to get back to them that day with progress.

Coach So you don't have time to deal with every contact with parents that happens? Who says you must deal with every contact within a day?

Headteacher (*long silence, then smiles*) I suppose I do.

Coach So I think what you're saying is that you think all enquiries from parents must come through you and that you need to deal with them yourself and inside one day.

Headteacher Well yes, I'm the headteacher.

Coach How does that expectation feel?

Headteacher Impossible. I can't do it all and I can't do it all in one day.

Coach What have you learned?

Headteacher That I think I have to do it all myself and it all has to be done in a day! That phrase Rome wasn't built in a day sounds quite funny now! A bit of a silly expectation really.

Coach So let's go back to your original target and look again.

What the headteacher does next is to redefine his original target and comes up with this one:

I have parents who know their concerns are dealt with effectively. I prioritize the issues and give parents a clear and realistic time by which we will investigate, deal with the issue and get back to them. I have this outcome in two terms.

The coach checks again how committed they feel to this target using the 1–10 scale.

In this section the coach has helped the headteacher to take a more objective look at his progress and to recognize that work has already begun towards the goal he has set and that he has already had some success here. The coach challenges the truism that he is 'constantly feeling that we are not doing a good job'. Crucially in this section of the model, the coach helps to begin to identify two self-limiting beliefs: 1) that the headteacher must deal with all parental concerns himself; 2) that all parental concerns must be responded to on the day the school is first alerted. These generalizations take no account of the complexity of the concern, the urgency (or triviality) of the concern, or the pressures that he is under in any one day. With these realizations dawning, the coach moves on to the ideas section of the model to begin to look at the practical ways in which the headteacher can achieve the target and overcome the unhelpful beliefs that he has adopted.

Ideas

The ideas section of the STRIDE model is all about generating creative solutions. Questioning in this section is used to encourage lateral thinking and enable individuals to come up with a range of possible courses of action to meet their target. Encouraging people to really let go of their thoughts and say or write down anything that comes into their head is an important part of this process. No idea is too ridiculous because every idea will allow associations to be made and thus generate further ideas. It is frequently our experience as coaches that from some of the most outrageous thoughts come some sound new avenues of thinking which ultimately lead to solutions.

With an amassed collection of ideas, it is important to check each idea back against the target. Will this idea achieve your target? Consider also the advantages and disadvantages of each idea. As the coach you are facilitating people to make their own decisions and so questions which explore each idea will help them to weigh up the pros and cons of their options.

Case study: ideas

Coach	So what's next?
Headteacher	I need to find some solutions.
Coach	What are your thoughts?
Headteacher	This is where I'm stuck. I'm so used to trying to cope and trying to fit things in that the idea of doing it differently is too hard to consider. Don't know. I just don't know. Help!
Coach	Just remember, Gerry, you do have some answers to this. What strengths do you have right now that can help you move this forward?
Headteacher	(*pause*) I'm a lateral thinker. I'm very experienced in dealing with parents. I come up with great solutions to problems for people.
Coach	How would you feel about a question here to help you think laterally?
Headteacher	Yes, great.
Coach	Remember that we are considering ideas here, so any idea is valuable however simple or unusual it might seem. Gerry, if you

didn't have to deal with all the enquiries on the same day, what could you do then?

Headteacher   I could ... I could ... (*pauses*) ... I could ask some questions, consider the likely timescale needed (a realistic one) to get back to the parent and tell them when I would get back to them. I could weigh up the urgency in all that. I could actually write it down.

Coach   OK, that sounds interesting.

Headteacher   Yes it is actually, really important. That feels so much better, so much more manageable.

Coach   So you could further enhance your prioritization process, here's another question ... Gerry, if you didn't have to deal with all the concerns that parents bring into school yourself, what could you do then?

Headteacher   (*silence, looking up into the air thinking*) Well that's quite easy because I could really use my other staff to refer specific issues on to. I could further skill-up my receptionist to recognize issues and ask questions and, do you know, that's a biggy because it's about how I manage my school. That's ... that's a big shift for me. I don't know if I'm ready for all that yet.

Coach   That's OK. One step at a time. We're just exploring ideas here. What other ideas are there?

Headteacher   Well, I think we could make a time for parents to contact us that's better than all day, anytime. I'd be much freer in the morning than in the afternoon, especially with my teaching commitment as it is now.

Coach   In the future, having used this approach, how successful are you in achieveing your target?

Headteacher   (*pauses*) Yes, I see this happening. Definitely.

In this exchange the coach has enabled the headteacher to think in resourceful ways about the possible means to make forward progress towards the target. Interestingly, he had already begun to solve the problem in the reality section when they redefined the target.

Early in the strengths section the coach recognizes that the headteacher has slipped into a negative thinking cycle: 'I just don't know'. The coach quickly reminds him that he has the solutions to his challenges within him, then asks a great rescue question: 'What strengths do you have right now that can help you move this forward?' Straight away he is back into a resourceful mode of thinking and begins resolving issues again. The coach then uses a really helpful questioning device – the incisive question (see below): 'If you didn't have to deal with *all* of the enquiries *on the same day*, what could you do then?' The first part of the question temporarily suspends the limiting belief that he has to deal with all enquiries himself and the second part encourages him to look towards solutions. Notice the word 'could' in the second half of the sentence. This reinforces the notion that at this stage nothing is ruled out as a possibility, these are just ideas. Using the word 'would' in the same place can close down thinking as it implies that the person must come up with answers that will work. The ideas section is about identifying a range of options.

In this section another interesting belief is beginning to emerge – the belief that the way the headteacher is currently managing might need some development. At this stage the headteacher seems unwilling to address this. Notice how the coach allows this to be recognized without following it up. This is likely to be an issue to revisit with the headteacher, but the coach's instinct is to hold back on this right now given the short amount of remaining time in the session and the close proximity the coach feels to the headteacher committing to some useful steps. This is an important judgement call – to coach is allow the individual to take manageable steps.

Holding silence is important during the ideas section, as is recognizing when individuals are really stuck. Where there are blocks in the way of progress, specialized questioning is a helpful way to move forward. Specialized questions that help to ease individuals around limiting beliefs are called incisive questions and are explored further in Chapter 7. Here are some useful incisive questions to be going on with:

- What could you do if you didn't have to live with the consequences?
- What might you do if time were not a factor?
- What might you do if intelligence were not a factor?
- Could you do if money were not a limitation?
- What could you do if you thought you were worth it?

Once all ideas are explored, taking individuals forward in time to a point when they have achieved the target using a strategy will check for any incongruence in the methodology. Questions like: 'What is success like using this strategy?' and 'Going into the future, how successful are you now that you have used this strategy?' will check the potential success of an idea. These are important at the latter end of the ideas section of STRIDE. You are then ready to move to the decision phase when individuals will commit to taking action to achieve their target.

I have some great ideas to add. Can I offer them?

Coaches often find themselves wanting to offer ideas in this section. The default position is that we do not do that. This is because the core premise of coaching is that the person being coached will find their own solution, ideally suited to their needs. That person will be able to work out what their next achievable step is far better than the coach, because the coach does not have the individual's unique insight into their limiting beliefs. It is the case, however, that while we would not want to knock an individual from their self-reliant course, we can offer additional ideas and these may be effective. Offering additional ideas is a matter of approach.

When you have ideas to offer:

- Listen to your own self-talk. Be clear why you are offering the ideas. Is it out of a genuine belief that they may be helpful, or is there another agenda?
- Always allow the individual to fully explore ideas for themselves.
- Ask permission before offering ideas and make sure you get it.

- If permission is given but you sense it is not complete, explore that with reflection and questions.

- Be clear that your ideas are 'just ideas and have no more validity than theirs'.

- Review all ideas at the end and remind the individual that it is their choice as to which ideas will best move them forward.

This may seem pedantic, but by now you have established a strong coaching relationship that can be damaged by a 'suggestion-culture'. You may also find that the person you coach looks to you for solutions. This undermines what you are trying to achieve with coaching.

The authors very rarely offer suggestions while coaching. In their experience when the coach really believes that those they coach will come up with solutions, they do. Their strong advice is to stick with the purity of coaching and let people find their way.

Five tips for the ideas phase

1   Remember this phase of the model is about possibilities, not realities.

2   Use the language of might, could, possibilities, options, ideas.

3   Use inspirational tones and energy in your voice.

4   Respect and congratulate every idea, however realistic or outlandish – it is, after all, only your perception!

5   If you do feel that there are ideas you have to contribute, wait until the person has concluded, then ask if it might be helpful if you added some ideas, too. Confirm that they are only ideas – just options for consideration. If they have new options that emerge as you speak, let them say what comes to them. Wherever possible let them take credit for great ideas – it is not about you showing what a great coach you are, it is about them finding solutions.

Decision

In this part of the coaching session, the coach will review the target with the individual and assist him to decide on the most appropriate course of action to move forward.

Case study: decisions

Coach   OK, Gerry, can you recap for me what you've learned so far today?

Headteacher   Yes. I've worked out that things are going pretty well for us at school in relation to dealing with parental concerns/complaints. We can do better, particularly when it comes to meeting expectations about getting back to parents following their enquiry. I've realized that I've set myself some pretty tough targets in my head for getting back to them all on the same day and for dealing with them all myself, and I'm a bit daunted by what this means in terms of my management style. I've also realized how important it is to take some time out to think about what I'm thinking, but don't know I'm thinking, if that makes sense! (*both laugh*)

Coach	Yes, it makes sense. We all need time to consider our thought processes. Sometimes when we feel like we have the least time to do it, that's the time we need to do it most. That's great work, Gerry. Your target is: I have parents who know their concerns are dealt with effectively. I prioritize the issues and give parents a clear and realistic time by which we will investigate, deal with the issue and get back to them. I will have this outcome in two terms. From the ideas you have looked at you have: prioritizing workload and sharing some of the workload. What will you do?
Headteacher	Well, the prioritization has to happen straight away. Now I think about it, it is specifically what has caused the two recent complaints. I'd made a promise to parents that I'd contact them that day, other things got in the way and I didn't get in touch. It wasn't life or death, but if I'd been clear when I might get back to them, I'd have had a less demanding deadline and it would have been realistic. If I prioritize first, before I promise, I'll get it right more of the time … no doubt about that.
Coach	What will that give you?
Headteacher	Freedom to plan my time. It's so silly that I didn't do this earlier, but I've just got on a roll with it and the behaviour has stuck. I'll consider each issue and decide how important it is, check with my diary and commit to a time to get back to the parent.
Coach	How will that move you closer to your target?
Headteacher	Parents will be clear that they will get a time for me to contact them which is realistic and I can achieve it. It's got to be better.
Coach	How will you decide the priority?
Headteacher	I'm ahead of you on that one! I'm going to use an urgent/important tool I got from a course a few years ago that helps me decide priorities. I'll also use my experience of how long it takes to deal with the issues that come up.
Coach	What else?
Headteacher	(*long silence*) Well, there's something pretty big on the horizon here that's about how I manage my school. I'm going to find that hard to look at.
Coach	What might make it easy?

Headteacher	I don't know. I'll need to think about that — it might be a topic for next time we meet.
Coach	That will be a great focus. What could get in the way of the prioritization happening?
Headteacher	(*thinks for a long time*) Yes, a good question. (*pauses again*) I think guilt could get in the way. I might feel guilty about not getting back to people straight away.
Coach	How might you deal with this?
Headteacher	I think, right now, remembering how much better things will be when I've prioritized things. That's what I'll hang on to.
Coach	That's great. When exactly will you begin this priority process?
Headteacher	I'll do it first thing on Monday.
Coach	So you will be a prioritizing headteacher from Monday? Why not from now?
Headteacher	Yes, why not? I'm a prioritizing headteacher right now! (*both laugh*)

In this section the coach has invited the headteacher to commit to a course of action and has helped him to begin to examine a broader issue about how he manages his school. The coach has also helped him to examine what might prevent him from achieving the actions he has decided on. The coach will have noted another interesting limiting belief — the guilt that the headteacher refers to. This may form part of a pattern that the coach makes the headteacher aware of later in his coaching experience. At the end of the section the coach encourages him to begin now and uses the term 'a prioritizing headteacher'. In this way he is encouraged not only carry out the action of prioritizing but also to be a prioritizing individual.

Evaluation

In this section the coach will explore with the headteacher his commitment to the decision and relate it back to the target. It will also represent the starting-point for evaluating progress in the next coaching session they have together.

Case study: evaluation

Coach	So, Gerry, you've decided to be a prioritizing headteacher and to prioritize parental concern enquiries and you have an approach to do this. On our one-to-ten scale, how committed are you to working in this way?
Headteacher	I'm right up there at a ten on that.
Coach	That's excellent. You know it's a pleasure working with you. I've enjoyed the openness in looking at how you operate.
Headteacher	(*smiles*) Thank you.

Coach	I've a question you might like to consider over the next week, before we meet again. How would you feel about considering a question?
Headteacher	That would be fine.
Coach	OK, Gerry. What is it to be an excellent head?
Headteacher	I like that. I'll give it some thought.

Five ways to get a measure of commitment when you coach

1 A one-to-ten score: 'On a scale of one to ten, where ten is totally and one is not at all, how committed are you to carrying out that action?'

2 A percentage score: 'On a scale of one to one hundred per cent, where one hundred per cent is sure and one per cent is not, where are you?'

3 Hand score: 'Show me with a finger score, how dedicated to this action are you?' (Where five fingers is completely and one is not at all.)

4 Red, amber, green cards: 'Give me your commitment by holding up your cards: red for not committed, amber for halfway committed and green for totally committed.'

5 Stakes – works well with youngsters: ask children to think of activities – one they love doing, one they feel OK about doing and one they hate doing. Ask the question, 'Which activity will you stake on you being sure that you will do what you have agreed to do?'

Extending coaching with an inquiry question is a useful way of promoting further thinking between coaching sessions. It can often stimulate a helpful focus for the following session. In the next chapter there are list of example inquiry questions. Although these example questions can be helpful, more often than not the right question to extend the person being coached comes from the realizations and beliefs that have been uncovered in the session. With practice, and a little trial and error, coaches come to trust the intuition in questioning, and the inquiry question is no exception.

The evaluation aspect of coaching is most important at the beginning of the next session spent together. This time is an opportunity to celebrate success when individuals have completed tasks they agreed to. It is also a time for evaluating aspects of the commitment that have not been completed. It is here that the coach needs to be particularly careful about avoiding judgement. If the person they are coaching has not achieved the actions they set themselves, there will be a reason – there may have been unforeseen external factors that need to be explored and ways around them identified. It may also be the opportunity for the person being coached to explore a limiting belief that has emerged as they have pushed forward towards solution. Such failures are not actually failures in the eyes of the coach. Everything that happens is feedback. The best coaches realize this and remind others of this.

Consequently the next coaching session can move a little more forward in helping the person being coached to further understand and work with their limiting beliefs to enable them to move closer to their targets.

As you have seen from the example coaching dialogue in this chapter, a coach might move around within the model and therefore use it out of sequence; for example, to redefine a target following a new insight. In this sense one might view it more as a checklist than a sequential model. Either way it represents the key process elements of coaching excellence.

Schools have found the STRIDE model to be an excellent way to framework discussions about change. Two examples of different uses of STRIDE follow.

> *Our deepest fear is not that we are inadequate. Our deepest fear is that we are powerful beyond measure.*
>
> Marianne Williamson

The STRIDE model has enabled Anne Copley, former Headteacher of Oakgrove School, Stockport, to assist her staff to resolve behaviour problems with children in the challenging EBD setting within her school. She uses a mixture of planned time on a regular basis with her colleagues to discuss ongoing issues and also ad hoc opportunities to assist their thinking when incidents arise. Anne has noticed positive improvements in the way that students respond to staff and overcome challenges. She also notes that the STRIDE model goes beyond merely supporting staff through incidents, it has a long-term benefit to developing improved attitudes and skills in the EBD environment.

Oakley College, Tafira Alta, Gran Canaria aims to be a caring family school with a strong emphasis on developing self-confidence and learning. They are using accelerated learning and coaching as part of their approach to building this culture.

Non-directive coaching began with staff showing a very positive response to the training and practising it in their everyday lives to gain confidence in using it. They have used the STRIDE model across the school for meeting frameworks and review. They have become more focused on their successes than previously and use them as a springboard to further development. At the same time they have used the STRIDE format for questionnaires sent out to staff and parents as part of their school development plan review.

They plan to continue implementing coaching within the school because they have had such a positive response to date. Management staff are gaining confidence using it and cascading it down through to the staff and students. They have tried something that was very new to them. They liked it and are learning more about it as time goes on. In a short time frame it has become a very powerful tool in helping identify forward steps and overcome obstacles. STRIDE used in these ways is a flexible checklist for the brokering of change. In 2008, Oakley now have coaching embedded within their continuing professional development processes within the college and use it to support and develop colleagues.

Coaching in a hurry and self-coaching

Coaching in a hurry is more about a shift in the way we use the coaching techniques we have already learned than about any new tools. Where others have problems or performance issues, we can usefully support them by *beginning* the process of coaching until we are able to give them more time. Additionally, coaching can be most helpful if the 'little and often' concept is applied. This can be achieved by beginning to work through the STRIDE model and simply asking a few questions to help individuals focus on the target outcome.

Beginning coaching this way:

- helps the coach to support the individual while being clear that they have insufficient time right now – the individual receives, in effect, distal questions to go away and process
- assists the individual to move into a resourceful state of mind
- starts the process of solution for the individual straight away
- allows a lengthy amount of processing-time for the individual to think carefully about the answers

In schools we are often so very busy that it might seem that we cannot help others to help themselves. On the contrary, students and colleagues alike often go away very satisfied with a question or two to consider following an exchange like this:

> *I am tied up right now, but I will help you. We can meet tomorrow at twelve if that helps. In the mean time how do you feel about considering a couple of questions?' **(await reply)** 'OK, What exactly would you like in place of the problem? Be really specific. And second, what personal characteristics will help you get that result?*

It is the authors' experience with both adults and children that they will come to the meeting saying that they have already sorted their problem out and enthusiastically explain how. Naturally this starts a process that people are used to when they work around a coach, and one could argue that they are already experienced in the patterns of coaching for solutions. Self-coaching can become a habit of mind with the right approach.

You might like to consider these questions at this point:

- How could you do this with your own children, with your class and even with your whole school community?
- How can you help others to develop this self-coaching pattern to make 'coaching on the hoof' realistic and thereby preserve your own time management?
- How could coaching be used to promote personal resourcefulness among students across a whole school?
- What if every child in the school understood and used the STRIDE model with other students, over time?

Further approaches

Introducing students to the STRIDE model and the Change Cube model can provide useful frameworks for personal reflection and development. The 'self-coaching model' shown in Figure 6.3 can be a great way to promote personal coaching for solutions.

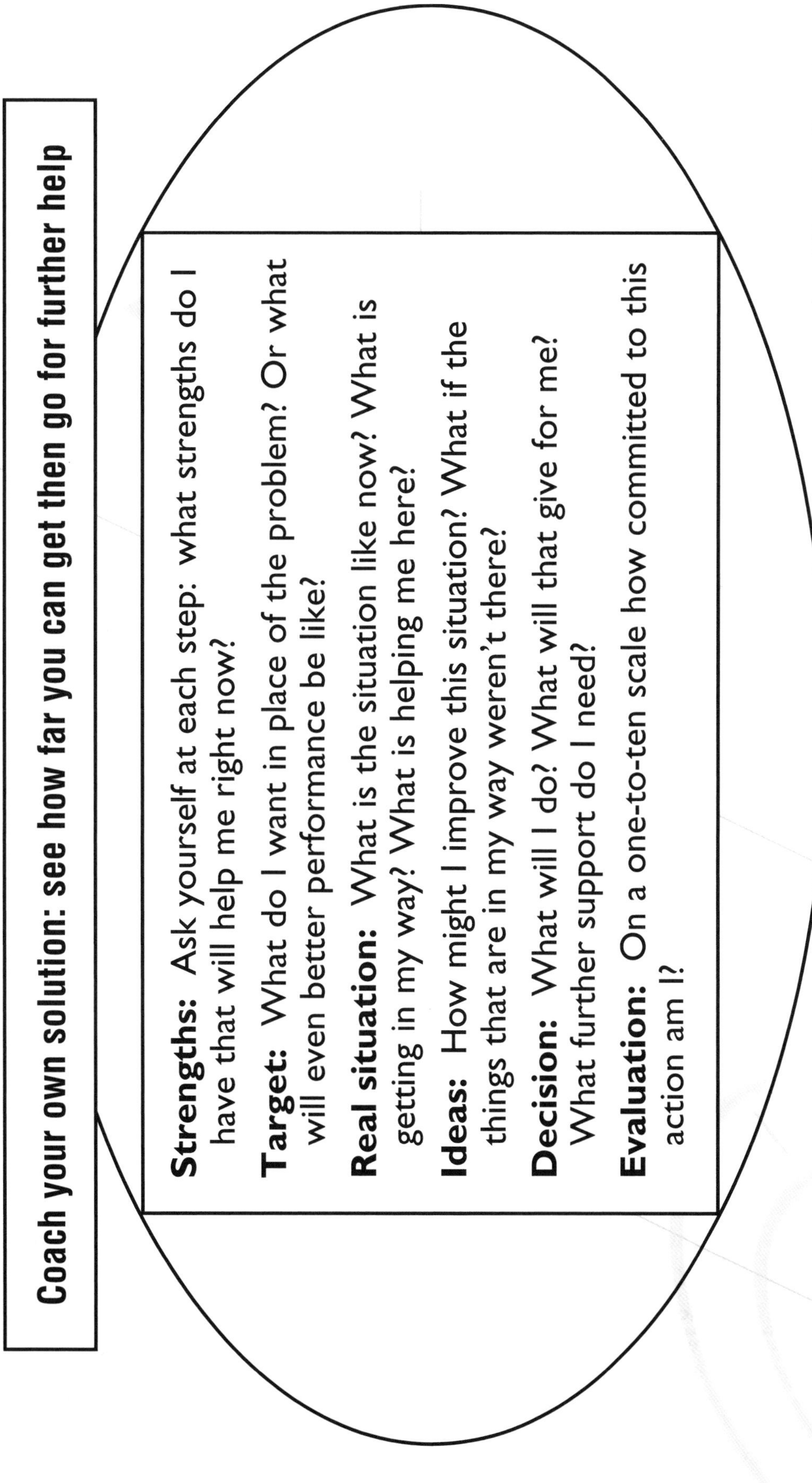

Coach your own solution: see how far you can get then go for further help

Strengths: Ask yourself at each step: what strengths do I have that will help me right now?

Target: What do I want in place of the problem? Or what will even better performance be like?

Real situation: What is the situation like now? What is getting in my way? What is helping me here?

Ideas: How might I improve this situation? What if the things that are in my way weren't there?

Decision: What will I do? What will that give for me? What further support do I need?

Evaluation: On a one-to-ten scale how committed to this action am I?

Figure 6.3 The self-coaching model

The self-coaching model

Displaying the self-coaching framework on corridor and classroom walls will promote interest and begin the process of children questioning and using the framework. Adding it to staff, student and parent handbooks creates a reference point which individuals can go to for self-coaching. Encouraging its use throughout the school and modelling its use in everyday problem solving can begin the process of embedding a coaching approach to thinking in school.

Another helpful tool in embedding self-coaching in school is to ask students to consider what might help them towards success and what they feel is getting in the way. This helps to minimize the thinking time when they meet with you for a more formal coaching appointment.

1   The areas to consider are as follows:
    - task
    - surroundings
    - others
    - me.

2   For each of the these areas consider how:
    - it helps me meet my challenge/improves my ability
    - it holds me back from meeting my challenge/improving my ability.

3   Try to consider five ideas in total for each area.

This format can be displayed again around school and becomes a great tool for thinking around a problem. Notice the reframe of problem to challenge.

When you meet someone for a coaching session you may often find that they have moved on from their original concerns. A useful question to ask then is 'How are things right now with your challenge?' Following this with 'What's changed since we last spoke?' helps you to point out some strengths they will usually display in beginning to solve their dilemma. This makes for great rapport and a resourceful individual from the start.

Speed Coaching

In the pressure cooker environment of an organization it can be a real luxury to spend 30 minutes working through an entire coaching STRIDE-based session. A really quick and useful approach to helping people when time is short is to use a '5 minute coaching' or 'Speed Coaching' system.

It works as follows:

1   Ask the person to define the issue in a nutshell (in 2–3 sentences, maximum).

2   Then ask them to scale their current feelings about this issue from 1 to 10 where 10 is a strong positive feeling and 1 is a strong negative feeling.

3   Now coach them for 3 minutes using only open questions which are in the reality section of the STRIDE model and which get them to understand more about their situation, e.g.:
    a What specifically do you believe about this?
    b Who says this is true?
    c What have you tried? What have you not tried?
    d How do you know when it's time to feel like this about this situation?

4   Once the 3 minutes are up, ask the person to scale their new feelings about the issue from one to 10 as before.

5   Finally ask them: whether you have gone up or down on your scale, what have you learned that's positive or useful about your issue. Draw this out of them and then leave them with the simple question to take away: what's next?

Regardless of whether the person feels better or worse about the problem, this short burst of coaching will have created a shift and this shift provides leverage for them thinking about the issue further. If you have provoked a positive shift in feeling then there is likely to be a next step generated for them to take. If they feel worse, then the fifth stage in the process will put them back into a resourceful state by drawing on the learning they have got from this. Very often the positive learning when someone feels worse after speed coaching is that they have to face up to doing something they know will make a situation better but they don't want to do! In the rare situation that they haven't made a shift, a useful question is: 'What question do not want to ask yourself, which if you asked yourself would create a useful shift?'. Such a session can help them to face a fear and make the necessary changes. You can also use the rescue techniques discussed earlier in this chapter, involving strengths, to build a positive state of mind in your coachee. This kind of technique can be a really useful 'corridor support' when you are needing to provide help when you are short of time and can be combined with mentoring-type suggestions too.

Creative ways to use the STRIDE model in and out of school

The STRIDE model is a versatile coaching framework that can be used for formalized coaching and informal exchanges in and around school. This chapter ends by considering some creative alternatives to the one-to-one discussion-based coaching explored so far. There now follow five alternative approaches to coaching with the STRIDE model.

Puppetry for coaches

Using puppets as a medium for coaching young children can be an excellent way to minimize threat and make personal change and learning an enjoyable experience. The web site www.PuppetsByPost.com provides an extensive range of high quality puppets for this kind of work, ranging from human to animal and fantasy characters. Equally, an old sock with eyes for buttons can be very successful with young children. Building the relationship with young children in this way can be magical and works well with the STRIDE model and the coaching questions outlined in the Chapter 7. Modifying the questions for the age group provides a fascinating way to focus children's thoughts onto understanding and changing learning behaviour. Children can be given puppets themselves to use to respond to questions posed by their coach.

Limited language coaching

Coaching does not have to be a language-rich process. Much can be gained from developing pictorial representations of each part of the STRIDE model. For example, asking a child to draw their current view of themselves in a situation and then their preferred view of themselves in the future when the problem is resolved/their performance is enhanced is a powerful way to promote thinking about change. In one example a young girl called Laura was having difficulties with her maths work. Her teacher asked her to draw herself being successful with her maths (Figure 6.4a) and then she asked her to draw how things were now (Figure 6.4b). Laura drew herself and another girl called Sarah. Sarah appears equal in size to Laura in the preferred future, yet much bigger in the real situation now. The teacher was able to explore the differences in the pictures. What Laura understood at the end was that when she did maths, she worried a great deal about how others were doing and Sarah in particular. This worry was paralysing when she saw that Sarah had finished her sums. Sarah's size in the second picture related to her ability as Laura saw it, and also the impact Sarah's success had on Laura. The teacher was able to ask Laura to draw ways to make Sarah feel smaller while Laura did her maths – she drew herself without Sarah in the options phase.

Figure 6.4a Limited language: Laura's current experience   Figure 6.4b Limited language: Laura being successful

Coaching can be used in managing behaviour positively by using the STRIDE model. The example below is taken from a classroom where a pupil is displaying particularly challenging behaviour. The focus of the conversation is about putting things right, NOT what went wrong. It follows the STRIDE model; time has been given away from the group to let the pupil settle before coaching begins.

Teacher	(approaches pupil, smiles and sits down next to him)
John	F*** off. I don't want to work over here.
Teacher	(choosing to ignore swearing) What would you prefer John?
John	I want to get back to working with my friends.
Teacher	I agree it's much better to be with your friends. Something's gone wrong. What do you need to do to fix it?
John	I'm going back over there to work with my class.
Teacher	Good idea but what do you need to do to get back to working with your class?
John	I suppose I have to say sorry.
Teacher	How will that fix what went wrong?
John	I don't know, I'll just say sorry.
Teacher	How was it when you left the class, when you came over here?
John	Joanna was really cross with me for interrupting her and swearing at her.
Teacher	How can you put that right?
John	I'll say sorry.
Teacher	I'm interested in what you might do as well as what you might say. What else might need to happen? How will you fix things?
John	I tipped a table over, I could clear up the mess I left.
Teacher	What's going to be different when you go back over?

John	I'll get on with my work.
Teacher	How easy is that to do? What will that look like exactly? Show me what you will do. (*At this point teacher encourages physically rehearsing what is going to happen.*)

During the physical rehearsal, the teacher asks further questions to move to the decision phase of STRIDE model:

- How will you say things?
- Who might stop you from getting this right?
- What might other pupils say or do to mess this up?
- What if...?

The teacher responds to John by praising his strengths in thinking through a solution and reinforces this when he carries out the agreed actions.

In this situation language exchange is minimized and coaching is enhanced by the student being encouraging to physically rehearse the actions he will take. The reality phase of the STRIDE model is kept to a bare minimum and there is no revisiting of the emotional aspects of the incident that led to his movement away from the rest of the group. This is important in order to move into and remain in a resourceful state of mind and re-focus on learning.

Stepping outside yourself

This can be helpful for some people who find talking about themselves very difficult. It is a successful technique for people who like to be active during their thought processes. It can enable an individual to step outside difficult experiences and dissociate from them temporarily to gain insight. In stepping outside yourself, the coach places two chairs at a slight angle to one another and invites the individual to sit in one. The coach then asks the individual to define their goal, as themselves. Following the STRIDE model, the coach judges times when the individual is finding the thoughts awkward or emotionally difficult and invites them to take a break and be an observer – someone who might support them in this situation. They then sit in the other chair and the coach asks questions of them in the third person. This can be useful when coaching problems involving relationships with other people, and works well for dealing with bullying situations among young people in school where the emotional trauma is often very profound. It is important to have time to carry out this process and to associate the individual with themselves in the original chair at the end of the process once helpful and positive solutions have been found. It is similarly important to point out that all solutions and insights have actually come from the individual – this is very affirming for them. In the *Coaching Solutions Resource Book* (the companion volume to this text) there is a scripted tool entitled 'Points of View' which takes you through a dissociation process for use with colleague and learners. It is very useful for assisting people to resolve conflict between themselves and others.

Walking the talk

An excellent approach to coaching suitable for adults and young people is to take a walk and use the STRIDE model on the move. This can range from two teachers having a mutual coaching session while on duty around the school grounds at lunchtime to taking a group of children to the local park or outdoor centre.

Coaching in alternative environments

There can be real benefits to taking people out of familiar environments and coaching them. Coaching in the mountains and coaching afloat on a sea-going yacht are two options for this kind of individual or team-building experience. For more information about coaching at altitude and coaching afloat contact info@visionforlearning.co.uk and info@in2uition.co.uk respectively.

Summary

The STRIDE model is one way of structuring a coaching session. It is a flexible model that gives guidance on the process of positive change.

Its core components are:

▶ Pay attention to the strengths of the person you are coaching and maintain a resourceful state of mind through this.

▶ Carefully define the target for development and revisit as necessary throughout the process.

▶ Explore the real situation and what the individual has tried. Listen carefully for evidence of limiting beliefs and probe these.

▶ Explore ideas using questions and brainstorms.

▶ Make a decision about the best course of action from the ideas an individual produces.

Finally, place the decision under evaluation using a 1–10 scale or other device so that the confidence and commitment to the course of action is tested. In the next coaching session the evaluation continues as the coach explores the success the individual has had with their agreed actions.

Additionally:

▶ A person being coached will not always follow the phases of the STRIDE model in the order prescribed by the model. STRIDE should be seen as a checklist rather than a rigid sequence.

▶ Coaching with the STRIDE model does not need to take place in one lengthy time period. The model can be broken down as steps, and working towards a solution can take place a few minutes at a time over a period of hours, days or even months.

▶ A self-coaching model is outlined. It is simple and can help people being coached to take their own steps towards resolution. Mulling over a problem subconsciously for yourself can provide new insights, setting the intuition running.

▶ There are many creative ways to make the STRIDE model come to life for young and older people alike. Some of these approaches are outlined in this chapter. This is by no means a prescriptive list and you may well have further valid ideas – go ahead and try them using STRIDE as the framework.

Questions

1   How might you use the STRIDE model in your role?

2   You are using the STRIDE model with a colleague. When they reach the options stage they decide that maybe they made a mistake with their goal. What would you do? What may your reflexive listening be aware of?

3   How would you check the level of commitment that a student has to changing their behaviour?

4   You are coaching a colleague through a difficult issue relating to their personal organization. How would you broaden the range of solutions they might choose from the ideas section of the coaching model?

5   Someone you are coaching for the first time, despite your best efforts to work through the model, seems to dart around looking at the different aspects of STRIDE. What do you do?

6   After coaching your team through to a solution, they all commit to the actions you decide together. A week after the action was due to be completed, you become aware that one person has not carried out the agreed action. What do you do? How would you apply the nine principles of coaching to this situation?

Masterclass

▶   When asking for an evaluation of the action agreed, ask the individual how they would like to score it. Some people are happy with a 1–10 scale, others prefer percentages. Some want to avoid numbers altogether and go for a more qualitative scale; for example, red–amber–green scale.

▶   Ask permission to pose more challenging questions by using a phrase such as, 'How would you feel if I played devil's advocate here?' or 'How would you feel if I asked you a direct question here?'

▶   Allowing people enough time to think through questions properly is a foundation of excellent coaching. Allowing silence is really important. Before starting coaching, explain that coaching is an opportunity to really think about the questions asked of you and that it is OK to take time to really think before answering. Inviting people to write things down as they think can help them feel more comfortable about this.

▶   Grow and learn alongside people you coach and model and respond to the spiritual aspect of the learning journey.

▶   Celebrate the attainment of the goal and the joy of the climb.

▶   Laugh alongside those you work with – making serious progress can be a lot of fun.

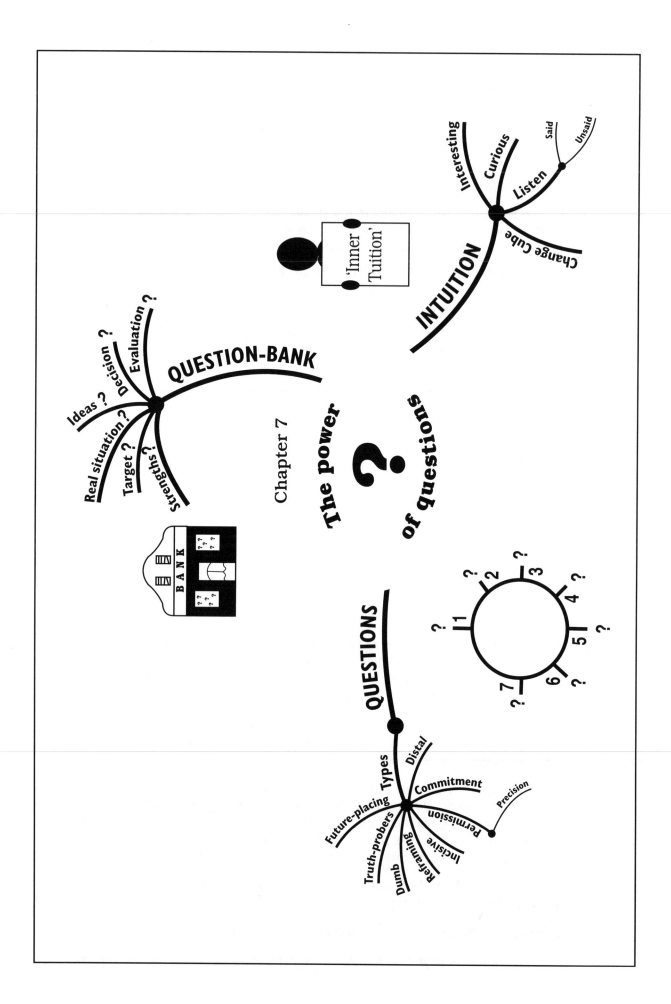

Chapter 7

The power of questions

IN THIS CHAPTER YOU WILL LEARN:

- about eight types of questions
- why open questions are best and why 'why' is to be avoided
- which questions to use and when to use them in coaching
- that the best questions are the ones that come from your own curiosity

PREVIEW QUESTIONS:

- What kinds of questions might help a person who felt unable to improve their performance through lack of resources in their job?
- What are the core questions that every coach should have at their disposal?
- Why do simple questions create greater insight than complex ones?
- What is the difference between a leading question and a curious question?

Shine that light over here

A man was searching for his house keys under a lamp post. As he scrabbled around on the pavement one of his neighbours asked him what he was looking for.

'I've lost my keys,' he said. The neighbour got down beside him and helped him look. After a while some more passers-by joined in and try as they might, they could not find the keys.

'Are you certain you lost the keys here?' said one of the group.

'No, I lost them over there by the wall at the back of the house,' replied the man.

'So why are we all wasting our time looking here?'

'This is where the light is ...'

The right question at the right time

The right question, asked at the right time and in the right way, will open up thinking pathways. If you do not ask the right question, a lot of time can be wasted scrabbling around in the dark. Asking questions is such a natural skill and from a very early age children utilize this skill both to find out about the world around them and to drive their parents mad! So what do we do? We tell them to stop asking so many questions! Lo and behold they stop asking questions and their curiosity ebbs away. As suggested in Chapter 4, try to rediscover your child-like curiosity to maximize your coaching effectiveness.

Open questions implicitly reinforce the coach's belief that the person being coached holds the solutions to their challenges within them. In short, the curious open question asserts and helps to maintain the individual's independence in finding resolution. In addition to the open questions described here, there are also phrases that can elicit helpful openings for individuals; for example, 'Tell me something about ...' or 'Describe to me ...'.

Coaching questions seek to uncover truth, clarify meaning, test commitment and open avenues of thought. It follows therefore that there are different types of questions that will suit these outcomes.

The most useful types of open questions for coaches

The key useful questions were discussed briefly in Chapter 4 and in this chapter we will explore them in more depth and identify when they are most useful.

There are eight key question types that are of use to coaches. They are:

- Future-placing questions
- Truth-probers
- Simple questions
- Reframing questions
- Incisive questions
- Permission and precision questions
- Commitment questions
- Distal questions.

Future-placing questions invite people to put themselves into the future at a time when they have achieved the goal they aspire to. These questions encourage people to pay attention to what they will be, see, hear and feel when they have achieved their goal.

They have two key purposes. First, they get people in touch with what they want to achieve and really motivate them – people imagine already having the quality, skill, result and so on. Second, they help people to look back at what they need to do to achieve that desired situation, that is, what the steps to success are. These questions can also help us to see whether we really want what we think we want or need! Sometimes in this virtual reality people do not like what they see and they come back and adjust their goals. All of this gives them more information about where they really want to aim. Of course, some of what we aim for in schools is imposed and exploring the future can help to uncover resentments and value-mismatches that exist about imposed targets. These might then be resolved through further exploration.

Examples of question that do this are:

- What are you seeing, hearing and feeling now you are actually doing this new role?
- What is it like to be person 'X' who already does this?
- Put yourself six months into the future. Standing there, having achieved this goal, look back. What decisions did you make along the way to achieve this?
- What do you see, hear, feel, now that you have achieved your target? Looking back what steps did you take in order to be this successful?

The last two questions work well together. They form the basis for future-scaping, which is explored further in Chapter 9. These two questions allow individuals to associate strongly with the achieved goal and then look back at the steps they took from a position of having achieved it. Looking back like this allows individuals to plan a path to success without being derailed by limitations that occur when we look from the present towards the future. This may seem a little strange if it is the first time you have come across the idea, but it can be a very powerful technique to motivate individuals towards targets.

Truth-probers These questions are designed to help individuals make large insightful steps forward and to move towards a deeper understanding of how and and why they behave the way they do. Truth-probers are often used because the coach's intuitive listening tells them something is not being disclosed that is holding back the person they are coaching from making progress. People need time to ponder on truth-probers and process for a meaningful response. Individuals may not always disclose the underlying issue to their coach, but these questions can still have an impact. They are delivered with an emphasis on the underlined word.

Examples of truth-probers include:

- What do you <u>really</u> want?
- What's <u>actually</u> stopping you?
- What's the <u>truth</u> here?
- What <u>else</u> is there here?
- How will you look back on this?
- What memories do you need to start creating now?
- What gives you <u>most</u> anxiety here?
- What difference will this <u>really</u> make to you?
- What are you <u>tolerating</u>?

Truth-probers take people out of comfort and into stretch and tend to disable the cruise control so they acknowledge underlying factors in their issues. Use these type of questions if you think someone is withholding details that are holding them back from progress. Always be sensitive and ensure you really have rapport with them.

Simple questions Whitworth et al. (1998) talk about the curiously named classification of question 'the dumb question', so-called because they usually feel too 'dumb' to ask. We prefer to refer to them as simple questions. This type of question is characteristically very short and simple. They often emerge in the coach's mind but are not articulated. Their power lies in creating a kind of wide-angled lens to view an issue through. Because they have very little content or context they encourage lateral thinking and can bring useful insights.

Examples of simple questions include:

- What do you want?
- Where are we?
- What's next?
- What's needed?
- Where do you want to go from here?
- What do you see?
- What did you learn?
- What do *you* think?

Simple questions are very useful in the initial stages of the STRIDE model when defining targets and, similarly, as a way of encouraging reflection throughout the coaching process.

Reframing questions Sometimes people present a limiting viewpoint of their situation, and as coaches we recognize the limitations this can put on their progress. We can challenge this and refocus them in the positive. Similarly a coach can draw on a person's strengths. Recently a colleague ('D') of Will's presented the need to reframe questions. 'D' would often say 'It's a waste of time, I'm no good at making decisions.' The response from Will was 'What strengths do you have right now that can help you overcome this issue?' There was some silence and then 'D' began to think about his strengths and said 'I could use some of my self-belief to stop giving myself a hard time and look for some new ideas to help me here …'. The result was that 'D' was back into a resourceful state of mind again.

Examples of reframing questions include:

Individual	Why do I always miss the boat?
Reframe	• What does getting the boat look like?
	• What can you do to be a success?
	• How do those that catch the boat respond to challenges like this?
	• What could success do for you?

Covey (1989) in his chapter on being proactive talks about the basic paradigm of determinism. He explains the transfer of responsibility that happens when we talk to ourselves: 'I am not responsible, not able to choose my response.' Covey goes on to point out that reactive language such as 'I must' or 'I have to' reinforces 'a paradigm that they are determined (in other words it is all mapped out for them – no choice) … they feel increasingly victimized and out of control, not in charge of their lives or destiny'.

Will uses reframing questions quite frequently when people uncover an unhelpful negative attitude to an issue. For example, when 'K' said, 'I just don't have any time for anything these days', Will replied, 'What do you have time for?' The dialogue went as follows:

K   Well, I have time for work – I have to spend so much time just keeping on top of it all.

W   You say you have to spend so much time keeping on top of it all; who makes you spend this time?

K   I suppose it's me.

W   Who could help you change this?

K   Well, I suppose I could.

W   Where have you changed something in the past that seemed like it had no solution?

K   When I was decorating the bathroom and the bath was too long for the space – we'd missed the need to leave space for the pipes – I looked at it again and found a way to raise the bath so it missed the pipes.

W   What mental resources did you use to solve this problem?

K   My common sense.

W   *What does that sense tell you now?*

K   *That I'm putting in too many hours at work and I can change that.*

Use reframing questions in the real situation phase of the STRIDE model once limiting beliefs have been identified. This encourages more lateral thinking styles as you move people into the ideas phase.

Incisive questions These are questions that temporarily lift limiting beliefs or external constraints that are perceived to be preventing progress and enable the generation of new avenues of thought. Such questions get the individual to consider new options by stimulating creative-thinking pathways.

The questions have two parts and usually begin 'What if …'; for example, if someone says that they don't have enough time to sort out a problem, the coach might reply, 'OK, so what if there was no limit to the amount of time you had, what would you do then?' The first part of the question suspends the limitation, while the second part encourages the search for solutions.

Examples of incisive questions include:

- What would you do if there were no resource constraints?
- What would you do if it didn't matter what others thought?
- What could you do if it didn't matter what others thought?
- What would you do if teachers never gave your work a grade?
- What would you do if you privately knew the answer to this?
- What if you didn't have to live with the repercussions of this decision?
- What if there was a time in the past when you overcame a similar problem. What did you do then?

All suggestions are treated with equal value by the coach or individual during this incisive stage of coaching. Sometimes even the most absurd-sounding ideas generated by this method trigger other thoughts that lead to new, realistic solutions for people. Softening the 'would' to a 'could' or 'might' makes the question less imperative and further stimulates new ideas. This is a very useful type of question to use in the ideas phase of the STRIDE model.

Permission and precision questions These are important when individuals are seeming to avoid an issue or when a theme or pattern has emerged. Permission questions help to establish whether an individual is willing to explore a potentially difficult area. The precision question directly challenges what the individual says. Such questions cut through generalizations and mistruths about experiences. This is best illustrated with an example.

One person while being coached was avoiding the issue of delegation in his role. He talked about work pressure and seemed to feel that he could do nothing to alleviate it. He described how a member of his staff made mistakes that took him hours to rectify. His coach asked him what he had said to the member of staff after he had rectified the problem. He became quiet and said he had said nothing to her. When asked what had held him back from explaining the error, he replied that he did not want to upset her. He also explained that his second in department was taking lots of time off with her six-month-old baby and he was having trouble coping without her. The coach asked how much the second knew about the pressures he was under and also how much his boss knew. He said that neither knew very much. When asked what held him back from telling them, he replied that he did not want to pressurize her when she had a baby, nor did he want his boss to feel that he could not cope as this would upset her. So a theme was emerging. He disliked upsetting people at the expense of his own work–life balance. His coach sensed he was sensitive about this issue from his tone of voice during the questioning and so asked his permission to look a little closer at this. 'How would you feel about exploring the idea of your impact on other people's emotions?' He paused, thought about it and then said, in an excited tone as if he was taking a great risk, 'Yes, let's do it.' Once permission has been granted the percision questions can then begin. Precision questioning is designed to 'slice' through to the underlying belief. For example:

- How exactly do you think they will be upset?
- What precisely do you think your second-in-department would think if you explained?
- What specifically do you perceive as being upsetting to your boss here?
- What fundamentally is the impact on you of withholding this information?

In this example, the individual being coached seemed to have a belief about upsetting people that was holding him back from dealing with his balance issue. The coach challenges the generalization here that upsetting people is likely to happen if he is open about his feelings. In these questions the words 'specifically', 'precisely' and 'exactly' focus very closely on the beliefs operating and challenge them. This style of question will usually encourage an individual to question the limiting belief and adjust it. It is not always necessary to use permission questioning with precision questions. This will depend on circumstances and is a judgment call for the coach. The precision question can come into play in any phase of the STRIDE model.

Commitment questions These questions tie down the person being coached to specific action points and check their level of commitment to a chosen path. Questions like 'What will you do?' and 'When will you do that?' are examples of such a commitment gathering process. Checking the level of commitment using a percentage scale or alternative (see Chapter 6) follows the commitment question.

Examples of commitment questions include:

- When will I know you have been successful?
- With whom will you make your commitment?
- When will you first use your new way of doing things?
- When will this start?
- What will this give you when it is achieved?
- What could get in the way of you completing this?
- How might you prevent this derailing you?

The last questions in this list are important preparations for the possible negative effects of what the person is striving for and the possible blocks that might prevent completion. These questions fall in the decision phase of the STRIDE model.

Distal questions Those questions that extend beyond the coaching session into the time between one session and the next are termed 'distal questions'. They are designed to continue the processing of themes from the coaching session. One member of staff spoke of 'thoughts of not being a good enough teacher' as a key feature in his working life. The distal question to him for the week to follow was 'How am I already a great teacher?' By the following week he had a page of ideas and he started thinking in a more balanced way about his strengths and weaknesses as a teacher.

Examples of distal questions include:

- What helpful thoughts do you bring into your classroom?
- What thoughts would you choose to leave outside the classroom?
- What is it to be a good teacher?
- What does being a great listener actually mean?
- What do I need to let go of so I can be even more effective?

Distal questions are characterized more by the timing of their asking than by their structure or content, although they are likely to have a range of answers that are specific to the person thinking about them. They are typically asked near the end of coaching sessions so that they can be processed over a longer time period. Will's experience is that these questions revolve consciously and subconsciously in people's minds and create really deep insights over the days or weeks between coaching contacts.

Beyond questions: some useful coaching statements

Statements that open up dialogue: 'Tell me more about …'
These demonstrate value for the person being coached and respect and help to develop the sense of independence in the individual.

Statements that clarify: 'I think what you are saying is …'
This statement is important when a coach wants to check the meaning of what an individual has said. In other words the coach wants to match their understanding of what the person has said to them.

The questions in action

In the following dialogue, a range of the question types described in this chapter is used.

A student (Tim) spoke to his teacher one day about some concerns with exams. He seemed detached from his usual relaxed state. He got straight to an issue and skipped the greeting that he usually exchanged with his teacher. As his teacher listened to him she began to sense that the issue he brought to her was not what he really wanted to talk about. The dialogue proceeded as follows:

Tim	I want to work on exam worries. (*silence*)
Teacher	Tell me about your exam concerns.
Tim	I'm worrying about whether I'll pass. (*note that tone of voice suggested no enthusiasm or even real worry about exams*) I just don't seem to be able to get down to do the revision. I get stuck before I even start. I just can't get to concentrate.
Teacher	(*noticing the tone and the reticence to talk more fluidly – normally Tim talked freely about issues*) What really concerns you, Tim?
Tim	(*long silence*) Telling my parents. (*silence*) Yes, telling them.
Teacher	What is it you might need to tell them?
Tim	That I don't want to go to university. I feel such a pressure to go on to university but it's not what I want to do with my life. My parents are forcing the issue and I have other plans. I feel nervous about telling them.
Teacher	What do you feel confident about?
Tim	I actually feel relieved I've told someone because this is what I really need to do – I mean not go to university – but telling mum and dad is going to be a nightmare!
Teacher	If you thought they'd be OK about this, what would you do then?
Tim	I'd finish my exams, but apply for the electrician's apprenticeship I that really want to do.
Teacher	When could you do that?
Tim	I can do it now.
Teacher	What exactly do you think would upset your parents?
Tim	(*pauses*) I'm not one hundred per cent sure. I suppose they might be disappointed in me, that I'm not a good son. I know I have to do this.
Teacher	OK, so if you have to do this, what might be your first step?
Tim	Before I say anything to them, I want to really get my facts right. I'll do some more research on the apprenticeships and get the forms and stuff.
Teacher	When will you do that by?
Tim	I'll send for the information by Friday.
Teacher	Great Tim. How would you feel about coming back to me when you have the info? Perhaps we can talk again.
Tim	That would be very helpful. Thanks.
Teacher	How would you feel about thinking about something over the next few

*days that might help? (**Tim nods**) A question: How might your parents already be proud of their son?*

Three sessions on from this Tim talked to his parents. To his amazement they explained that they had realized he might not want to go to university. They said that it was not what they had planned but they respected his decision. Tim's sense of relief was enormous. He felt that he had achieved a great deal in asserting his needs and his confidence grew considerably.

There were some key elements in getting to the real issue here:

1   Sensing the signs of unusual reticence in someone the coach knew.

2   Noting the tone of voice that lacked conviction when Tim talked about the surface problem.

3   Using the dumb question to allow opening of the topic. The coach sensed the lack of commitment.

4   Challenging with the truth-prober question: What really concerns you?

5   Using a reframe question to bring Tim out of his unresourceful thinking: 'What do you feel confident about?'

6   Using the incisive question 'If you thought they would be OK about this, what would you do then?' allowed Tim to consider options while suspending the fear associated with the issue.

7   Using the precision question 'What exactly do you think might upset your parents?' helps Tim to consider what his parents might be thinking and begins to challenge his concerns about them being upset.

8   Asking the commitment question 'When will you do that by?' adds a measure of commitment to Tim taking his next step.

9   Ending the conversation, the coach asks a distal question: 'How might your parents already be proud of their son?' This is designed to assist Tim to stay resourceful in thinking about his relationship with his parents and maintain confidence in his chosen career direction.

In conclusion, using a range of questions can provide ways to reduce anxiety about change and unblock thought pathways. When we are relaxed we think more rationally and can assert our needs more accurately, calmly and authentically.

So far in this chapter a range of useful questions have been described by type and use. In the following pages a set of questions are organized in relation to the STRIDE model so that you can relate them to the coaching model described in Chapter 6. Use whichever way of classifying and recalling questions suits you best.

Coaching questions for use with the STRIDE model

Strengths

(Important in helping to maintain self-esteem at high levels – the skill is in picking up an individual's strengths and feeding them back throughout the coaching process.)

- Remember to look for and draw attention to the strengths of the person being coached throughout. Affirm the positive.

- Useful question: What strengths do you have that could help you here?

- What would your most trusted colleague/friend/confidant say were your greatest attributes?

Target

- What do you want?

- Go ahead to a time in the future when you have achieved your goal. What is it like?

- What will it look like? Sound like? Feel like?

- When do you want to have achieved it by?

- What excites you about this goal?

- Think into the future when you have achieved this. What do you feel like?

- How will you know when you have achieved this target?

- When will you accomplish this target?

Real situation

- What is the current situation?

- What do you feel about this right now?

- What is missing here that you would like to have?

- What are the problems this is causing?

- What have you already tried doing to improve things and what were the outcomes?

- How does it feel at the moment?

- What are the current obstacles to achieving your target?

- What resources do you need to overcome your obstacles?

- Look back at your target. Is it still what you want/need?

Ideas

- What might you do if you could move yourself a step forward now?
- What could you do if you didn't have to explain it to anyone else? How would that feel?
- What could you do if resources/time/parents/school/teacher/students/friend and so on were not blocks here? (Insert the limitation they have identified.)
- What could you do if you did not have to live with the results of your actions?
- Brainstorm one of the options you have come up with. What other ideas are sparked off?
- If you secretly knew what the answer was, what would it be?
- If you had answers lurking just below the surface and you shared them now, what might you share? And what else?
- From your options, which is the quickest/easiest/cheapest/most comfortable/ least comfortable/most effective thing to do?
- Now go through each option. Remind yourself of your target. How will the option you have chosen move you closer to your target?
- What is the benefit of doing the thing that you have chosen?
- What will you know that's new by doing this?
- What impact will it have on you/your colleagues/your role/students and so on?

Decision

- What are you definitely going to do?
- What are the steps?
- Go forward to the time when this is already achieved. Looking back, what did you do to get there?
- When will you take these steps?
- Who else (if anyone) should be involved in this process? What will they do? How will they know this?
- When will you review your progress towards your target?
- What are the barriers to you taking that first step? How likely is it to stop you? What can be done to overcome it?
- How sensible is your timescale?

Evaluation

- Have you been successful?
- How have you made forward progress?
- What's not gone as planned? What did you learn from this?

  (Many of the real situation questions can work here too.)

Questioning and intuition

Life is more a matter of choosing than of knowing. You can never know the eventual destination of your path, but you can always choose in which direction to take the next step.

(Mike Stover, 2002)

While the last two chapters have outlined specific types of questions and suggested some clever questions to overcome sticking points with those you coach, there is no compulsion to use such prescriptive lists of approaches. Indeed coaching can become stifled and wooden, holding people back when the process feels scripted. Coaching is most fluid and most successful when the coach simply sets out to be curious. Using the Change Cube and STRIDE model as a checklist for the process, you can follow your instinctive curiosity about what to ask next. Sticking to open questions is still important. Using the Change Cube model will guide you should you feel you need it. It is a most effective way to enhance your coaching practice. Remember that the Change Cube focuses on exploring and re-adjusting four factors:

- perceptions
- self-talk
- emotions
- state (physiological readiness).

The intuitive coaching approach helps you consider the ways in which the person you are coaching is experiencing interference with their desired outcomes. Coaches who work in this way still root their practice in the nine principles of non-directive coaching.

Dilts (1990) says that changing our behaviour is 'not necessarily about losing the content of the belief but about re-arranging the relationship'. Asking innocent questions of those we coach helps them to explore their choices and make informed decisions. Any successful leader, teacher, parent or learner is accomplished because they are fully aware of their choices at any given time in a decision-making process. A critical awareness within the coach's head is important and the following questions should be asked by coaches of themselves:

- What is my own agenda here? How is this helping this person I am coaching?
- What are the emotional responses that I am having?
- How might my own perspectives influence this situation?

With time and practice you will become adept at separating out the voices of your own emotions, your own self-talk and your own interferences in the process of supporting those you coach. What you are left with is the sharpness of pure intuition, which is swift, analytical and pattern-seeking. It will serve you and those you coach well. Your coaching will move to a higher level.

If the STRIDE model is the way into coaching, intuitive coaching is the height of performance. Intuitive non-directive coaching is the subtle blend of rational and intuitive processes and reflective practice in the support of others.

Summary

▶ Coaches use a range of questioning styles within the structure of the STRIDE model.

▶ There are eight core questions that coaches will find useful to challenge and support individuals to make progress.

▶ This chapter contains a bank of questions appropriate to each phase of the STRIDE model that can be used as a guideline for beginner coaches.

▶ Curiosity is the key mindset for coaches to adopt in finding the right question at the right time for those they coach.

▶ Our emotions, self-talk, perceptions and physical state both interfere with and enhance our performance.

▶ The intuitive coach recognizes the importance of them, enables the individual to explore them and to understand the choices available and ultimately to decide on a course of action.

▶ The Change Cube provides a framework for supporting intuitive approaches to coaching.

Questions

1 What kind of questions would be best suited as responses to these statements/ situations by coaches:

▶ People always put my achievements down.

▶ This is quite upsetting for me to think about (coach has noticed pattern of avoiding commitment to start a revision programme).

▶ I'm not very good at making the right decision.

▶ Coaching time has come to an end, and the individual has been exploring how to relate better to a colleague whom they perceive as highly critical.

2   What has struck you about the rational STRIDE model of coaching and the intuitive approaches outlined in this chapter?

3   What do you see as the next level of development for your coaching with regard to questioning?

4   Provide three questions that might be of general use in any coaching situation for each part of the STRIDE coaching model.

Masterclass

▶   Drop your agenda. Be in the moment with the person you are coaching. If you have a series of questions planned ahead in your mind, the individual will sense it. This will at best slow down their progress and at worst damage your relationship.

▶   Read through the bank of coaching questions – pick out five questions that strike you as interesting. Decide how they might be useful. Practise them in your head each day. This will grow your intuitive collection of questions – when you most need them, these questions pop out of your memory to great effect.

▶   Be curious and ask those innocent questions that pop into your head as you coach. Trust your intuition to develop questions that will help individuals explore opportunities and choices.

▶   Be prepared for the individual to move around within the STRIDE model and to come back to the target and redefine it periodically within a session and over several sessions.

▶   Take the longer-term view with questions. Be prepared for the greatest insights to happen over days and weeks rather than seconds and minutes.

▶   Be happy in the belief that every question you ask is helpful and that some may be the most helpful that the individual has ever been asked. But do not expect them to give you credit for it!

▶   Always have your rescue question ready for those times when the individual gets stuck in an unresourceful state of mind.

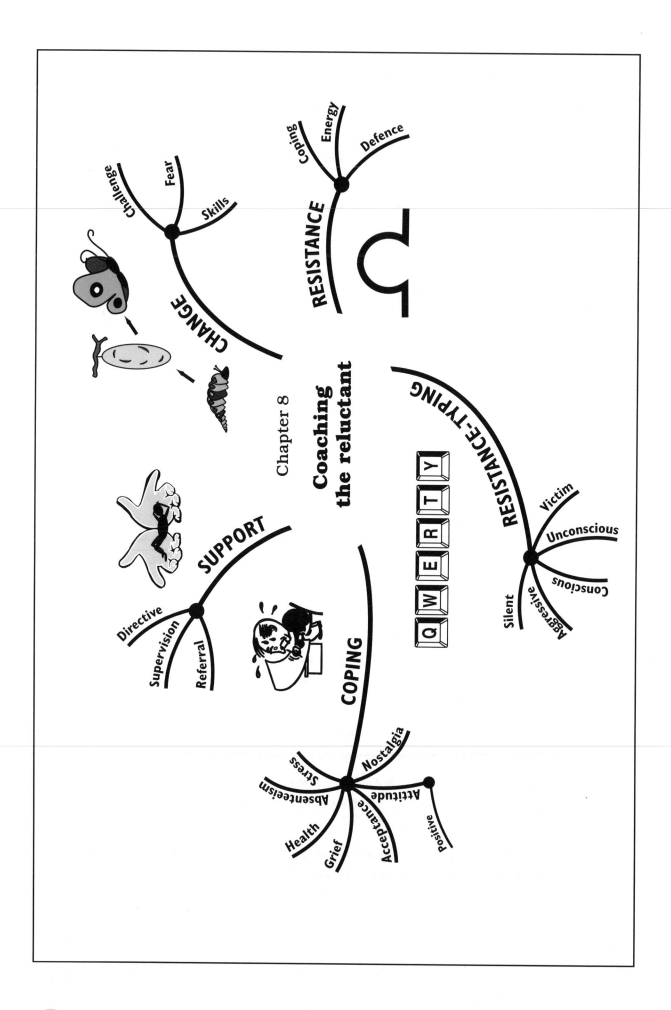

Chapter 8

**Coaching
the reluctant**

Chapter 8

Coaching the reluctant

IN THIS CHAPTER YOU WILL LEARN:

- to understand what resistance is
- to understand the factors that create resistance
- to understand the change process
- to develop the coach attitudes to deal effectively with resistance
- to have a range of strategies to deal with resistance

PREVIEW QUESTIONS:

- What is resistance?
- Why do people resist and what are they resisting?
- What causes people to be resistant?
- As a coach how can I react to resistance? How do I actually react?
- What can I do to prevent, understand and deal with resistance?

How tight is your shackle?

Francois Bizot had been in Cambodia for six years researching Buddhism. In October 1971 his researches took him to a monastery in the Oudong region thirty kilometres north of Pnom Penh. It was here that he and his two companions were captured by the Khmer Rouge. For three months he was held in chains in a remote detention camp near Angkor. Accused of being an agent of American Imperialism, a spy and a Lon Nol sympathizer, Bizot survived. His two companions did not. While in the camp Bizot was interrogated daily and at length. His every word was written down as he and his interrogator, a man called Douch, tried to outwit each other. If Bizot lost the battle of wits, it meant his death.

Bizot describes how, in confinement, humans attach themselves to the most derisory objects, even 'to the instruments of one's own torture', simply because they are there every day and they become a familiar and permanent part of the landscape. To move position, to shift to new piece of ground, to be chained to a different tree, caused Bizot terrible feelings of distress. Bizot describes how he became familiar with the tree to which he was attached and to the piece of ground in front of him. He became familiar with the feel of the heavy iron chain that held him.

One day a new prisoner arrived in camp with his young daughter. She looked about nine years of age. As her father was taken away, the child was transferred to a communal dormitory and given a place recently vacated by an old woman who had died. This was where the sick prisoners were kept. The girl curled up in the corner. She would not eat.

Bizot spent many days trying to persuade the guards to allow him to share his food with the girl. He had a daughter of a similar age. Eventually they agreed. He sent her milk and sugar heated with water in a bowl: she did not touch it. The food lay untouched all day. Bizot had secured the right to bathe in the river from time to time. As he was led to the river later that evening, he paused by the girl and tried again to engage her in conversation. She turned her back on him. On the way back he tried once more. Again, he received the same response, but this time noticed that she had drank the contents of the bowl. Over time, the child grew bolder but would not speak.

Eventually she overcame her shyness and would come and sit beside Bizot as he compiled his journal for Douch. The child's silent presence made him feel renewed vitality as if 'the flame of life that now burned in her little body … had dispersed daylight all over the camp'. She would watch him write, carefully scrutinizing the marks he made, accompany him to the stream and eat her food alongside him. At the same time she was taken to the self-reproach sessions and communal singing that were part of the Khmer Rouge indoctrination programme for everyone in the camp.

Bizot was chained – painfully – by the ankle. One evening his little protégée arrived and sat beside him. She slipped her tiny finger underneath the chain link between the irons and his badly bruised ankle. Moved by her concern, he did his best to minimize the pain by nodding his head in a gesture of 'denial and smiling reassurance'. She skipped away and, to his astonishment, returned with a bunch of keys. He looked at her with a sense of anticipation as she undid the heavy padlock. With some difficulty she then retightened the chain. The little victim had become the persecutor.

(Based on a story by F. Bizot)

What is resistance?

When people resist they put energy into defending their usual coping strategies. Coaching is primarily about change. Naturally when change is in your own control it is easier to deal with than when it is imposed by others. It is easy to make assumptions about the motivation of others to change. To do so we only have to look at life from the privilege of our own prism. We can construct a whole universe of 'musts' and 'shoulds', of 'ought to's' and 'why don'ts', of 'right ways' and 'wrong ways' by never asking 'what if?'

Bizot is plunged into demoralization because he has, understandably, shaped his understanding of what he sees around him through his own prism. To understand the motivation of others, and thus the response to change, we need to position ourselves in a variety of possible starting-points.

Within institutions, change brings a mixture of emotions. These emotions will vary over time and between those within the organizational culture. For example a change of headteacher will invoke in a variety of responses in people, such as:

- aggressive behaviour towards others and the headteacher
- excitement at new possibilities
- highly productive attitudes as new culture emerge and opportunities become obvious
- depression at loss of old (in some cases traditional) working practices

- fear of unknown, of success, of failure
- secretive working to cover errors, reduction of openness
- obsequious behaviour to make favourable impressions upon the new head
- acceptance from the beginning
- withdrawal
- rigidity – continue as have always done.

With this range of emotions and attitudes, resistance inevitably emerges in some groups and individuals. Zeus and Skiffington (2003) identify this resistance as being more likely in people with certain behavioural approaches. Those people who exhibit the following approaches are often predisposed to resisting change:

- The Perfectionist: low ambiguity-threshold – those who find imprecision of tasks or instructions challenging. Uncertainty is difficult for them.
- The Two-Parters: those who can accept institutional changes but find it hard to make the personal change in behaviour that goes along with it.
- The Power-Seeker: those who need to exert power and find it more difficult to do this in changing times.
- The Control-Seeker: those who perceive that external factors control them (they feel out of control within the changing culture).
- The Extreme Thinker: those who have extreme feelings of paranoia, narcissism, obsessive compulsive feelings and passive/aggressive polarity.
- The Cynic: those who are naturally suspicious of outsiders in the case of a new leader or external performance coach being brought into the organization or new ideas.

Among the coping strategies brought about by any change we have:

- positive mental attitudes
- acceptance and excitement
- grief over the loss of old practices
- stress brought about by resistance
- health-related problems
- absenteeism
- wallowing in misplaced nostalgia.

In summary, some people react well to change and others experience a range of behavioural responses that can be destructive to themselves, to others and to the organization.

As a coach it is so important to recognize that people react in different ways and to acknowledge that their emotions and their reactions are not directed personally at you, but at the situation, at the change. We can sometimes feel that aggressive behaviour is directed personally at us, but we must remember that it is often directed at us merely because we represent the institution that is imposing the change.

It is helpful to think of this kind of response as feedback. Assume the position that 'everything is feedback and from feedback we can improve – no feedback is no use'. We have a choice about how we react to the feedback. Emotions in coaching terms are information and often provide powerful insights into beliefs. We can learn a great deal of useful information through listening to emotional responses. We gain important levels of trust when we listen and acknowledge the depth of feelings of the people we are coaching.

The number one rule for dealing productively with resistance is to listen and acknowledge the emotions. Use this as a way into understanding the beliefs and values that underlie the emotional expression. For most of us, strong emotions such as anger come from finding ourselves in situations where the beliefs and values that we have long held are at odds with the organization or person who has power over us. How we approach this depends largely on whether we see change as an end or as a beginning, as a problem or an opportunity.

A coach helps others explore the new beginnings and the opportunities that change presents while respecting the emotions around these points. Coaches can so often help the transition by challenging the 'all or nothing thinking' we met earlier that says 'I have to give up everything from the old culture to fit in with the new culture.' Acknowledging those factors from the old ways of working that are productive and that individuals might wish to transfer or adapt to the new way of thinking can smooth the transition.

Coaching through resistance

Managing resistance is really about managing change. To some degree, most people experience fear, loss, grief and other powerful emotions when change occurs in their lives. An important attitude for coaches to adopt is that resistance can be part of the change process. This is not to trivialize the emotions and thoughts, but to help the coach understand why some people may behave in ways that appear irrational or overtly emotional at times. Assume that resistant people do want to change and, in the interim, it is just that they are working out how to do it. For a whole range of reasons they find it difficult. For example:

- Challenges to long-held beliefs – some which might have nothing to do with teaching, but to do with their past as students themselves, as children and so on.

- They fear losing face by having to comply with a concept or way of working that they have been openly critical of.

- Fear of failure – they believe (often unconsciously) that they cannot make the changes – they have concerns about their ability to cope with new behaviours.

- Fear of success – a concern about what might happen if they are successful – what the implications for their lives might be; for example, recognition, criticism, shifting relationships, more or less time on their hands.

- They lack some skills that would enable them to make the transition effectively, such as time management, negotiation or ICT skills.

- They fear losing control of their lives through change.

- They have other pressing issues outside of school, such as a challenging teenager, elderly sick relative or alcoholic partner, that create stress.

So how do you actually deal with the resistant colleague or student?

Replace the word 'change' with 'learning' and look for examples of success with learning. Successfully changing is really just about learning to do things differently. There are institutional and individual aspects to change that can be dealt with separately.

Supporting change in any institution:

- Announce changes early, simply and, if possible, to everyone at the same time.
- Explain clearly why the change is needed, what the outcomes are likely to be, and the likely benefits to the stakeholders in the organization, including the students.
- Acknowledge concerns and then reframe them.
- Be prepared and able to provide support and further discussion opportunities to help minimize resistance phase.
- Decide on a reasonable time period for the change to be implemented and consult people wherever possible on this.
- Where resistance is heavy, explore this with individuals, using your leadership structure to do this (we explore how below).

Supporting change among groups:

- Do the above.
- Provide opportunities for people to voice concerns.
- Provide subsequent opportunities for groups to meet again after time to assimilate the message.
- Provide clear and unambiguous written summaries of what is proposed and how it has been and will be shared.

Supporting change among individuals:

- Do the above.
- Accept that all the responses you get from the individual are informative and not personal.
- Should you feel that they are personal, you have the right to challenge their statements. Do this in a business-like way, avoiding an emotional response.
- If you think you might react emotionally, then put the feedback to one side and deal with this later.
- Be prepared to acknowledge their emotions – listen carefully.
- Be prepared to show that you believe in them and their ability to adapt successfully.
- Hold to your belief that the individual has the solutions within them.
- Hold to your conviction that this person will make the best choices for themselves.
- Remember that people change at their own pace – avoid forcing the pace and be aware of your own frustrations and manage them.
- Recognize that when we meet resistance it is often a helpful sign that the individual is close to uncovering an important belief that holds them back from useful change.

If these mindsets are too difficult for you to create and maintain, do not coach the person, get someone else to do it.

Throughout the coaching of resistant people it is helpful to keep the Change Cube (see page 68) in mind. Remember that to help individuals to adjust behaviour we must influence beliefs and to do this we can explore perceptions, emotions, self-talk and physiology. Using this model as a basis for questioning can help people to experience the change differently. Some useful questions are:

- How could you contradict what you are saying/seeing/feeling?
- In what ways, now that you think about it, is this expectation helpful?
- Whom *will* you benefit? How is that helpful?
- What might the longer-term benefits of this be?
- If you could secretly see positive things in all of this, what might they be?
- How might you let go of the feelings here and move on?
- In what ways might you be able to accept this?
- How could you turn this to your/the student's/the department's advantage?

Dealing with resistors in formal coaching sessions

Resistance comes in many forms. There are five key categories as shown in Figure 8.1.

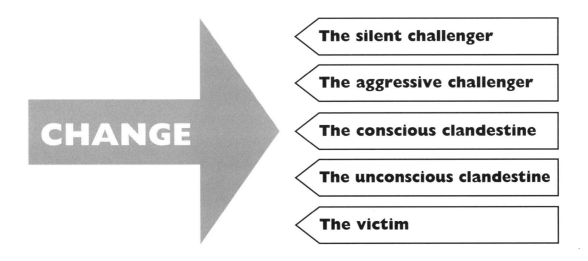

Figure 8.1 Categories of resistance

The silent challenger resists through quietly smouldering with emotions bubbling below the surface, but these are visible in body language and detectable in tone of voice. They say very little, find it difficult to express emotions and are often the most difficult of individuals to challenge.

- Where the resistance shows as frustration and there is little openness, gently challenge the behaviours you see by drawing attention to them. A useful question here might be 'What are you experiencing right now?'
- Where there is no acknowledgement of a problem, you might probe deeper: 'What I'm noticing now is that you … (say what you see or hear).' A deeper challenge then is 'I am sensing some resistance from you – what are you resisting?'

The aggressive challenger resists with accusatory and sometimes personal-sounding language, may swear and raise voice, is cynical about the process of coaching or a specific change. They are often highly critical of others, particularly those in positions of power, and may have an arrogance about their own performance.

- Begin by listening – allow them time to release their emotional load.
- Acknowledge their feelings and the aggression often dissipates.
- Probe the reasons behind the emotions.
- Useful questions:
  - What is this emotion telling you?
  - What is this emotion creating?
  - What do you want to do with this emotion?
  - If you didn't have this emotion, what would you do now?
  - In what ways is this emotion useful to you right now?

- If you find the language or tone of the challenger uncomfortable, do not be afraid to give them that feedback. You might use this approach:
  - This is what I am noticing/hearing …
  - This is how it makes me feel …
  - This is what I would like to happen now …

- Challenging critical statements about others is also useful. For example:
  - What evidence is there for that?
  - How would that person feel if they heard you say that?
  - In what ways does this person's behaviour actually help you?
  - So what? – this question is rarely used as it is very challenging, but can be highly effective. Be cautious with this kind of challenge, but it can work if you have enough rapport with the individual. It cuts through the emotional and into the rational.

If you sense that the trust is insufficient, you will need to build more before challenging further. Helpful leads here take the individual away from thinking about the resistance and reframing. For example: 'Tell me about what's working well for you at the moment.' In some people this will lead them into a resourceful state and so to communicate with you; for others it will not. Exploring the successes can lead the coach to ask questions later about the perceived resistance. Where individuals choose not to move to a resourceful state, coaches can ask further questions about how they are feeling. A simple question 'How are you feeling right now?' may well help the individual to engage with you again.

Always remember that the aggressive resistor may well be experiencing a clash between their own values and beliefs and those of the institution or change. Be firm and challenge the resistor, but remember that they may be frightened. Encouraging them to talk through their fears is a key goal. If they have been forceful in their resistance, they can often be full of guilt about the way that they behaved towards their coach after the event. As coaches it is important that we respond in a way that helps them to acknowledge their success and release that guilt so they can move on.

The conscious clandestine resists by appearing open with you, exploring issues and identifying actions. This resistor will often score very highly when you check commitment agreed actions. They will not, however, carry out the actions in full and usually appear vague when probed for more detail. They want to please when with you but find it difficult to carry through actions. Often these resistors appear to make immense progress in coaching sessions but little between sessions. They are aware that they are resisting change, but tell you what you want to hear.

- This kind of behaviour is difficult to spot and may only present itself after a pattern of not carrying out agreed actions.
- Do not try to distinguish between unconscious and conscious clandestine individuals.
- Wait – there will be beliefs underlying the behaviour that over time will manifest themselves

The unconscious clandestine appears to go along with the process of coaching, however, usually appears unmotivated by the process. They may find it difficult to access their creativity in the ideas phase of STRIDE. Such resistors may agree actions, but tone of voice might suggest a lack of commitment or interest. They appear to make little progress in coaching sessions and carry out few of the agreed actions. They are not aware that they are resisting change.

- To some extent everyone belongs to this category.
- We all have beliefs – and behaviours that stem from them – of which we are not consciously aware. Coaching can help us to learn more about these beliefs and in some cases adapt them.
- We should not be judged for what we do not know about and we must always remember that coaching is a process that respects this.

The victim is caught in a cycle of unresourceful thinking. They believe that other people or environmental factors prevent them from progressing. They demonstrate a reluctance to explore possible solutions and seem to come up against many excuses as to why a course of action will not work. Although they might reluctantly commit to action, they carry out actions only if fair weather prevails. They feel that they have little or no control over their lives.

- This behaviour set often comes from deeply held beliefs about a person's self-worth. The victim requires sensitive handling and coaches must tread very carefully.
- Re-frame to help build self-esteem and trust.
- Challenge unhelpful generalizations – 'They made me feel like this' or 'She caused me to miss the bus by keeping me talking too long'. Ask 'Who exactly made you feel like this?' followed by 'How specifically did they make you feel like this?'

- Challenge nominalizations – 'No one likes me' and 'Everyone thinks like me'.
- Reach back into the past for positive experiences when they were successful.
- Use the incisive questions that temporarily lift the limiting thoughts and allow people to see past them. In response to 'They made me feel like this' a coach might reply 'If they hadn't made you feel like this, how might you feel?'
- Coach, do not counsel.

Coaching, resistance and supervision

The professional coach should always consider whether a person who is resisting coaching needs more specialized therapeutic support. Some of the signs that should be looked for are:

- obsessive behaviour
- failure to meet goals despite a range of coaching interventions and confronting of the failure over time
- being under treatment or supervision for depression or other mental health issue
- if someone is consistently intensely emotional in coaching sessions
- where coaching interventions fail to bring individuals into resourceful states of mind, that is, where they remain in a negative thinking cycle for most of the coaching session and there is evidence that this state of mind exists for protracted periods in their life
- the disclosure of unresolved distressing experiences; for example, bereavement, abuse, serious medical condition or psychological trauma, victim of criminal act and so on (when working with children you have a legal obligation to report such disclosures to the relevant child-protection agencies – check the policies that your institution has which interpret these legal positions).

It is difficult to produce an exhaustive list of all the signs of referral. Likewise the need to refer to therapeutic counselling also depends on the seriousness or number of issues that have been disclosed or made obvious. Coaches must use their judgement and make informed decisions about when to refer and when not to. This is a considerable responsibility, and coaches are advised to develop a network of supervision as exists in therapeutic practice. This consists of a regular meeting with another coach where issues could be discussed in confidence – usually once per month, though other meetings might be arranged in certain circumstances. It is important to have a code of ethics about this and it is usual to withhold the individual's name from any discussion. The supervision provides that necessary support for judging responses to difficult circumstances presented by individuals. Additionally it provides an opportunity for you to let off steam when individuals raise issues in yourself, which does happen. These may be resurrections of personal issues that you should work through with your supervisor or unproductive emotions you experience when with an individual. Frustration at slower-than-expected progress is one example of an such issue. For the sake of your own mental well-being and effectiveness as a coach, be sure to set up a supervisor arrangement.

Directive approaches

So far this book has covered a range of different kinds of resistance behaviour and techniques that can be employed to help individuals to overcome their resistance. However, it is important to reiterate that while most people really want to change, there may be those who are unwilling to resolve the tension between their values and beliefs, or to overcome their fears about change. While coaching can make it more likely that people will overcome resistance, it cannot guarantee it. Where an individual becomes stuck in a resistant state it may be necessary to exert directive pressures upon them to motivate change. Careful coaching, which focuses on the strengths, is the best way to broker change. Only you can decide at what point coaching has run its course and more directive methods need take over. However, if we want really lasting change in others, we have to invest in valuing them, building trust, and recognizing that each person starts from a different point and requires varying degrees of support.

Some important caveats to this chapter

Describing five types of resistor is merely an attempt to categorize resistance as a means to suggest effective methods of helping people overcome their resistance and make important changes. It could be regarded as judgemental to categorize people in this way. Indeed, very often people display a range of behaviours that might rest in a number of different resistor types. Some individuals move between different categories in the course of a day, depending upon the experiences they have. Others change their resistance over the course of time or of coming to terms with change. It must be stressed therefore that these categories are simply a convenient framework for analysing how best to intervene, rather than as blanket labels for people. The latter should be expressly avoided.

Getting people into coaching

Getting people started on the road to change is eased by a number of factors:

- Be transparent about why coaching is being offered.
- Understand the process of coaching and its intentions.
- Coaching is developed in the organization as a process for improving on good practice rather than for those with serious weaknesses.
- Allow people choice about who coaches them.
- In cases of historical reluctance, employ an external performance coach with a confidentiality promise.
- When someone presents a problem, ask for permission to use a coaching approach.
- Create proper time and space for coaching.
- Get your most motivated people coaching first and use their enthusiastic responses to it to recruit the less-motivated individuals.
- Examine your own attitudes towards reluctant individuals.
- Consider being in the shoes of the reluctant individual and try to see it from their point of view – what would you need in that situation?

Summary

In this chapter we have learned:

▶ *When people resist they put energy into defending their normal coping strategies.*

▶ *Coping strategies include positive mental attitudes, acceptance, excitement, grief, stress, health-related issues, absenteeism and nostalgia.*

▶ *Resistance is an integral part of a process of change for many people.*

▶ *Change can be viewed as learning.*

▶ *To develop this learning, steps can be taken at institution, group and individual level in schools.*

▶ *Reluctant individuals who are resisting change fall into five key groups. Different manifestations of reluctance to change require different strategies. These are outlined in the chapter.*

▶ *Coaches involved in working with challenging individuals should consider setting up supervision structures to support them in delivering high-quality coaching.*

▶ *There are key considerations in getting individuals to commit to coaching in schools. These are outlined in the chapter.*

Questions

1. Using the five categories of reluctance in this chapter, what characteristics does the individual who most challenges you exhibit?

2. How well are you currently managing them?

3. What insights do the frameworks and tips in this chapter provide for you to deal with this individual?

4. What are the key changes that you need to make to the way you coach them?

5. How do you react to change and what kinds of behaviours do you exhibit in the face of change? What do you resist? How can this insight help you to help others whom you lead?

Masterclass

▶ Always be prepared to let individuals express emotions – do not take it personally.

▶ A useful phrase in emotionally charged situations is: 'I can see that this is affecting you deeply.' Avoid phrases such as 'I know exactly how you feel … I feel just the same'; such comments serve to frustrate rather than alleviate emotional tensions.

▶ Do practise excellent listening and match your body language to the person who is upset, and gradually change it to the body language of a more alert and positive person. People shift their body language and this can affect the way they feel.

▶ Do not be afraid to state what you are seeing and hearing to a person whose behaviour is intimidating. Use the formula 'OMD': **O**bserve: 'I am noticing X about the way that you are behaving'; **M**akes me feel: 'It makes me feel Y'; and **D**irect change: 'I would prefer it if you Z'.

▶ Remember that reluctance is a symptom of beliefs at odds with the changes taking place. Expect change to be gradual and use the nine coaching principles to work alongside the individual concerned.

▶ Seriously consider bringing in an external performance coach to work with particularly challenging individuals. A performance and life-style coach who is entirely independent can bring about real changes in individuals because they can explore wide avenues of possibilities with absolute confidentiality. In some cases resistant individuals alter their perceptions and manage the shift to new practices; in other cases they make decisions to move to new roles or institutions.

Where now with coaching?

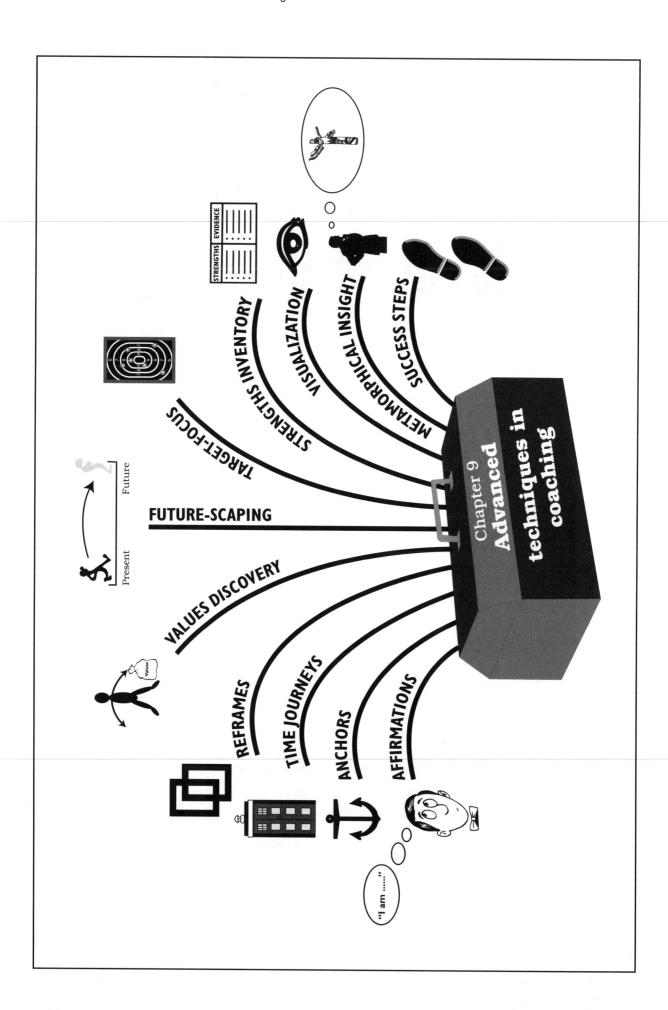

Chapter 9

Advanced techniques in coaching

IN THIS CHAPTER YOU WILL LEARN:

- specific techniques for working with the emotions, perceptions, self-talk and state factors identified in the Change Cube
- the blueprint for using strengths inventories, anchoring, reframes, success steps, affirmations and visualization

PREVIEW QUESTIONS:

- How can you work directly with perceptions?
- How can you meet the requirements of a person who needs to work with self-talk?
- What is the effect of associating with past successes and how can these be used to meet future challenges?
- What is a strengths inventory?
- What is anchoring?

Take the path of wisdom

The story goes that on a certain day Gandhi and a companion entered the gates of a great city in order to share their teachings with the inhabitants. Almost immediately a follower of the Mahatma, who lived in the city, approached and told him, 'Master, you are wasting your time and energy here. The people here are hard of heart, and resistant to change and the words of truth. They are dumb and ignorant and have no wish to learn anything. Do not waste your gifts upon them.'

Gandhi smiled at the man and replied, 'I have no doubt you are right.'

Some minutes later another adherent approached Gandhi saying, 'My Lord, you are indeed most welcome by all in this fortunate city. The people await and anticipate the jewels of learning that will fall from your lips. They are hungry to learn and eager to serve you. Their hearts and minds are truly open to you.'

Gandhi smiled and replied, 'I have no doubt you are right too.'

His companion turned to him and said, 'Master, how is it possible you can say one thing to one man and something completely different to another? The sun and the moon can never be the same thing, and day cannot be night.'

Gandhi smiled at his friend and replied, 'I have no doubt you are right. And you may also consider that both men spoke truly according to their own values. The first expects to see the bad in everything. The second sees only the good. Both men perceive the world as they expect it to be. How can you say either man perceives wrongly since all humankind perceives the world as they choose to experience it? Neither man spoke falsely; just something incomplete.'

Nick Owen, 2001

Techniques for multi-sensory coaching

So far this book has focused on language as the medium for effecting change. The language used when we coach can be linked to the visual (what we see), the auditory (what we hear, internally and externally) and kinesthetic (what we do and feel). Those we coach use metaphors as they speak that indicate the kind of sensory thinking they are using: 'That's a bright idea' is an indication of a visual representation of experience; 'That sounds right' might be an indication of an auditory representation; 'I felt the weight of the problem on my shoulders' could be an indication of a kinesthetic representation of experience.

These sensory representations of experience can be linked to the Change Cube concept (see Chapter 5). In the Change Cube we have the perceptions (visual experience), the self-talk (the auditory experience) and the physiology and feelings (the kinesthetic experience). Some of us experience our world more through one sensory system than the others – through what we see, or what we hear, or what we touch and feel emotionally. In our coaching experience, changing the approach to coaching so that it makes use of a different sense often unblocks a pathway and allows a person to make progress.

This chapter looks at some specific tools that coaches can use to help individuals move quickly towards goals. The first part of the chapter outlines tools that can enable us to work even more effectively with the sensory system. The second part introduces some important tools for creating focus, defining and prioritizing values, and dealing with time.

Working with the senses

As we work with individuals we become more aware of their preferred sensory preferences. Sue Knight (1995) outlines the use of eye-movement cues as a way of interpreting how an individual is representing their world. Broadly speaking it is upwards for visual, sideways for auditory and down to the right for kinesthetic with eyes moving down and to the left for self-talk. Follow the Sue Knight reference for more information on this. Listening carefully to an individual's language (as described above) also gives us information about how they are thinking. The ability to identify another person's sensory representational system grows with experience.

Below are some techniques that can help access sensory systems more effectively:

- Anchors – useful kinesthetic approach to creating resourceful feelings
- Affirmations – helpful auditory approach to building confidence and using internal dialogue
- Reframing – helpful auditory tool for changing negative thoughts to positive ones
- Success steps – an important kinesthetic resourcefulness building activity, well suited to working with young people
- Visualization – as the name suggests, a great way to access visual representations of experience
- Metaphorical insight – a multi-sensory approach to exploring and supporting individuals towards change.

Anchors

This activity is ideal for creating positive energy/confidence for forthcoming challenges. It works by associating a physical action to a strong positive experience from the past. It interacts with emotions in powerful positive ways and can alter physical state. Anchors can be used with both individuals and groups.

The approach:

- Ask the individual to identify a future event that they want to feel more confident about.

- Think about how you would really like to feel when this event occurs.

- Think about a time when you have had this great feeling in the past.

- Imagine that past experience vividly – what did you see, hear and feel.

- Now when this past event feels really strong, use a physical anchor – for example, pinch thumb and finger together, curl your toes or press an earlobe – to anchor the feeling.

- Ideally repeat this process at least ten times daily until the event has arrived. Each time you do it, ensure that you are fully associated with the picture, sounds and feelings of the past success.

- Now imagine the challenging new event and practise 'firing your anchor' to bring forth resourceful feelings. Use this anchor before, during and after the event.

Children can use this successfully as a calming activity before entering examination rooms. A number of schools give students a small polished glass bead that they squeeze as an anchor in preparation for GCSE exams. It is anchored to feelings of success for six weeks prior to the exam taking place. The school makes sure that students go into the exam room several times in the weeks leading up to the exam so they can practise firing their anchor in the room where they will sit the exam.

Affirmations

An auditory approach used for reinforcing confidence and appropriate responses. Affirmations work with our self-talk to influence behaviour. They are useful for working towards how you want to be by focusing on the self-talk you will have when you are successfully operating as you desire.

The approach:

- Decide what you want to focus on.

- Create and write down a sentence that describes the attribute you want.

- Write the sentence in the following way: make it personal (I am always a confident person), make it say what you do not want (I don't want), make it in the here and now (I *am* always …).

- Create about three affirmations – write them down and say them to yourself at least three times a day or when they are required, such as when you need to feel confident. For example, in a classroom where a challenging child has triggered a teacher's emotional response in the past, the teacher writes an affirmation for herself 'I count to five in my head and respond with intelligence.'

Affirmations can help by reinforcing the thinking or behaviour that we have identified as most appropriate before a familiar challenging situation.

Reframing negative self-talk

This useful technique has already been explored in the Chapter 4 but is worth revisiting here. Reframing challenges negative beliefs/self-talk encourages individuals to reverse the talk and experience the perceptual changes it brings.

The approach:

- Write down negative self-talk that comes into your head in a given situation; for example, 'I can't do this …'.

- Decide what the opposite of this self-talk is: 'I can do this if …'.

- Challenge the negative self-talk with the positive opposite each time it crops up.

Success steps

These are ideal for developing resourceful feelings to cope with stressful events. They work by influencing emotions and physical state, and are especially good for those with a more kinesthetic preference for learning.

The approach:

- Identify something you want to improve; for example, feeling more confident.

- Place a piece of paper on the floor, this is your confident place – it's brilliant there.

- Stand on the paper and draw up all the feelings and self-talk that tells you that you are in that confident state.

- If you can, imagine a time when you felt this good before and relive it – intensify the feelings.

- Listen to the self-talk you get in this situation.

- Step off the paper and take five deep breaths, then step back on to the paper in to that brilliant feeling again.

- Repeat this at least five times, each time saying the simple statement 'I feel confident/ energetic/successful …'.

- Check that the feeling comes back again when you say the phrase once more. If it is not strong, repeat the above five more times.

At the point where an individual has strong feelings of success each time they step onto the paper, ask them to tear off a corner of the paper and take it with them as a reminder of the goal and the feelings of success.

Visualization

Using internal images can be very powerful in rehearsing successful outcomes. This technique focuses its approach on the perceptions factor in the Change Cube. It has been used extensively in NASA training for astronauts and by athletes, including the successful England Rugby Team in 2003. The more you practise it the easier it gets.

The approach:

- Take some deep breaths and relax.

- Decide on a target, which could be a skill or feeling, and create an ideal performance in your mind.

- Describe/see/feel what you can see, hear, feel when you are performing in this optimum way. Make it as accurate and vivid as you can. Make it positive.

- Decide on a realistic goal to move you one step closer to this excellent performance.

- Repeat this visualization each day over a 6–8 minute period.

- As time goes on and performance improves, adjust the details to revise your visualization.

Visualization can be a helpful tool for those who process information in pictorial form readily. It can be developed for use with auditory stimuli. Never force someone to try to visualize if they say 'I can't picture it' as this can lead to escalating stress levels. In this situation another technique may be more suitable, such as circle of success or affirmation.

Metaphorical insight

Working with people to explore the metaphors associated with their reality brings new insights and useful developments in understanding. It is the ultimate sensory experience for those being coached, as the use of specialized language techniques allows the individual to work in their own preferred sensory representation without influence from their coach.

The language used by the coach for this approach is loosely based on David Grove's excellent 'clean language' concepts. David Grove, a New Zealand psychotherapist, developed these approaches to help individuals deal with trauma. Reported in Lawley and Tomkins (2000) 'he [Grove] realized many clients naturally described their symptoms in metaphor, and found that when he enquired about these using their exact words, their perceptions of their trauma began to change'. Clean language is designed to avoid making assumptions about what a person means by using as much of their own wording and phraseology as possible. The effect can be replicated in less intense work-based experiences using similar approaches. Lawley and Tompkins (2000) detail the process of symbolic modelling, which involves the use of clean language to facilitate change, and details of their book and video demonstrating the process are to be found at www.cleanlanguage.co.uk.

The metaphor allows a person to be detached from a problem as they explore it, which is very helpful where an issue is emotionally charged. This method works especially well where individuals have issues involving other people and where emotions are running high.

To gain access to the metaphorical domain it is essential that the individual feels relaxed and that you have a strong rapport with them in order to allow them to think metaphorically. Always begin by suggesting what you have in mind and gaining permission. Explaining the process and the possible benefits of it is a way of gaining a deeper insight into the challenge. You can then use your coaching skills to follow your curiosity and explore the metaphors the individual come up with.

Useful phrases here are:

- What kind of _____ is this?
- Where is the _____ in this?

An example of a metaphor that one person developed:

> Geoff: My issue is like a round shape in a sandy beach, which can almost be
> seen but not quite – buried by the sand; it is like a cloud with four
> layers to the edge; it is like a bag of flour that has a little margarine
> in it. He is like a furnace with a poorly fitting door.

Using the above example as an illustration, the following dialogue might be typical:

> Geoff   My challenge is like a round shape in a sandy beach.
>
> Coach   So it's like a round shape in a sandy beach. And what kind of round
> shape is it like?
>
> Geoff   It's like a large stone but it's like skin and it's moving.
>
> Coach   Tell me about the skin.
>
> Geoff   It belongs to someone who is buried in my beach.
>
> Coach   Who is buried in your beach?
>
> Geoff   It's Margaret and she's spoiling my beach.

In this particular example Geoff very quickly gets to the issue in this metaphorical way. Not wanting to admit that a colleague was stopping him progressing, he was able to say the person's name and validate his concerns through the detachment of the metaphorical process. This can be used within the STRIDE model to explore the real situation and continued into the ideas section of the model if you wish. People can go into a trance-like state with this kind of dissociation and it is helpful to bring them out of this domain by firmly saying 'Look at me (use their name), in your own time now you are back with me today and it is (say time and day of the week).' Then ask them what they have learned as a result of the metaphorical insight.

This is a great technique to use when you sense that there are some barriers to talking about the root of the issue. It is known as the fiver approach because there are five stages to this kind of insight (see the next page).

Fiver insight approach

1 Relax using the process outlined below.

2 With your eyes closed, think about your issue for a moment.

3 As you do this, ask yourself (or get your coach to ask you) this question:

- What is this challenge like?

Other questions that can help here:

- What thing is this issue like?
- If this issue had a shape, what would its shape be like?
- If this issue has a colour, what colour is it?
- If there was a sound, what is the sound?
- If there is a feeling, what is the feeling?

4 Go on exploring the ideas you come up with to discover more about the metaphor you have in your mind using your curiosity to ask questions such as:

- What kind of _____ is this?
- How is this _____ like this?
- When is this _____ like this?
- Where is this _____ like this?

Pay attention to the details noticed and explore them with further questions (or get your coach to do so).

5 Complete the process by asking yourself:

- What have I learned from exploring this metaphor?
- How might this information support me to find solutions?
- What will move me one step closer to success here?

Relaxation method for use prior to the fiver insight

- Sit down quietly in a situation where you will not be disturbed.
- Close your eyes and focus on your breathing.
- Notice your calm breaths in and breathe in through your nose then breathe out through your mouth.
- As you breathe out through your mouth, notice that any tension inside you is leaving your body.
- Repeat this process of breathing in calm and breathing out tension. Continue for as long as it takes for you to notice your shoulders dropping down as tension reduces and for you to begin to yawn.
- Allow yourself to yawn, stretch and relax.
- Once you are feeling more relaxed you are ready for the fiver insights.

Further useful advanced coaching tools

Strengths inventory

Ideal for developing high self-esteem and a positive attitude, this tool also interacts with self-talk and can alter negative internal dialogue. Ask individuals to make a list of:

- positive qualities and positive experiences they recall.
- things they have seen, heard and felt about themselves throughout their past.
- things others have noticed and commented upon.

Building up an inventory over a period of time provides a useful reference for boosting self-esteem at times of particular challenge. A sample is given in Table 9.1.

Table 9.1 Sample strengths inventory

Strength	Where experienced	Noted by whom?
Polite to others	As we came into class today	Teacher congratulated me
Can now draw a face and get the eyes in the right place	In art class today	Me – it looked right
Was sure about what I wanted	In the dinner queue	Me – I made my mind up quickly and spoke clearly

The example in Table 9.1 is of a young person's strengths inventory but it is equally useful for adults to keep a note of their successes and strengths. They may not feel comfortable recording them in this way, but keeping a file of feedback is helpful. One colleague of Will's kept a drawer in a filing cabinet full of records and mementoes of the best that had happened to him in his career. On a bad day he would go into the drawer and delve for reminders of his successes and values. On the day of his retirement, he was asked why he came into teaching. He replied 'I entered teaching to change the world.' A colleague asked 'And did you?' 'No,' he said 'but I did change thousands of worlds.' He had the evidence of this in his filing cabinet.

The target-focus tool

This is one of the core tools of the performance coach in helping people who have a general sense of disorganization or lack of focus. It is one the authors use a great deal to help an individual get an holistic view of their situation and then to identify key areas for development. It is an excellent starting-point for any coaching you do and is particularly useful for:

- assisting teachers experiencing stress to focus on key areas of concern
- students approaching key times, such as the build up to exams/SATs and so on
- leaders focusing on how best to develop their areas of responsibility
- anyone keen on improving their work–life balance.

It can be left to the individual to determine the areas for consideration or the suggestions given here can be used and/or adapted to suit their needs. Providing some suggestions for the individual can get them started quickly, and they will then often develop their own categories, just using some of those suggested. It is most important that their freedom of choice is communicated throughout.

Suggested categories that can be used as triggers for the most important professional and personal aspects of focus include:

- environment
- leisure
- personal growth
- professional development
- career
- money
- health
- friends
- personal life
- budget
- teaching and learning in department
- educational trips
- meetings

- personnel
- developing others
- resourcing
- curriculum
- specialist college status
- PSHE programming
- UCAS applications
- new GCSE course
- work–life balance
- fund-raising
- vision
- time management
- organization

The approach:

- Identify your work sectors; for example, teaching, office, leadership, finance, time management and so on.

- Write each one into the toolkit frame (see figure 9.1) along the base of the toolkit.

- Score each sector between 1 and 10. Use your intuition. Make your decisions based on your 'gut feeling'.

- Consider the following questions:

  - What do you notice about the pattern of scores you have given?

  - What, if anything, surprises you about your scores?

  - Which area would you change immediately if you could?

- Begin with the highest scoring area and work through the STRIDE model toolkit.

An example of how to fill in the frame is provided in Figure 9.1.

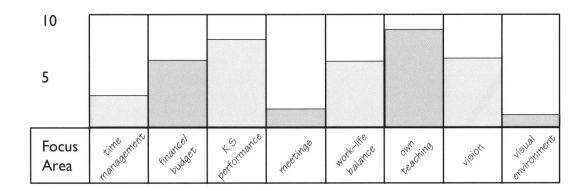

Figure 9.1 An example of a completed target-focus frame

When the exercise is completed, it is often useful to ask the person being coached whether there is also another category that they now feel they would also benefit from looking at. Doing this can open some additional understanding for them.

Let the individual use the outcomes of this activity to decide the areas for focus in future coaching sessions. For even greater insight, encourage people to go on to break down an area of the tool they wish to focus on into further categories and invite them to score these also.

Future-scaping

Future-scaping is often used to enable individuals to really connect with their targets and to work out the steps to get them to the end goal, but with less interference from our limiting beliefs. The instructions for the process are given on the next page and an example for the footprints is provided in Figure 9.2.

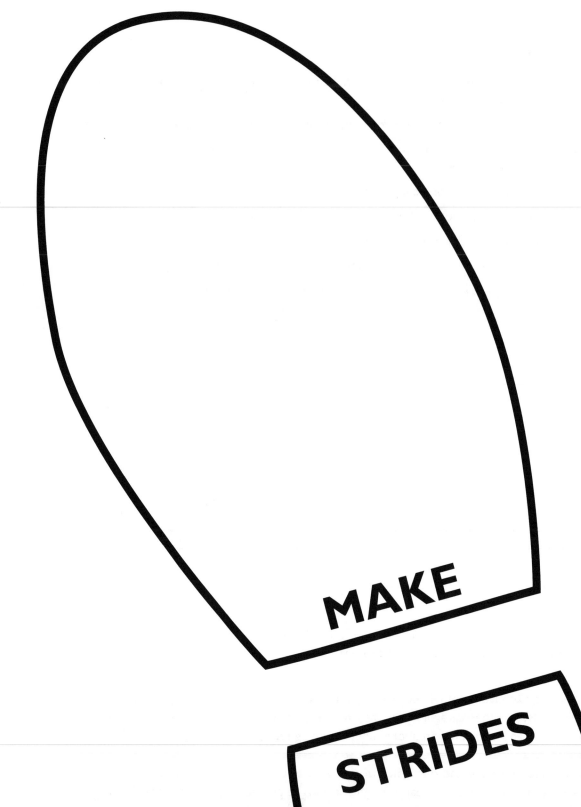

Figure 9.2 An example footprint for future-scaping

There are just a few key points to pay attention to when doing this:

- When you take the individual into the future, allow them to determine the future time they move ahead into.

- Once they are in the future, you must use the language in the present tense to enable them to really associate with the success.

- As you get them to look back, be sure to use the language of the past tense (even though it is actually in the future!) 'Now when you look back into the past, what steps did you take in order to be so successful now?'

- Ensure that you do re-orient individuals into the present again, with date, time and place.

- Allow enough time for you to fully debrief this.

When you have completed the future-scape, you can explore the reality of the situation and begin to uncover any limiting beliefs by getting the individual to be in the present and look forward at the steps they identified in the future-scape. Ask the question of each step: 'What, if anything, might get in the way of you achieving this step?' Use your coach's curiosity to probe the responses with open questions. This process often brings up new ideas for tackling a problem and so may also benefit the ideas phase of the coaching model.

The benefits:

- Individuals will get a really strong idea of the benefits of achieving their target.

- They will be able to check whether what they are aiming for is what they really want.

- They will be able to look back in the past to a time before they achieved this target and look at what they did to become successful.

- They will avoid the interference of limiting thoughts that can stop them making progress.

The approach:

- Invite the person being coached to relax using the relaxation technique given on page 154 (or use one of your own).

- Ask them to close their eyes and travel into the future to a time when they have already achieved their target.

- Ask them to tell you what they experience at this time when they have already achieved their target:

  - What do they see?

  - What do they hear? In their head? Said to them? Said about them?

  - What do they feel?

- Once they feel like they are really there, already successful, ask them to turn around and look back at the steps they took to become successful.

- Invite them to detail each step they took in as much depth as they can.

- Record what they say in a form that suits their learning preference, that is, for visual, draw the steps on paper, for the auditory write them down and read at the end, for kinesthetic, put them onto cards or onto footprints like the one in Figure 9.2 so they can hold them and arrange them after the visualization is over.

- Ask them to walk back in to the present again and to open their eyes when they are ready. Say the date, day, time and location they are in clearly to re-orient them fully.

- Now review with them the steps they took.

This exercise can be used to help the planning stage of target-setting. Using footprints like the one in Figure 9.2 adds an even more powerful dimension if the they actually walk into the future physically along a timeline in the room. When they look back and tell you what they did to get there, you write the steps separately on footprint templates.

Values discovery

The emergence of a clear understanding of a person's personal values is the basic foundation for making decisions and setting goals that will meet their needs. This exercise is a powerful way of helping people who find themselves in conflict or lack a feeling of balance in their work and/or home life. It is a great activity for them to do as a homework exercise and to bring to the next meeting.

Repeating this exercise with their perception of values of the organization they are working in can prove most useful. It can reveal interesting insights for individuals into the nature of conflicts and concerns and is an excellent starting-point for discussion when personal values and organizational values are compared.

Repeating the exercise every three to six months is a useful exercise and uncovers some interesting learning. Essentially this approach can be used to identify strengths, to develop areas for target setting and to explore reality. It is one of the most potent ways of building self-esteem and of uncovering beliefs which are limiting progress.

You can experience various degrees of willingness to engage with the exercise and your skills of rapport building and timing will allow you to judge the best time to invite the person you are coaching to do it. Similarly the degree of disclosure is very much left to the individual by setting it as a homework task and being clear that they can choose what they want to share. The tool can be used within a coaching session; allow 45 minutes to do it properly.

This activity helps individuals to begin the journey towards aligning personal and professional values, as well as those of the organization. This does not mean changing values to fit, but rather finding ways to honour values and still meet goals – although it does happen that values are questioned and re-appraised as a result of this experience.

Trust your curiosity to explore the outcome of this exercise using open questions. Permission questions can be of use and make it easier for the individual to respond; for example, 'May I ask you about …?' 'How would you feel about us exploring …?'

Always begin and end this activity by focusing on the strengths of the individual undertaking it.

Values discovery tool

What are values?

- A value is something you naturally feel is important to you.
- There is a big difference between wants, needs and values; a value is something you are drawn to and is not influenced by your wants and needs.
- Values, if honoured, lead in directions of new opportunity.
- Values help you set more effective and appropriate goals.
- When your goals are in line with your values, conflict is eliminated and your goals become easier to achieve.

Consciously being aware of your values and the degree to which the direction you are moving in is in line with your values is important. The exercise below can be adapted for most age ranges. It is probably the most important tool you will use with yourself and the people you coach. It identifies strengths and begins a process of thinking about what you want to achieve and why you want to achieve it. It is strongly recommended that all coaches carry out this exercise at least once every six months and use it to reassess the appropriateness of their own goals.

Getting to know your own values

To begin with, here are some examples of values identified by people during coaching. This is neither an exhaustive list nor a recommendation of what is best – your values are your values and no one can make them up for you!

- honesty
- love
- community
- money
- fun
- power

- independence
- others
- flexibility
- freedom
- order
- collaboration

- knowledge
- health
- integrity
- fairness
- learning
- adventure

Seven steps to learning more about your values

1 Make a list of personal values that you hold dear – the question to ask to reach each value is: 'What is important to me?' Remember these are not wants or needs, they are simply things you feel are important to you.

2 When you have around ten such values write them onto cards (one on each card). Begin to arrange them in order of priority, with the most important at the top and the least important at the bottom. Do this quickly and as intuitively as possible. The idea is to get an approximate hierarchy, as the next step is to refine the priority list.

3 Now starting at the second value, take each value and test it against the one above and below it. Ask the question: 'Is this value really more important than the one

below and less important than the one above?' Move cards as necessary to fine tune your priority.

4   Repeat this process until you have refined your priority list of values.

5   Once you are happy with your list copy the hierarchy into the table below:

	Priority ranking	Value	Honour score out of 5	Feelings/ thoughts
1				
2				
3				
4				
5				
6				
7				
8				
9				
10				

6   Now, trusting your instincts, score each value between one and five based on how well you are currently honouring (living by) that value in your life as a whole. Record the value in the third column. Five represents fully honouring the value and one barely honouring it. As you do this, note down in the fourth column any feelings or thoughts that come to you as you do the exercise.

7   Now consider the table and its contents using these questions:

   a) What are my strengths?

   b) Where in my life am I honouring my values?

   c) Where am I honouring my values least?

   d) What is the impact on me of honouring the values in question b?

   e) What is the impact of moving away from honouring values in question c?

   f) What did you notice about your recordings in column 4?

   g) Based on what you have learned here, what is next for you?

Time journeys

This approach is designed to explore the strengths of an individual, but is also helpful in considering target-setting and reality because it has a time dimension to it.

Useful for almost any age group, the metaphor of a journey is most adaptable. For coaches exploring the outcomes of this with others, there are some interesting opportunities for questioning to uncover beliefs that may be limiting.

Questioning can be based around the attributes individuals record:

- Tell me about this strength.

- What is it about this strength that makes it so important in your past?

- What makes this strength part of your past but not of your present?

Additionally, questioning about the picture they draw of their journey can be revealing:

- How come your past is so much larger than your future?

- What is the significance of the turn in the road/river?

- What possibilities are there beyond the end of the road that you have here?

Where people give more emphasis to past or future or present in this metaphor, we sometimes uncover beliefs about where they spend their thinking time. This can help them to overcome problems related to motivation, stress and performance, and attitude.

- Think for today – don't worry about tomorrow.

- Think for the past – dwell on how good things used to be or how bad your lot is.

- Think in the future – ignore the pleasures and practicalities of the present.

Even the most innocuous of activities can provide great insights into how people think and where they spend their thinking time.

Helping others to create solutions is about so much more than tips and pointers, it is about understanding how we think and challenging it – sometimes that is enough to alter our habits significantly from within.

Again this tool can be used with individuals and teams including team-building and understanding motivation and planning in classrooms. It is a great way to plan with a group in the lead up to examinations.

The approach:

- In this activity you might like to consider your past, your present and your future.
- If your life is a journey, begin by drawing the road or river along which you travel. Next, mark out sections of the journey that represent your past, your present and your future.
- Now take each time frame (past, present and future) and in any order think about and record the attributes that make you strong and resourceful in each.
- In the past, it is about experiences you have had where you have shown strengths.
- In the present, it is attributes you are currently using or have available if you need them.
- In the future, it is attributes/strengths you will be likely to develop or would like.

The *Coaching Solutions Resource Book* is the companion volume to this book. It contains over 80 photocopyable tools for use with colleagues and learners, in a highly accessible and user-friendly format.

It can be purchased at www.continuumbooks.com

Summary

The techniques outlined in this chapter are useful additions to the coaching approaches already discussed in this book.

▶ *Learning is most effective when it is multi-sensory.*

▶ *The tools in this chapter provide a variety of alternatives to discussion-based coaching by providing varied visual, auditory and kinaesthetic sensory stimuli.*

▶ *Between them the techniques provide for influencing beliefs through the key factors in the Change Cube of:*

  ▷ *perceptions*

  ▷ *state*

  ▷ *self talk*

  ▷ *emotions.*

Questions

1   What kinds of uses would you put visualization to in your coaching?

2   Which techniques would be most effective in:

   ▶   preparing students for a more relaxed approach to exams?

   ▶   helping a largely auditory-processing boy to feel more confident about making a phone call?

   ▶   developing a clear idea of the appropriate uses of a smash shot in badminton prior to a big match?

   ▶   planning a lengthy piece of coursework for a student who told themselves regularly that they cannot do planning tasks?

   ▶   helping a person in conflict with the organization?

3   Which techniques outlined here would you prefer to use for your own development?

4   To what extent might you impose your own preferences for these techniques on people you work with? How might you guard against this?

Masterclass

▶ *When working with individuals in coaching relationships, listen carefully to the sensory language they use to guage which advanced coaching techniques might be most suitable for them.*

▷ *The use of visual predicates, such as 'focus', 'clear', 'bright', will indicate a preference for visualization.*

▷ *The use of kinesthetic predicates, such as 'I felt it weighed heavy on me', 'I felt as light as a feather', may predispose them to circles of success and also anchoring.*

▷ *The use of auditory predicates, such as 'It went with a bang', 'That sounds like a good idea', may mean that reframes and affirmations will work best.*

▶ *Making anchor actions as subtle as possible means that they can be used anywhere and at anytime. Gently clenching the fist of one hand is possible in many situations. A nurse who needs an anchor as she is drawing up an injection will choose a curling of the toes since her hands are otherwise engaged.*

▶ *With all these techniques the more they are practised, the more effective they are when called into action. Start using the ones you are most comfortable with first.*

▶ *Achieving states of relaxation before developing any of these techniques enhances the rate at which they become established. They are best introduced towards the end of a coaching session, when the individual has had time to relax.*

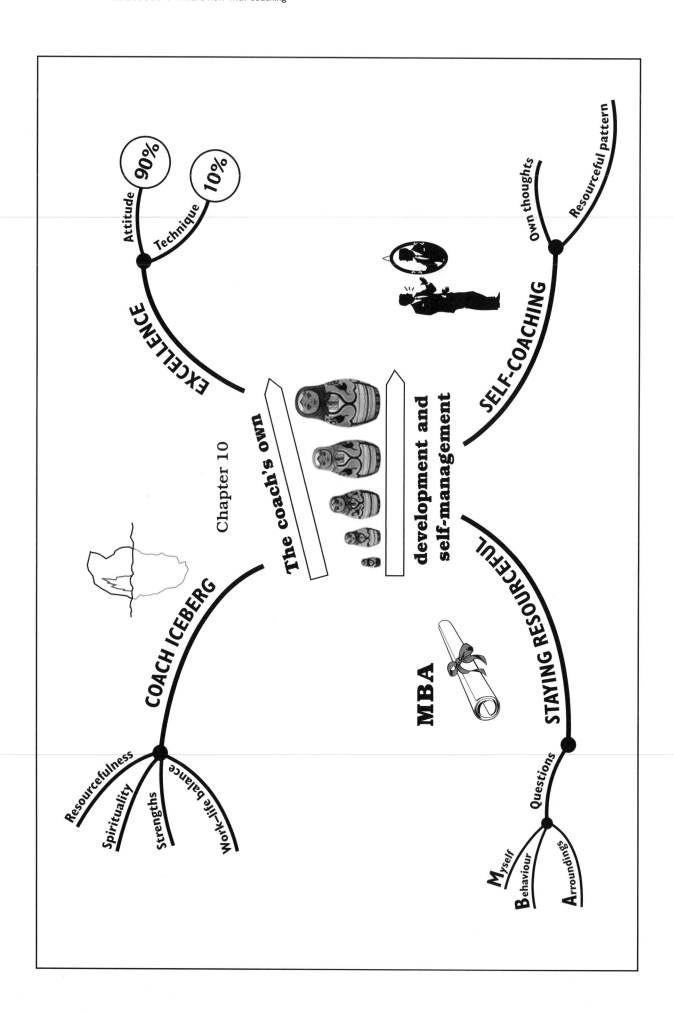

Chapter 10

The coach's own development and self-management

IN THIS CHAPTER YOU WILL LEARN:

- to understand the responsibility of being a coach
- to gain insight into the state of mind of the coach
- to be able to manage your state of mind effectively as a coach
- to gain techniques for self-coaching
- to know how to further enhance your coaching capabilities

PREVIEW QUESTIONS:

- What is your responsibility as a coach?
- What states of mind make for an effective coach?
- How does one achieve the right state of mind?
- Can you coach yourself? If you can, how?
- How can you become an even better coach?

How do you look at things?

At five years of age a boy watched his younger brother drown. Within the year glaucoma plunged him into permanent darkness and his parents were too poor to afford the medical help that might have saved his sight. He was the only blind child in his hometown. His parents struggled to make ends meet. During his early teenage years both his parents died. Alone now, he was sent to a state institution for the blind. As an Afro-American, he was not permitted access to many activities, including music. Given the obstacles he faced, one could not have predicted that he would one day give something back to the world.

As a musician, Ray Charles was revered worldwide. He said of his past:

> *My mom, to me, was the most fantastic woman in the world. As I think of her today, she didn't have a lot of what people say you're supposed to have. I mean, she didn't have a college education. She only went to fifth grade. We were in a very small town and very poor, and there were no such things as psychologists to teach her how to raise a kid who was an oddity in that town. I was the only blind kid in this little town, so that made me odd to all the other kids. But my mom, she somehow knew that there's nothing wrong with my brain. I just couldn't see.*
> *(Quoted in Brooks and Goldstein, 2004)*

Walk the talk

The question that every first time coach asks themselves is: Do I need to be perfect to coach? The answer is no! However, to be an effective coach you do need to grow your credibility as a person who practises what they preach. This means that coaching yourself and using others to coach you is part of being a successful coach. This is because being a successful coach is really the same as being a successful individual or manager or teacher or student. It is about taking time to reflect and to notice when an attitude or behaviour is working well, when it could be enhanced and when steps should be taken to make that improvement. It is why maintaining yourself in a resourceful state of mind is imperative. The natural ups and downs of life occur with each week, month and year that go by. Managing our time, workload, physiology and emotional state of mind is vital to being at our best for those we coach.

How to get an MBA in success

You might like to take a few moments to complete the following questionnaire. Consider the questions and pick the most appropriate answer for you. At the end of the questionnaire follow the instructions for reaching the overall score and an interpretive explanation can be found.

While this questionnaire can be of use, it is by no means an accurate diagnostic tool, and if you have concerns about your level of resourcefulness over a period of more than a few days, you should seek the advice of a suitably qualified health professional.

How resourceful am I today?

1 As a percentage of my maximum energy level I currently have the following level:

   a) 76–100 per cent

   b) 51–75 per cent

   c) 26–50 per cent

   d) 0–25 per cent

2 If a colleague came to me right now looking depressed and anxious (and he often does) I would:

   a) smile, listen and commit to coaching him through

   b) smile, listen, and think 'oh no not again', but commit to coaching him

   c) match his facial expression, half-heartedly commit to helping, but feel that it is a waste of time

   d) make an excuse to go and see someone you do not have an appointment with to escape from the encounter

3 In the middle of a really busy term, knowing that you have a stack of work to do, the opportunity to go on a personal development and coaching course is passed your way. You have wanted this for a long time. Do you:

   a) get really excited and immediately recognize the longer-term benefits of the course and think of ways to reschedule your workload so that you can go

   b) decide that you might like to go, but put off making the arrangements because you are so busy

   c) decide that the immediate issues you are dealing with are too pressing and so decline to consider the possibilities that the course might bring

   d) think, 'oh no not another thing to worry about, even more I HAVE to do, how ever will I fit it in?'

4 You have only ordered enough exercise books for half of your department's students. You are around 400 exercise books short at the start of the term. Do you:

   a) immediately think 'OK this is a reality, there's got to be an easy solution here' and get on and find it. Excuse your mistake, understand why it happened and think of a strategy for next time to enhance the ordering system.

b) feel quite nervous and realize that this is a potentially embarrassing situation. Worry about it overnight and then go to your associate deputy to talk it through.

c) be self-critical and blame yourself for your stupidity. Admit to everyone that you have made a foolish mistake and apologize profusely. Make a quick decision to tell all students they must bring their own exercise books in by the end of the week or else! Communicate this decision via messengers to classes before the end of the school day.

d) feel like resigning from your post. Go into a cupboard to take a bit of time out and compose yourself, be genuinely upset. Feel that this one error of judgement means you are entirely unfit for your role.

5 Your boss comes to you with a project that they want completed by the following week. It is a huge undertaking where you communicate with 12 members of your team and them asking questions of students in each class that they teach. Your boss explains that the project will net the school a useful sum of money, but admits that the project has been on their desk for six weeks, as other other pressing matters have got in the way. Do you:

a) listen to the them, consider the proposal and ask them to leave it with you for 24 hours so that you can see what might be possible. Realizing immediately that it will impact on another job they have asked for, for tomorrow, you ask them which is the greater priority to help you plan your workload. You agree this and go back the next day to negotiate further.

b) perceive that with information that they have given so far, there is no point in considering it as you just do not have time. So you tell them there and then very clearly.

c) become angry and feel that this is an unfair request and your emotions are expressed in the conversation, as you explain this sense of unfairness you feel.

d) become upset internally, assume that this MUST be done because the boss has asked for it. You already have enough work in the next week to keep you out of bed until 2 a.m. each day. You feel powerless. You agree to do it, with a growing sense of panic inside.

Totalling the questionnaire

You will now need to find a numerical value from the choices you made. To do this allocate points to your responses to each question as follows:

a) 20

b) 15

c) 10

d) 5

Add the points together for the whole questionnaire.

Interpreting the questionnaire

Totals of:

80–100: you are amazingly resourceful and practising in your own work what you preach as a coach.

65–79: you are resourceful most of the time and practising reframing techniques with your own thinking will help you to prepare better for coaching others.

35–64: you are resourceful some of the time, though you might benefit from some coaching yourself to help you manage some areas of your work even more effectively.

29–34: you should seek the support of a colleague to help you to develop greater feelings of resourcefulness and to prepare you for coaching others before you do so. You may also find the suggestions in the 'Managing yourself' section of benefit.

25–28: you may be finding your work overwhelming and you should definitely seek support without delay. You may find coaching others leads you to feel less resourceful. You may wish to get some support from someone at work or outside of work, particularly if these feelings have gone on for more than a few days. You may also find the suggestions in the 'Managing yourself' section of benefit.

Managing yourself: get an MBA in coping!

MBA stands for Myself, Behaviour and 'Arroundings'. Those in the teaching profession know only too well the physical, mental and emotional drains upon them that a high workload brings. Coping with the stresses and strains of the expected and the unexpected is largely a matter of approach and with a bit of adjustment workload pressures can shift from punishing to exciting. Most of us like to feel we have some control over our lives. As workloads increase, the time we feel we have for the volume of work we have to deal with can sometimes seem to shrink. Yet we all have 24 hours a day to deal with it. So how do some people manage to stay calm in the face of adversity, while others feel the strain? It is largely a matter of, first, attitude and, then, approach.

As we grow up we model the strategies that our parents, teachers and close friends use in the face of pressure. Some of these models are excellent and help us to learn patterns of behaviour to manage workloads and still feel in control. Other models provide us with strategies that tend towards a coping strategy that makes us feel hopeless and unable to progress. The ability to cope with large numbers of competing factors is something we can learn, just as the inability to manage is learned.

If you are serious about further enhancing the way you manage your workload (and as a coach it is important to do this), you will need to start by formulating a workload-related goal. What do you want to achieve? Imagine you already have what you want to achieve in terms of your personal effectiveness; take yourself forward in your mind to the time when you have that workload balance you seek. What are you experiencing when you have things how you want them. What are you feeling? What are you seeing? What are you hearing? Really intensify that feeling of success. Now what is it that most motivates you about having this balance? The process of moving closer to an even more successful approach to dealing with workload pressures starts with this motivating goal and continues with an MBA.

M is for Myself

Looking after 'number one' is perhaps a cliché; something that can be shrugged off as selfish, self-indulgent and unimportant. Yet, without the appropriate level of balancing in terms of your physical needs (food, water, sleep) and your social and emotional needs (stimulus-free time, rest, interaction, diversion and laughter), your emotional and physical reserves dwindle. What was once a challenge and an exciting prospect becomes a problem and a source of fear. This kind of depletion of your resources can shift even the most positive of thinkers into a cycle of negativity. The number one priority is to stay on top and you can do it by looking after yourself.

Things you can do for the 'Myself' of MBA:

- Take time away from your pressures – even a few seconds periodically within a busy day helps.

- Build in moments within the day when you notice your heart rate, breathing rate and levels of tension. Consciously slow your breathing down.

- Get enough sleep – monitor how much you need, do not kid yourself you can survive on less. If you have difficulty sleeping, take steps to find out why and deal with the root cause.

- Take regular exercise – at least three times a week for about twenty minutes.

- Eat regularly – a little and often is better than larger meals. Balance carbohydrates fats and proteins. Too much carbohydrate sets up a cycle of high, followed by very low, blood sugar levels. This adds physiological stresses to your body and can make you feel tired and irritable.

- Reduce (or better still, cut out) caffeine. Drink water regularly throughout the day. One of the first signs of dehydration is irritability. Caffeine exacerbates water loss.

B is for Behaviour

 If you do what you've always done you'll get what you've always got.

Great habits of mind lead to behaviours that support us towards performing at our best. One of the early realizations of those we coach is often that they possess far more choices in their lives than they first realized. We can sometimes feel that everything that is requested of us is a 'must do' or 'should do' activity. When we realize that actually everything around us is a 'could do' activity, we understand that we have choices in everything we do, everyday. Knowing that we have a choice helps us to react in ways that balance our needs with those of others. Whenever Will finds himself up against difficult odds, he always remember the words of Victor Frankl. He faced unspeakable torture at the hands of the Nazi regime in the Second World War while interned in a concentration camp. His insight into what he calls 'the last human freedom – the ability to choose how to respond in any given situation' is a powerful attitude of mind. When we focus on putting a gap between stimuli in our environment and the decision to react to it, we can fill it with time to choose. This gives us space to consider the range of options and pick the right one. Moving from being a 'must do' and 'should do' thinker to a 'could do' and 'might do' thinker can really help you cope better with the demands of the day. Considering how the choices we have link to our primary goals can help us to react in ways that ease our pressures. Many people react in repetitive patterns that actually compound their workload difficulties. For example, in haste they offer to take on additional tasks rather than questioning the necessity of the task or the timescale or whether it is they themselves who are really the best positioned to do it.

Improving performance is largely a matter of slowing down and noticing your behaviour. Once you have noticed a pattern, you can plan alternative behaviours and try them out next time the same stimulus occurs. Of course, remembering why you are striving for change is important; go back often to the goal and relive the experience of having already achieved the goal. Do this at least once per day. This helps you stay in touch with your workload balancing amid the daily pulls on your time.

Changing your behaviour will change the workload experience. Here are some ways to help you do this:

- Focus on your goal and revisit it in the way described above at least once per day.

- Decide how much of the 24 hours in each day you want to spend working, and fit your work into that time. Only you can make the boundaries.

- Plan and prioritize: carve out one hour each week to plan. Work from priorities, prepare to be flexible with the plan, and highlight what is realistic. If it is not realistic, then choose to drop it, delegate it, reprioritize, or re-negotiate the timescale. You have 100 per cent of your work time and no more! Each week consider your long-, medium- and short-term plans.

- Take a few minutes everyday to look at your long-, medium- and short-term plans and plan what you will do that day to move them forward.

- Decide in which areas of your work 80 per cent perfection is enough and go for that target.

- Start to notice the ways in which you can minimize your workload (ask questions of yourself, such as 'How could I make this easy and still do it right?').

- Give up excuses such as 'I am a naturally disorganized person' or 'I'm a teacher, it goes with the territory' – that is all they are, excuses! Take control. Everyone is a natural organizer, just let yourself do it.

- Stop and think carefully each time someone attempts to delegate work to you. Probe the nature, timescale and relevance of the task. Be prepared to ask for time to think it over before agreeing. Be assertive.

- Handle paper once – sort it into 'Do it', 'Pass it on', 'Bin it'. Be ruthless and leave the guilt behind – think of your goal.

A is for 'Arroundings'

'Arroundings' is a made-up word, but for good reasons: it draws in the physical surroundings and the distance your consciousness extends around you. There are things in our environment that we can control, such as having a great filing system and a place to work. Managing workload effectively is also about being able to move between the big picture and the details, moving back and forth to balance the immediate pressures of the day with the longer-term goals, including those of our own health and well-being. When we keep the longer-term goals in our minds it allows us to notice the opportunities to fulfil these goals each day.

Approaches to managing your 'arroundings':

- Use a metaphor to switch your thinking between the bigger picture and the details regularly during the day. For example, imagine you are a bird flying over your head. What will you see if you fly low (the detail)? Then what do you notice as you fly higher and see the bigger vista before you?

- Create an effective and logical filing system for emails in your computer and in a filing cabinet for your paperwork. If you do not have a filing cabinet, then make one with a box and some dividing cards, that way you have a place to file papers and a way of finding them again. It really helps the one-touch paper rule.

- Change the small things that cause you regular concern. I had a nail in my shoe once that was sticking into my foot. I left it for two weeks. It never damaged my skin but I felt it regularly and it caused me great annoyance. The day I took control and sorted it out was fantastic. It is the small details which add up and drain our resources.

Coming back to the question posed at the beginning of the chapter, 'Do coaches have to be perfect?' Still the same answer. But, intention is everything. A good friend, and one of my greatest coaches, Tom, has a neat way of considering mistakes and learnings. When I perceive that I have screwed things up, he asks me a great question: 'Will, what was your intention when you set out with this?' Almost invariably I will come back with a brilliant intention, and he affirms this. 'So the intention was spot on,' he will say. 'So you found a way that almost works. What's the next step?' I am straight back to feeling good and go to the next step. On the occasions where my intentions were adrift, I soon realize and there is some great learning there too.

The coach Will owes much in balancing his working life and finding the direction for his passion for coaching to Anne. Anne has a great question that Will uses on himself regularly now: 'OK, you know what you want, now what will pull you towards it?' This is a liberating question when you feel stuck. It is asking what will make things more motivating and it really works for me!

This now leads us on to another important point about self-management for coaches.

Can you coach yourself?

One of the most inspiring aspects of longer-term coaching is that as the relationship grows between you and the person you are coaching, you begin to think together. A fluidity develops and before long the coach asks fewer and fewer questions and the individual asks their own questions. This is the true genius of coaching in that others develop a 'coaching pattern to their thinking'. The sad part is that the individual will soon realize that the work they had to do with their coach is done. Reframing this, it is a closing door that opens a new one to another person in your organization who is ready for your expertise.

The more you coach others, the more the patterns of thinking are instilled in your own way of life. Coaching others profoundly and positively affects your own outlook and success. Coaching yourself is almost unavoidable and can be most beneficial. There is, however, no substitute for occasionally inviting in a coach to work with you and to ask you the questions you dare not ask yourself and stretch your rubber band of possibilities. As far as giving yourself some quality time to recharge and renew, there is nothing like getting a coach working with you for a few sessions.

As an approach to self-coaching and considering your own health and well-being, try the following day chair test on yourself.

The 'day chair test'

- You must have a powerful positive anchor set up in advance to do this (Chapter 9) – you can use this at any time to come out of the day chair experience.

- Sit down quietly for 20 minutes.

- In the first five minutes focus on your breathing – as you breathe, focus on breathing in calm and breathing out tension.

- Tense the muscle groups beginning with feet and working up to head and tongue. In each case tense and hold muscle groups as you breathe in and relax as you breathe out.

- Fire your positive anchor to check it is working.

- Move rapidly through the decades to a time when you are old and sitting in your day chair.

- You are a spritely, cheerful and healthy old-age pensioner. You are active and positive and love life to the full.

- Now that you are old, in this great state of health look back on your life and describe to yourself the steps you took to be this healthy at this age.

- Be as specific as you can and describe the timescales for the steps you took.

- You can also do the day chair test by looking at the ill health you might have in the future based on your current lifestyle – always have your positive anchor ready for this one! Fire it if you need to. Looking at what you did not change through your life is also a powerful motivator. Carrot and stick may well be useful approaches with this.

- You only get one life; it is yours and what you choose to do with it is your affair, but remember that the choices you make now shape your future of tomorrow – remember the day chair – you'll be sitting in it quicker than you think!

Ten questions to personally move you forward (or someone else)

1 If I could take up any challenge knowing that I was guaranteed success, what challenges would I begin with?

2 If I could ask any question relating to my life knowing that I will be given an answer, what would my questions be?

3 What would I need to do to turn my problem into a solution?

4 For me, with this challenge, what exactly does success look like? Describe it.

5 How does the other person see it?

6 What am I going to do about it?

7 How does behaving in this way help me achieve …?

8 In what ways can I contribute to a solution?

9 What will I think about this in five years' time?

10 What is the next question?

Developing your coaching skills

 Coaching is 90 per cent attitude and 10 per cent technique.

In developing our own attitudes we need to be able to accept challenges to our ways of thinking. We have already impressed the importance of the nine coaching principles (see page 19).

When coaches begin with non-directive coaching they can sometimes lose their nerve with the third principle. This becomes a self-fulfilling prophecy. The moment the coach believes the individual is stuck, they can go into 'suggestions' mode and start throwing all kinds of lame solutions at the individual. Occasionally they suggest something that the individual thinks might work. More often than not the individual takes a suggestion and half-heartedly implements it. It does not work well and the belief begins to shift for the individual: 'This coach says I have the solutions, then gives them to me and hey, they don't work anyway – this is a waste of my time!'

To develop your skills in coaching try the following recommendations:

- Get some quality, non-directive coaching training.

- Get a coach for yourself to experience being coached and periodically revisit them. Use different coaches to experience the range of coaching styles available and incorporate practice you like in your style.

- Coach everyone you can to practise your skills – be upfront about what you are doing and ask their permission.

- Use the coaching principles as questions to gain feedback on the attitudes you bring to coaching – make it part of your periodic review process with those you coach mid- and long-term. The better you get to know them the more honest they will be.

- Gain feedback regularly from individuals and work on building the belief that all feedback is extremely valuable information. Whatever it is, good or bad, it is bound to help you be even more effective and bring new levels of freedom to your coaching.

- Read everything you can about coaching. Develop your awareness of the huge range of definitions and styles of coaching. Be individual and evolve the style of coaching that best suits your values and beliefs.

- Visit the websites listed in the back of this book.

- Listen to other people talking and practise the coaching interventions you might use were you invited to coach them at that moment.

- In the words of Ghandi 'Be the change you want to see in the world.' If you have been hooked by the coaching bug, then use it well, use it morally, teach others what it is and share your enthusiasm. For the sceptical, as your confidence grows, offer them a chance to experience it, and rise to the challenge of the resistant individual.

- Recognize that this book is only the tip of a very large iceberg.

The coaching iceberg and staying resourceful

The coaching principles and strategies outlined in this book are powerful interventions for positive change in education. Based on proven approaches used in a variety of organizations the world over, the non-directive coaching iceberg has only just begun to come into view. This book describes pragmatic and creative approaches to thinking and problem solving, yet there is another level on which coaching has a fascinating range of possibilities. Deep insight coaching and insights into values, creativity and possibility are a natural extension of what is described here. While venturing at this point into what might loosely be termed the 'spiritual dimension of coaching', it is prudent to point out that this does not have to be a dimension of coaching for you in your school. It is, however, worth consideration. This spiritual dimension is an essential part of remaining in the right frame of mind for coaching. Maintaining your own sense of balance and relaxation as a coach is the way to really clear your mind and be the blank canvas that the people you coach need you to be. Clearing your agendas and interferences is not only essential to function as a coach, but also for your own health and well-being.

There is also a bigger picture here. Sadly there is evidence of the terrible impact of negative press and an over-zealous inspection system that has emphasized fear and judgement, and assumed weakness rather than building on a platform of strengths. This does not make sense in terms of developing excellent educators. Happily there are clear signs that approaches to improving performance are changing for the better. Schools can lead the way in this by adopting positive coaching approaches as part of their culture.

If education is really about preparation for life, then it must be about congruence with values as well as balance, fulfilment and learning. If we expect to help young people to shape their lives for the better, we need to provide role models for them that portray this. This means teachers who are in balance in their lives have a congruence with their values, feel fulfilled in their work and are the lead learners in their classrooms. Of course, many teachers are, but for those that are not, schools will need to provide support for them to achieve this.

There will be much more said about this in the coming months and years, with a growing emphasis on work–life balance and job satisfaction as routes to optimum performance and a healthier, happier nation. Coaching is already acting as a catalyst for delivering a healthier, happier and more effective workforce and the signs are that the use of these approaches is growing in schools.

How do you currently open your mind to balance? If you read this and dismiss it, you may be in need of this insight more than you realize.

Summary

In this chapter we have explored the importance of looking after oneself:

▶ Without taking physical, emotional and spiritual care of yourself, your capacity to coach effectively diminishes.

▶ Communication with others can be distorted by the effects of over-stretching your resources.

▶ Assessing your current state of resourcefulness can be done with the questionnaire on pages 171–173

▶ Using the MBA acronym there are three areas to consider in self-management: myself, behaviour and arroundings.

▶ Suggestions are given in the chapter as to how to balance your needs with your work.

▶ Self-coaching is possible. There are advantages to using a personal coach periodically.

Many people perceive balance as an end point in their lives. Balance is in fact an ongoing item on your 'To do list'. Each day you make conscious and unconscious decisions about the balance that you maintain and grow. Each decision we make has implications for balancing or unbalancing our lives in the days, weeks, months and years ahead. Ultimately the balance we achieve now can affect the length of our life and its quality in the future.

Questions

1   On a scale of one to ten (ten is peak awareness), what is your current level of awareness of your MBA needs during a typical day at work?

2   How much time each week do you take (other than sleep) when you clear your mind of everything and just relax in the moment?

3   In what ways are you looking after yourself well at the moment?

4   What kinds of problems do you think you may be storing up for yourself in later life based on your current behaviour?

5   What would you like to change about your lifestyle currently?

6   What could you do to move yourself closer to this change?

Masterclass

▶ *Balance in coaching is about the whole of our lives. To support colleagues in school to improve their performance will almost certainly involve changes in the rest of their lives. Be aware of this when you coach and maintain open questions that allow all aspects of life to be explored. Remember:*

▶ *To assume that your role as a coach focuses purely on work is to close avenues for positive change across a person's life – but do not probe for this!*

▶ *You need very strong rapport and trust before many people will bring home-life into work-performance conversations – but do not shy away from these issues with individuals if they bring them up.*

▶ *To support others effectively in maintaining a focus on their development is about maintaining balance and a sense of fulfilment in your own life. We must strive to live what we believe.*

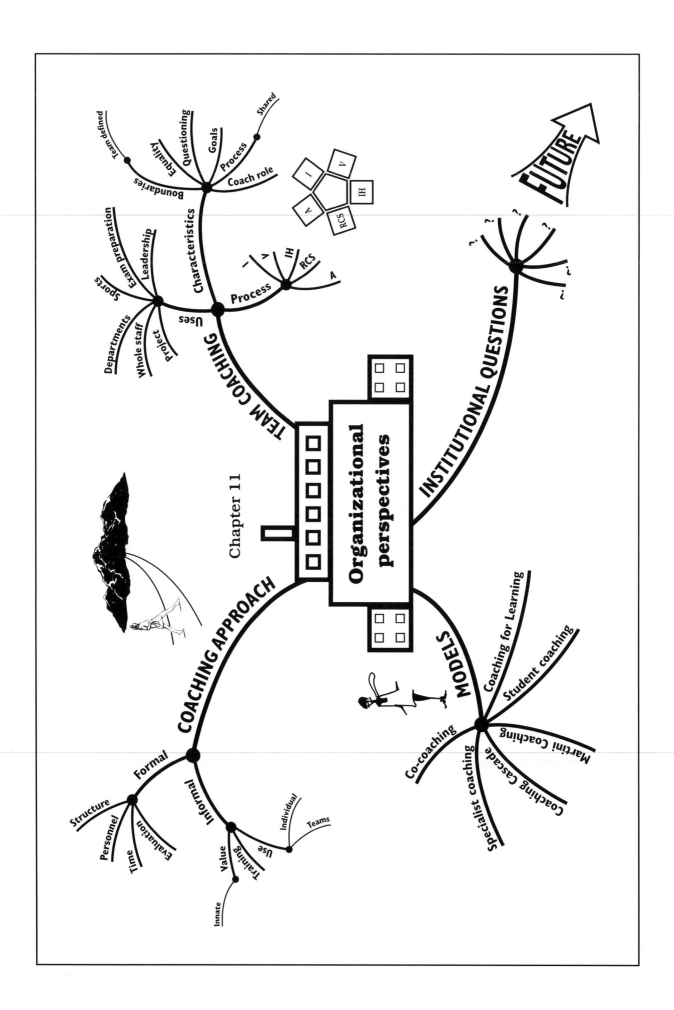

Chapter 11

Organizational perspectives

IN THIS CHAPTER YOU WILL LEARN:

- how organizational culture develops and can be changed
- to consider benefits for a whole-organization approach to coaching
- to understand a range of possible organizational models using, developing and maintaining coaching
- to understand the team-coaching process and approaches
- the benefits of networking
- how some organizations are bringing about change and improved performance through coaching

PREVIEW QUESTIONS:

- How could coaching be beneficial across a whole organization?
- How might teams be coached?
- How might an institution utilize coaching to resolve problems and develop a solutions-focus?
- How can institutions structure the development and maintenance of high quality coaching practice?
- Where might this approach lead?

Old habits die hard

There were five monkeys who had lived together for some time in a large cage in a municipal zoo. One day their keeper changed.

The new keeper decided to try and dissuade the monkeys from eating their food at the end of the cage furthest from the general public. So when some of the monkeys tried to do this he hosed all the monkeys with cold water. Quickly the monkeys realized that taking the food to the far end of the cage led to an uncomfortable soaking so they avoided doing so. Any monkey who attempted to take their food there was quickly and violently apprehended by the others.

Gradually the monkey population aged and changed. Some died, others were moved, but most just forgot the old ways. One day the newest arrival grabbed his food and made for the far end of the cage. The others seeing what was happening, pounced on him, shrieking and biting and dragged him away.

The new monkey, badly shaken by the ordeal, eventually recovered himself and asked why he had been stopped from eating where he wanted. He was told 'That's the way we've always done things around here.'

Change, profound cultural change is possible.

Coaching teams and organizations

Old habits die hard. Sometimes it is easier to live with them than to challenge them. Changing organizational attitudes amounts to a change in culture and sometimes it takes a burst of cold water for a shift to happen, but more usually culture is recreated through processes which influence the conversations in staffrooms and corridors. Questions and practices which nudge equilibrium can give space to open up discussion and debate – a healthier approach than guessing agendas. In this chapter we explore some of the approaches to culture shift that organizations have taken in order to effect a more open and effective change-development agenda. Since the first edition of this text there have been major steps forward in the use of coaching in schools and colleges and we have captured some of the dedication and hard work undertaken by colleagues in the descriptions and case studies included here.

In his book, *The Naked Leader* (2002), David Taylor describes his work on a leadership programme for 40 staff. He worked with groups of ten for four successive weeks and asked the question of each group of ten:'How many of you believe that hidden agendas play a part in the team of 40?' They all put their hands up. The next question: 'How many of you have a hidden agenda?' No one puts their hand up. Conclusion: it is always someone else who has a hidden agenda!

Coaching is now being seen as one way to bring about a more open agenda in organizations. Its openness and non-judgmentalism provides a refreshing space for people to unwrap the real issues that threaten continual improvement, allowing people to be more honest about the challenges they face, and they can do this within relationships which are respectful and supportive. One school on the south coast of England has moved out of Special Measures following the use of co-coaching approaches to improve classroom practice. One teacher explained that the process of co-coaching (which involves being part of a pair or trio of teachers who meet regularly and coach one another) has enabled her to 'stop being afraid of saying "I can't handle this class" and turn this into an honest discussion which results in a clear plan and cast-iron strategies'. All too often in organizations there can be a wall of silence behind which teachers sit, unable to see a way forward and unable to speak out for fear of judgment. The principles of coaching discussed in Chapter 1 enshrine this openness and make for professional development that has integrity for all.

Some of the best developments occur when the talents that already exist within staff are fully utilized and shared. Through a coaching programme in your institution you can access the talents of more staff, focus on solutions, and develop observation and feedback skills that are essential for progress. In its first edition, this book had mainly theoretical perspectives to offer on the subject of whole-school coaching. There had been few positive UK examples of success, drawing mainly from experiences in the US. That has changed considerably. In this chapter we present a number of case studies and experiences, which demonstrate the positive effects of developing coaching structures and indeed coaching cultures within schools and colleges.

Organizational culture change and coaching

We can describe the culture in an organization as 'The way we do things here'. Changing the culture is about changing the way people conduct themselves. It extends beyond behaviour and indeed encompasses beliefs, mythology, complex perceptions and conversation. There is a sense with organizational culture that it is 'bigger than the sum of its parts' and commentators on organizational culture suggest that it can become unpredictable in response to outside influences. Like a pile of sand which is constantly added to and which will respond without warning with either small rolling sand particles or huge sand-slides as a new grain is added. Many organizational-change consultants agree that the way to change culture is to influence the daily conversations between people within the organization. But this is easier said than done. Change consultants rarely agree that you can influence this kind of interaction through top-down models of leadership, yet they do agree that influencing these daily conversational exchanges is the key to shifting the collective paradigms and how they play themselves out.

Emergence is a phenomenon which exists within organizations.

Kevin Mihata defines emergence as:

The process by which patterns or global-level structures arise from interactive local-level processes. This "structure" or "pattern" cannot be understood or predicted from the behaviour or properties of the component units alone. (Mihata 1997:31)

In an organization the agents that create cultural change are people. When people have sufficient rapport, emergence occurs. A new pattern of collective behaviour emerges. The French anthropologist Daniel Sperber has for many years used the Viral Model as a metaphor to explain cultural change process. We would like to draw on this metaphor to suggest an approach to changing culture towards a coaching culture in schools. It is not an elegant or tasteful model, but the metaphor does work beautifully, so we hope you will excuse its rawness in places!

Clutterbuck and Megginson suggest that a coaching culture has six main features which I have adapted slightly to meet the needs of an education setting:

1   Coaching is linked to educational drivers, e.g. our core business of learning.

2   Being a coachee is encouraged and supported.

3   Training is provided to develop coaching skills and quality.

4   Coaching practice and time invested in it by individuals is recognized.

5   The process of coaching is systemic – i.e. assume people are competent and there is constructive challenge of ideas.

6   The move towards coaching is managed over time.

Taking these features as a vision for a coaching culture, Sperber's Viral Model can then be employed as a methodology for influencing this to come about.

Benevolent infection

In organizations where Viral Organisational Coaching has been established, individuals responsible or passionate about developing coaching have created a benevolent virus – the concept and practice of coaching with its inherent benefits. Then they (the creator) have sought out individuals within the organization who are most likely to be susceptible to the virus and then infected them by talking about coaching. Crucially with coaching they have also coached individuals to give them an experience of the power of the process. Once these hosts are infected, the original creator of the benevolent virus can move on to 'infect' others. Those infected go on to share the benefits with others. Those who are infected are referred to as 'sneezers'. Sneezers require training and support to develop their skills and keep their infection-motivation high. The creator sees to this. After a time, the creator takes stock of the spread of the virus and brings together the small group of the greatest, most enthusiastic sneezers. This group becomes a focus group of infectors. Into this group, the creator also brings a member of the organization who is an active immunizer. Immunizers are those people who will resist the change. Through the participation of the immunizer in the sneezer group, their beliefs about coaching begin to change. In other words their immunity to the virus is suppressed and begins to allow the virus to take effect. The effect of an immunizer, who stops resisting a virus, is huge in the staff rooms, corridors, offices, car parks and smoking shelters through which they pass. It changes the conversations in these places, and crucially it changes the interactions between people, and consequently the culture.

This approach has been used extensively to shift culture within organizations. It is highly effective in situations where external parties are required to create coaching cultures in organizations where they are not the leaders, nor do they have a positive relationship with the leadership. Local Authorities and consultants can find this to be an excellent approach.

The broad steps to changing to a coaching culture are:

1 Build your own knowledge and skill levels.

2 Craft the benevolent virus – in other words craft the case for coaching based around four questions which will reach all of immune-suppressors:

    a Why is coaching worth investing in?

    b What is it and what does it do?

    c How does coaching work?

    d What are the possible outcomes if we invest in this?

3 Seek out your most likely advocates – your sneezers – and infect them.

4 Step back and support your sneezers – let them do the work.

5 Train and coach your sneezers.

6 When there is a nucleus of support, form a focus group of sneezers and invite in an immune-suppressor.

7 Structure the group activities to build motivation, skill and knowledge, and also approaches to advocating coaching more widely. Support your immunizers to overcome their objections. Bring in more immunizers gradually, taking the line of least resistance.

8 Conduct a small-scale study and measure the impact of the coaching.

9 Present the impact data to those who need to be influenced to invest in time and training to up-skill everyone who has training needs.

10 Once you have achieved this, you will be able to influence approaches to coaching which might include more formal structures such as trio coaching or cascade models.

Organizational models of coaching

There are a number of organizational models of coaching ranging from highly organized to ad hoc and from leader to learner. These fall into six categories. These categories are outlined below and then expanded upon in the text that follows:

1 Co-coaching Professional development Pairs or trios. Characterized by open professional dialogue through a coaching framework such as STRIDE. Good to great	2 Specialist coaching Particular focus of development, with coach having some experience	3 Coaching cascade A line management model of coaching where senior colleagues are trained in coaching and coach others down the hierarchy spreading the practice and supporting colleagues. Principally used for enhancing professional practice of teachers and leaders
4 Martini coaching Support for colleagues in their professional challenges, development, and learning on an ad hoc basis around school. So-called after the Martini beverage advert of the 1970s 'Anytime, any place, anywhere'	5 Student coaching confidence, improving performance, and Particular skills development. May be group or individual	6 Coaching for learning Coaching skills used with learners, within classroom practice for learning to learn, AfL, behaviour management, Skill development, e.g. PLTS, G&T

1 Co-coaching

Co-coaching or 'Collaborative Coaching' is a system whereby all or some members of an organization engage in dialogue and coach one another to explore and improve practice. It is characterized by high-level listening and reflecting skills on the part of the two or three people involved. There is a high degree of coaching and a small degree of mentoring, since the relationship is essentially equitable.

It is one of the most successful approaches to using coaching in schools and colleges. It involves the formation of teams of colleagues into pairs or trios for professional learning discussions. Co-coaching can:

- provide a genuine and meaningful forum for professional development
- share outstanding practice across an organization
- prevent teachers re-inventing the wheel, and reduce workload through collaborative working
- help to embed learning from training
- support colleagues through challenging periods or experiences
- shift organizational culture from teachers feeling that things are done to them to one where they feel they are trusted to use and develop their professionalism
- liberate tangible improvements in teacher and pupil performance.

The Mayfield model Born out of a crisis in teacher recruitment, Mayfield School, Portsmouth, has had a successful history of training teachers from a variety of atypical backgrounds and creating excellent practitioners of them. The Mayfield model was pioneered by Ian Cox and Mike Harbour and is aimed at further enhancing the performance of teachers and leaders in their classroom practice. The staff have been divided into 'coaching trios'. Each trio of staff has an experienced and trained coach, a newly qualified or graduate teacher trainee and another experienced member of staff. The school creates regular opportunities for these trios to meet and the trained coaches elicit discussion, goal-setting and solution-foci. One trained coach on the programme commented on how helpful it was to shift from a mentoring model to a coaching model. She explained that the coaching model took away the dreadful burden she had felt when mentees expected her to have all the solutions to their problems ready and waiting when they arose.

One of the important aspects of this institutional approach to coaching is the inclusion of all staff, regardless of experience, in the process of structured self-reflection. While the agenda for reflection remains with the individuals, the structure in terms of groupings and time resourcing was created by the school. Consequently the main barriers to coaching taking place are removed and the reflection process can take place with minimum disruption. There is a genuine excitement about meeting your trio and trust has built up quickly through the use of a non-critical/non-judgemental approach. This model used a mix of co-coaching and mentoring to support colleagues.

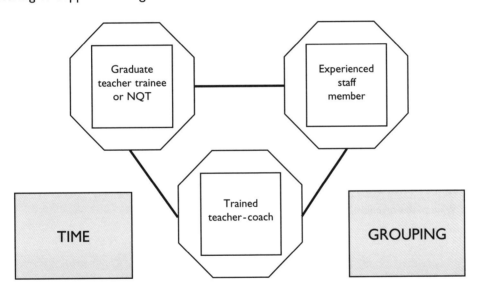

Figure 11.1 The Mayfield model

One school in Manchester, Newall Green, provides a co-coaching system which, while broadly focused on learner improvement, remains confidential and open to teachers to focus the agenda specifically as they see fit. It has enabled teachers to work together to develop their practice. A novel approach saw teacher A observing teacher B and then teacher B coaching teacher A on what they had observed in relation to teacher A's own practice. A pilot study involving the coaching of teachers of Year 9 groups showed improvements in 'value-added' scores for the pupils whose teachers were being coached. (Source: How to develop effective mentoring and coaching in your school, NUT Professional Development Seminar November 2005.)

Another trio-coaching model includes an element of coaching skills development within it. The model often attributed to Thurston School, Suffolk, operates when person A coaches person B. Person C then coaches Person A on their coaching and so they change places. This introduces a highly recommendable level of quality development in the coaching process.

From Will Thomas' work with a wide range of schools and colleges using coaching for development, there would seem to be a number of factors core to the success of co-coaching ventures. These factors also hold for specialist coaching models too. These elements serve to minimize resistance to coaching from colleagues or learners and create greater openness, transparency and trust.

A formal coaching framework involves a number of factors summarized by this diagram:

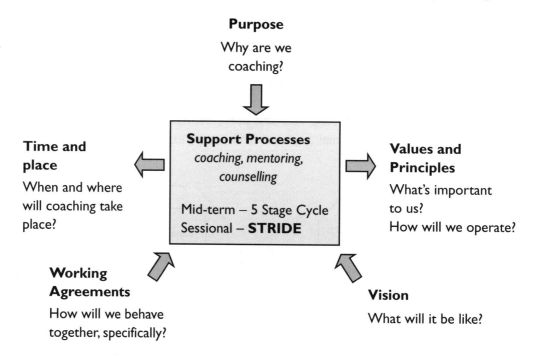

Figure 11.2 What makes organizational coaching work? – © Will Thomas 2007

The factors explained:

Purpose The core question 'Why are we coaching?' needs to be addressed at the leadership level and through discussion among colleagues. Clarity and transparency about the purpose make for easier feelings about engaging with coaching. It should make clear the separation of coaching from formal performance management systems. While coaching skills will invariably be used in performance management as they assist in making it more productive, any formal coaching models, in the authors' view, should be separate from such processes.

Values and principles As with any development in an organization, clarity about the values and principles that underpin its day-to-day operation is important. These need to be shared and be both implicitly and explicitly observable, with feedback on coaching quality linked to this. By using a set of defined principles for coaching we can provide a language for talking about development and the processes that underpin it, as well as support the growth of high-quality coaching. Using existing principles like those discussed in Chapter 2 or adapting them or developing new ones to fit your setting is likely to provide the foundation for positive experiences with coaching. The more collaboratively produced this is the better.

Vision Developing a vision of how coaching will operate, be seen, experienced and developed is also vital. Considering the 'coaching' organization in five years is a helpful way of planning for the resources that will be required. Imagining the conversations that will be taking place in classrooms and staffrooms between teachers, learners, parents, as well as what will be seen and felt by people, is part of that vision. Vision needs initial leadership, but is best developed collaboratively. Providing a vision gives leaders and teachers enough direction to set goals and creates a positive magnet to draw them towards those goals.

Working agreements Essential to all coaching structures is a set of clear agreements about how coaching will operate. These include aspects of confidentiality, behaviours throughout the coaching process, and boundaries of practice. In most cases these need to operate both at a whole organization level, e.g. global agreements about what is expected, and also at local level within coaching trios or pairs. Agreements made early on make it easier and more comfortable for people to address issues that might arise about approach and style, and thus allow for a more emotionally intelligent way to deal with concerns or conflicts.

Time and place Coaching must be given time for it to take place and appropriate places for it occur. In Will's experience, organizations that do not provide at least some time for coaching, e.g. disaggregated training days, spread throughout the year, or guaranteed non-contact time, seldom sustain coaching beyond a few enthusiasts, whereas those that provide either time for co-coaching to occur or invest in creating time for lead coaches to be available tend to build a sustainable system that works. Equally, appropriate places to coach are necessary. Free from disturbances, and conducive to relaxed discussion, coaching can take place almost anywhere. In some schools, colleagues use their classrooms where they have easy access to resources and exercise books to aid discussion about teaching and learning; in others they find quiet rooms, offices or corners of libraries at times when others are not around. Coaching can even take place in larger venues with many pairs or trios, provided that there is sufficient 'buzz' in the room for people not to feel conspicuous. The main point here is that physical and psychological comfort should be considered in setting the place.

In the centre of the model in Figure 11.2 are the Support Processes, the STRIDE model and the Mid-term cycle.

The support processes This refers to the blend of support offered to colleagues/learners which might consist of any variation of mentoring, coaching and counselling skills. This is discussed in more detail in Chapter 2. Suffice to say here that coaching is a foundation process for support, but the empathy and stimulus that can come from counselling skills and mentoring respectively are also valid aspects of support.

STRIDE model This model for structuring a coaching discussion is explained in detail in Chapter 6. It is a desirable framework in coaching discussions as it has built into it language and process that encourage problem-solving and resourceful thinking. It can minimize stuck and negative thoughts and result in quick, more thorough and more effective outcomes. With practice it becomes a free-flowing and conversational framework.

Mid-term cycle For co-coaching and specialist coaching approaches, it is useful to have a mid-term process cycle. We include one below as a suggestion. This is particularly useful when coaching involves observations or data collection. It provides a series of steps for colleagues to transition through and aids time-lining of events and appointment-making. A typical cycle might take place over a six-to-eight week period.

Such practice can form a core part of continuing professional development for staff, or indeed become the way that CPD takes place, through mutually supportive co-coaching relationships. It is certainly preferable to separate professional development through coaching from performance-management schemes, although in qualification it can be used as a tool within such schemes, provided it is made explicit that while the destination may be fixed, by the leadership team, the journey to that destination can hold choices. In this sense coaching can be used in a non-directive way to facilitate individuals towards choosing the most appropriate route, although it is unlikely that one approach to incorporating coaching across a school or college will be effective for all players. Organizations may take formal or informal approaches to using coaching.

2 Specialist coaching

This is defined by CUREE/DfES National Framework for Coaching and Mentoring as 'a structured and sustained process for enabling the development of specific aspects of a professional learner's practice'. It comes close to what we define earlier in our book as mentoring. It is characterized by coaching skills but also modelling of practice sharing learning

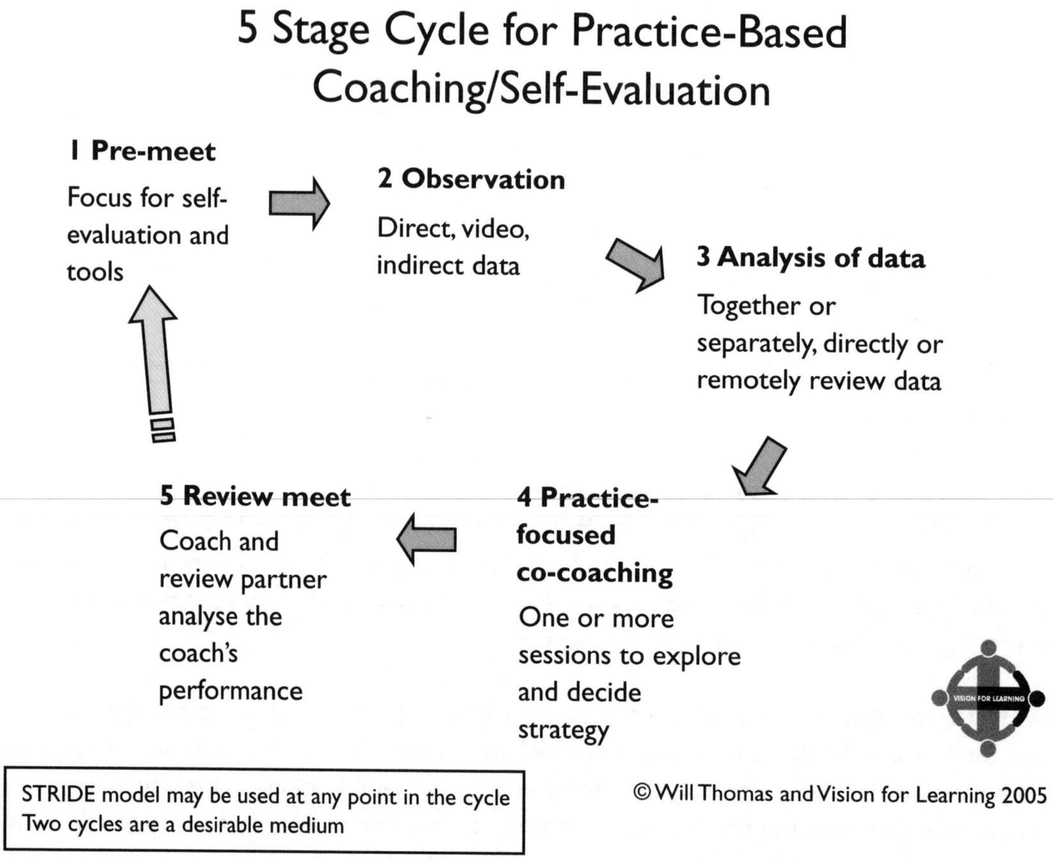

5 Stage Cycle for Practice-Based Coaching/Self-Evaluation

1 Pre-meet

Focus for self-evaluation and tools

2 Observation

Direct, video, indirect data

3 Analysis of data

Together or separately, directly or remotely review data

5 Review meet

Coach and review partner analyse the coach's performance

4 Practice-focused co-coaching

One or more sessions to explore and decide strategy

STRIDE model may be used at any point in the cycle
Two cycles are a desirable medium

© Will Thomas and Vision for Learning 2005

Figure 11.3 5 Stage Cycle for Practice-based Coaching/Self-evaluation

experiences; there is an expectation that the specialist coach has greater knowledge and experience in a particular field of practice. At Ravens Wood School in Kent, all staff have used coaching as part of their continuous professional development. Coaching in 2004 had become an established part of the culture and has been used with both specialist and co-coaching approaches to support ASTs ITTs, NQTs additionally for leadership development and for improving particular aspects of teaching. (Source: How to develop effective mentoring and coaching in your school, NUT Professional Development Seminar November 2005). The structures outlined in the co-coaching section above also work for specialist coaching. There is an inherent inequity between the two people on this approach however, and to minimize this, agreements need to be clear and revisited regularly to ensure the process remains empowering and promotes independence.

3 The coaching cascade model

The cascade model ensures the development of high-quality coaching practice and a learning culture that ranges from senior leadership all the way through to learners. Its aim is to develop an organization in which everyone is active as a learner. The core benefits are intended for end-users (students) but it also enhances the culture of the institution as a learning organization.

This model can be tweaked to be used with specific groups of students; for example, the C/D borderline, those with issues about self-confidence, and so on. It can also lead to every person in a school having access to learning the skills of coaching and experiencing the benefits of the process.

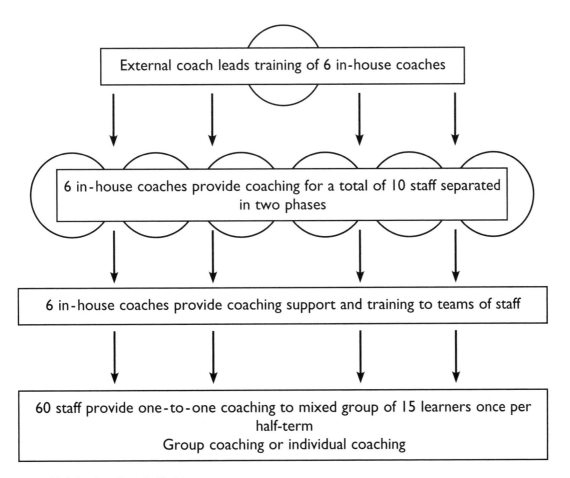

Figure 11.4 Coaching Cascade Model

4 Martini coaching

In the 1970s an advert appeared on television which advertised the popular drink, Martini. A scantily clad woman on roller skates delivered drinks on a tray in a café. The tag line for the advert was 'Martini, any time, any place, anywhere'. Using the coaching skills and frameworks outlined in this book, in corridors, staffrooms, pubs and classrooms for ad hoc conversations that support others is referred to as Martini coaching because it happens throughout the school day as required. The approach is used by many leaders as a 'way of being' within their role. One study showed that leaders who used coaching as a style of leadership created more empowered and independent workers and the leaders themselves were able to spend more time thinking strategically and less time fighting fires in the workplace. Most coaching that goes on in schools and colleges today is of the Martini variety and, through many conversations the authors have had with colleagues, they report that it has made a substantial difference to their success as a leaders and teachers. Steve Clark, Deputy Head and colleagues trained in coaching approaches at Bournville School in Birmingham use this approach.

5 Student coaching

Coaching using external and internal coaches has been employed by a variety of schools. South Bromsgrove Community High School used a trained coach to help young people to build confidence in school. Using non-directive coaching techniques, students identified areas they wished to work on during the sessions. Pre- and post-coaching evaluations of the students made by the teachers and the students themselves showed that benefits in terms of students' career plans, motivation, confidence and behaviour were noted during and after the period of the coaching. Trained teacher-coach Helen Barrett led a wider coaching programme for young people within the school using non-teacher volunteer adults to support the work. In the same school, Dee Gilmour led an innovative project with sixth formers who use non-directive coaching techniques to support younger students in making career decisions. In keeping with the philosophy of non-directive coaching, these sixth formers do not give advice but use their coaching skills to help other students to explore possibilities and overcome fears connected with career choice. The sixth formers have adult supervisors with whom they discuss issues that may need further support. Potentially, peer coaching could be used as a vehicle for all kinds of in-school and community support where individuals trained in the process of coaching can provide support in a wide range of helping roles. In the case of peer career coaching, the concept grew out of a growing concern that the traditional career service, now Connexions, has shifted its emphasis in recent years. The school saw peer coaching as a way to ensure career support for all in a sustainable way.

Chris Herrington was a learning mentor working in Kent. Trained as a coach, she worked with young people. In an article for *Coaching Chronicle* (2004), she explains that she is 'working with a school that caters for the top 25 per cent of the area's academically able 16-year-old boys'. She goes on to explain that 'they are often referred to me predominantly because they are not achieving their predicted grades' and this is often accompanied by challenging behaviour. She says that 'most if not all pupils [she works with] have incredibly low self-esteem'. In Chris' view she is '90 per cent coach and 10 per cent mentor'. With the inherent trust and value that coaching places in young people, it can have significant effects on building self-esteem and growing self-awareness.

The work of Jean Ramsey at The Cooper School is also worthy of note in the field of student coaching. A fuller case study is to be found later in this chapter. At her school they have linked coaching intervention to decreased exclusion rates and as a direct result of a group coaching approach they have enhanced the qualifications of formerly disaffected young people.

6 Coaching for learning

The use of coaching in classrooms has been increasing in recent years. Teachers have recognized the link between coaching styles of communication and the development of higher-order thinking skills like evaluation, analysis and creativity. The open-ended questioning and reduction in the use of closed questioning which steers pupils to teacher-determined responses benefits learners' academic and social skill development. Following a project funded by The National Union of Teachers and run by Will Thomas and Sarah Mook in 2005, a team of primary and secondary teachers trialled a range of coaching strategies for encouraging learners through coaching. A core part of the study was to get learners to coach one another.

Many of them used a variation on STRIDE to provide a structure for conversation among students and to assist students to coach one another.

The model is called GAME.

This model provides an easy-to-use structure for younger children. For older children STRIDE worked better. Here are some of the quotes from the NUT study:

> 'Sharon wanted to give her mixed-ability Year 8 students more insight into ways they could help each other to raise achievement in speaking and listening. Using GAME – "because it's simple and allows students to plan their own learning journey" – she videoed her students talking about their targets and how they aimed to achieve them in KS3 unit "TV scheduling". They were then able to discuss their performance with peers.'
>
> 'Jane introduced her Year 2 group to GAME. She wanted them to have an independent approach to solving problems without always needing her. The pupils used GAME in maths, literacy, and PE activities. The pupils learned that they could find solutions/answers for themselves. Jane found it particularly suitable for word problems in numeracy and making pupils think more deeply and use one another for support.'
>
> 'Linda read her Year 2 class Duncan and Delores by Barbara Samuels. They discussed how Delores might get on better with her cat Duncan, and examined pictures to discuss body language. They then discussed how humans use language to communicate and get on with each other and went onto explore Makaton symbols.'
>
> 'They played games where a speaker talks for one minute about anything they want and an observer rewards the listener each time they show good listening skills.'
>
> 'She found that children realized that good listening skills had to be learned.'

Many teachers are finding that in their day-to-day work in classrooms, they are moving away from their old practices of using closed questioning to steer students towards pre-determined answers and adopting coaching approaches which scaffold problem-solving and resourceful thinking but leave the specific actions and decision to learners. For many practitioners, coaching is becoming a core approach in relation to Assessment for Learning in the classroom, behaviour for learning approaches (see *Challenging Behaviour* by Anne Copley),

Good at...?
What are you good at?
What are your strengths?

Aim for...?
What do I want to aim for?
What will it look like when I'm successful?

Might do...?
What could I do to meet my aim?
What ideas could I use?

End up doing?
Based on my ideas, what will be the best thing to do?
When will I do it?

© Will Thomas 2007

personal, learning and thinking skills, to name but a few areas. Approaches to supporting gifted and talented young people, for whom highly structured and steered conversations are limiting to their expression, can potentially be greatly enhanced through coaching. Further support in the areas of using coaching for learning and coaching for behaviour can be found in Anne Copley's book *Challenging Behaviour* (2006) and Brin Best and Will Thomas' book *The Creative Teaching and Learning Toolkit* and *Resource Book* (2007 and 2008 respectively).

Team and group coaching

While coaching is highly effective as a process to enable individuals to gain personal and professional insight, resolve problems and enhance performance, it also has value when used with teams of people.

Team coaching

Coaching with teams can:

- build strong team identity
- build agreements about how the team will behave collectively and in one-to-one interactions
- explore and crystallize common purpose and values
- develop a collective vision and motivation
- grow a time line for implementing change
- overcoming obstacles within and outside the team
- resolve conflict.

Team coaching approaches might be used in a range of situations including:

- senior leadership team development
- preparation of students for exams
- sports teams
- department of curriculum teams
- whole-staff team development.

Rosshall Academy, Glasgow, used a team approach to developing a collective vision and set of values with their senior and middle leadership team in 2008. They found the process useful in affirming common beliefs and values and developing stronger sense of teamwork and ownership, as evidenced by feedback from colleagues on their time spent being coached as a team.

When coaching a team it is useful for both the coach and team members to have a model of team development. A number of models for team coaching approaches exist. The one that follows is born of team-coaching experiences in schools where the coach might be the leader or an external coach brought in to coach the team. Any school choosing to coach teams is opting to seriously improve performance. Teams are truly teams when the individuals within them work together towards common goals and values and as a result are bigger together than their individual contributions. Coaching teams is incredibly rewarding from the point of view of the coach as well as the team. The skills of coaching on a one-to-one basis transfer well into the team environment. Indeed the STRIDE model remains the principal approach for developing teams. There are some differences about coaching teams, however:

- It usually takes longer for breakthroughs to be made with teams compared to individuals – take the longer view.
- There are multiple levels of disclosure in individuals who are coached; these are multiplied by the numbers of people in the teams.

- Internal conflicts of personality can be directed straight at the individual concerned.
- Conflict is sometimes aimed at the coach, whether or not they are connected with the team.

Team coaches observe a cyclical process of change in the groups they work with.

We call this the Team Coaching Ecocycle (see Figure 11.5).

This team-coaching process model describes the processes that teams can go through when they are coached. It can help the team and the coach to understand the emotional changes that happen throughout team coaching experiences.

Icebergs In the early stages of coaching only a small proportion of the goals, aspirations, beliefs and values of individuals in the team are exposed. There is a reticence to share information about individual hopes and needs. Individuals are encouraged to share their personal and professional aspirations and concerns.

Volcanoes As coaching progresses, beliefs and judgements about members of the team and the institution begin to show themselves. At this stage of the coaching process, conflicts and personal and professional differences can surface. Sometimes coaches find themselves at the centre of blame for the emotional exposition that occurs. Staying calm and grounded in this phase is very important. The emotions expressed need to be acknowledged and it is important to detach yourself to some extent to avoid taking this projected hostility to heart.

Island-hopping Facilitated by the coach, the process of acknowledging what individuals within the team feel and perceive is followed by activities that help team members see issues from other colleagues' points of view. For example, pair colleagues up and assign them to chairs where they sit facing one another and state their viewpoint on an issue that has created volatility. Once they have both expressed this (usually in a tight time frame), they swap seats and place themselves in the position of their partner, arguing in support of their partner's views or needs.

Ripples in a calmer sea Following the island-hopping phase, much more of the iceberg is now exposed. Team members know more of the individual aspirations and concerns of others and are more empathic towards them. There are still sensitivities among and between the team members and these can create ripples. The team is generally calmer working together, but they can return to the volcano or potentially the iceberg stage at this point. Returning to the volcanic stage usually leads to important new insights and forward progress. Returning to the iceberg stage is not productive and when this happens the coach needs to bring the team back to their collective goals and challenge their commitment again.

Archipelago This is a stage of deeper connection between the group members and is indicative of progress. Working far more in tune with the needs of the common goals and with a greater understanding of the individuals in the team, this is an incredibly rewarding stage to be at. In the archipelago stage, individuals work more effectively as a whole and a synergy occurs. The whole is more than the sum of the parts. Over time, teams invariably return to the iceberg stage and further breakthroughs are required.

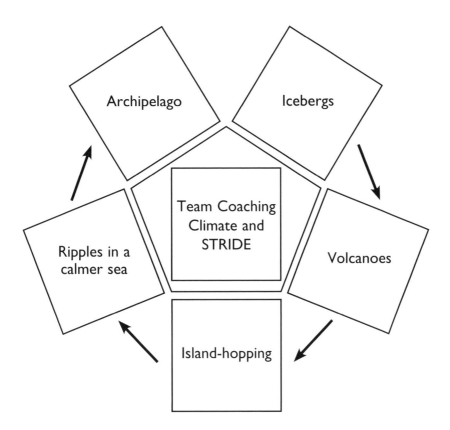

Figure 11.5 Team Coaching Ecocycle

It is desirable in team coaching situations to use a person as coach who is not part of the team. This frees the leader to be fully part of the process and to listen.

Quality development and measuring the impact of coaching

Mike Hughes, in his book *Coaching in Schools* (2004), suggests that it is not just coaching that brings about improved performance, but high-quality coaching. To this end it is vital that coaching has quality structures associated with it, if used in any formalized way in an organization. Since time and public money are invested in coaching, there is a clear need to justify the allocation of resources in a public sector organization. The impact of coaching, like other strategies implemented in complex organizations, e.g. Assessment for Learning or behaviour for learning, is notoriously difficult to measure. Best efforts in commercial settings have come up with measures such Return on Investment (RoI) and improvement in productivity (IiP). This balances the costs involved in delivering coaching with the outputs gained from it and productivity enhancements. RoI is usually an inappropriate measure for public sector organisations and schools especially, and IiP is difficult to guage in complex learning systems. Drawing on the work of John McBeath, on school self-evaluation, a best-practice approach to measuring the impact of approaches in schools comes from the idea of triangulation. What this seeks to do is present a three-part story which adds up to evidence of success. For example, taking the module test scores of a group of students before and after their teacher is coached and calculating the difference against a control group becomes one piece of evidence in the triangle, or indeed attendance statistics. A second might be the matching of teaching criteria of the teacher against agreed standards, over the period of coaching, and a third might be the quotes from interviews with young people about their experiences of the learning over the period of study. The data is a mixture of quantitative and semi-quantitative and qualitative data, which adds up, on balance of probability, to evidence of effectiveness. This unfortunately does not present the neat single statistic that politicians would have us believe is required; however, it is interesting to read Professor Jim Taylor of Lancaster University's management school who argues that school league table data is 'inherently misleading and potentially harmful'. He argues that raw scores tell us a lot about the performance of pupils but virtually nothing about the performance of schools. We would contend that raw scores tell us little about the specific interventions, policies and practices that create them. Nonetheless it is both desirable and often essential for organisations to measure the impact of their work. Triangulation remains the best approach currently available.

Where institutions are developing coaching it is desirable for those leading coaching to establish quality-assurance processes and best practice through up-skilling key members of the team and offering them opportunities for accreditation and feedback on their coaching. This can be done in a variety of ways, although the authors recommend that any accreditation should contain a significant amount of practical coaching, as opposed to a theory-based course. We suggest a minimum of 18 hours coaching training and experience for lead practitioners.

For further information on impact measurement and quality assurance of coaching Vision for Learning Ltd publish a very useful e-book and details of this can be obtained by emailing info@visionforlearning.co.uk or visiting their website at www.visionforlearning.co.uk. Equally for information on practical and Masters level coaching courses contact the same address. The Institute of Educational Coaching has become established as a leader in education-based coaching and provides resources, training and accreditation in conjunction with the University of Worcester. Their website is at: www.instituteofeducationalcoaching.co.uk.

Case studies in coaching

What follows are three case studies in coaching. Two of the case studies explore coaching developed in single schools and the third is of a large scale local authority project spanning 40 schools.

- Coaching case study 1: The Cooper School, Oxfordshire. Student support coaching
- Coaching case study 2: The George Eliot School, Coventry. Staff development coaching
- Coaching case study 3: West Sussex Local Authority: Coaching across 40 schools

CASE STUDY 1

Coaching at The Cooper School. Student support coaching
written by Jean Ramsey, lead coach

The advent of a new head teacher, Ben Baxter, at Cooper School and my enthusiasm for coaching created the ideal circumstances to bring about a sea change in the culture of our 11–16 mixed comprehensive in Oxfordshire.

In 2005 our GCSE results 41 per cent A–C indicated that we were an underperforming school and our Context Value Added score reinforced this label. Coupled with that, too many of our students were leaving with absolutely no qualifications whatsoever.

The exclusion rate was unsettlingly high and the governing body was gravely concerned. There was a rump of disaffected, disruptive students who were taking up a disproportionate amount of teachers' time and energy and diverting attention away from the course of learning.

School improvement is like a jigsaw and the headteacher saw that certain corner pieces had to be put in place. These pieces included:

- implementing workplace reform
- emphasizing teaching and learning
- revamping a very traditional curriculum
- tackling low self-esteem and low expectations through coaching

Coaching was seen as an approach to supporting school improvement. We began in a small way with a coaching champion, showing that coaching is effective and powerful for a few members of staff. This has had the effect of encouraging others on the staff to want to opt in to experiencing coaching and learning the skills.

The next stage was for the school to establish one day per week for me to coach students. Funding this has come through RATL (Raising Achievement Transforming Learning). Initially we were looking at those students on the C/D borderline in Years 10 and 11 and they were the priority. Then we looked at the more disaffected, disruptive students, some of whom were considerably younger. It was agreed that I would see the young people once a fortnight for 30 minutes. We have used the STRIDE coaching model as a structure for a total of six sessions. This scheme was introduced to the bulk of the staff through an early September 'Curriculum Development Meeting' and it was emphasized that coaching should take priority but that certain circumstances could be negotiable. I also had to liaise with the Learning Support Team to make sure that our resources were being used cost effectively.

The remit for the coaching-champion work was also extended to group coaching with those students who would, for various reasons, not be able to manage the full GCSE curriculum. We follow the MAGIC youth coaching course designed by Duncan Gee and the impact of coaching on these young people is equally profound. We had a cohort of 15 students and 10 of them will be awarded level 1 OCN. The visiting moderator reported that this was very impressive for a first round. At the time of writing, we are looking to get the young people up to level 2 in the next cohort.

To date, we only have one qualified coach in school. We see it as being very important that those involved in coaching have a suitable level of training, so that the integrity of the process is retained. Two of our student counsellors have attended coach training and they are very keen to continue developing their skills. Coaching at The Cooper School is well and truly on the agenda. We have begun now to train all the learning-support assistants in basic coaching skills.

We have collected quotations from the young people involved with coaching. On being asked 'Have the coaching sessions had any impact on your lives?', these were some of the responses:

- I feel happier
- Waking up is easier
- Mum doesn't shout so much in the mornings

- I can discuss things with my mum now our relationship is much more open; I can tell her what my feelings are

- Coaching has helped me to see what I am being like. I have sorted myself out and started to do my work by listening to the teacher

- Dad has noticed no after school detentions so he is saying I must be good in school

- It (active listening) means I don't have to keep asking questions because I understood it the first time.

- It makes me feel proud of myself.

We also have exclusion figures that show very clear downward trends:

2004–2005	119 fixed term exclusions	74 students involved	291 school days lost
2005–2006	104	68	277
2006–2007	97	54	239
2007–2008	48 (90)*	28 (50)	95 (220)

*figures in brackets were the head's targets for 2007–2008 which you can see we have exceeded.

2007–2008 of course is the academic year in which we formally introduced coaching to Cooper, although it has been operating in many less structured ways throughout the last few years. It is notoriously difficult to pin one particular approach, such as coaching to a set of figures, in such a complex environment as a school; however we feel that a significant credit must go to our student-coaching programme, given the young people we have targeted for support.

I believe that one of the reasons why coaching has been so successful at Cooper is that we (staff and students) have treated it very seriously. The young people value their coaching appointments and they can see how powerful taking small steps can be. We have strong communication and sometimes I think that a coaching session may be the first time an adult has actively and respectfully listened to many of our young people. I have a very supportive head who is prepared to take risks and I know I walk my talk.

Where now? We want Cooper to become a centre of excellence and a 'hub school' for coaching and school improvement. The coaching ethos is becoming embedded throughout the school and the wider community and we look forward to the day when there will be a full-time coach in every school in the land. A project I am involved in, in 2009, will see coach training offered to many partner schools in the area, enabling coaching to be experienced by students throughout their school career and for staff to have access to the effective and powerful skill-set that is coaching.

CASE STUDY 2

The George Eliot School, a Business and Enterprise College, Coventry
Staff development coaching
written by Chris Morris, Warwickshire Local Authority

Work on developing a coaching culture at George Eliot School began in 2007.

The focus for the school was on the following areas:

1 Aiming for greater whole-school consistency in the use of Assessment for Learning (AfL) practice in all lessons.

2 Using collaborative coaching as an in-house professional development tool to develop consistent AfL practice.

At that time, pockets of good AfL practice existed in departments, but there were inconsistencies. The headteacher, Tim Over, wanted to facilitate the sharing of good practice in a way that would bring about positive and sustainable changes.

Action taken

The support co-ordinator and headteacher considered the actions needed to make collaborative coaching viable in terms of cost and time. Governors were informed and gave the initiative their support. The head put £200 into each departmental budget for lesson cover so that teachers could meet, plan, observe and review together. He disaggregated a training day in exchange for a commitment from staff for five hours of coaching, and this was matched with five hours from teachers' PPA time. Digital cameras and wireless microphones were bought so that teachers could record their lesson if they wished, and use the recording to support their post-lesson coaching conversations. The head of ICT and ICT technicians organized this aspect of co-coaching.

The exact focus for co-coaching was decided upon as a result of pupil questionnaires and interviews, using the '8 Schools Project' pilot materials. Results showed inconsistencies in objective-led lessons, peer- and self-assessment and questioning. Training tailored to teachers' needs was provided as well as training for subject leaders on how to ensure consistent practices in their departments. Support was then given on basic co-coaching skills. Teachers paired up across departments. Subject leaders reported to the head on monitoring sheets filled in at departmental meetings on the progress made with AfL and/or co-coaching. The initiative started in September 2007, following pupil surveys in June 2007. The process was also supported by the support coordinator's residency for half a term and for half a day per week when staff would book time as groups or individuals on any aspect of co-coaching or AfL with which they needed further coaching support.

Impact and outcomes

The school had an Ofsted inspection in January 2007, which stated:

> "Teaching is satisfactory overall. An increasing proportion is becoming good or better because of the school's focus on peer [teacher]coaching."

In January, at an INSET day, teachers said of the co-coaching process:

> "It's given me back what I came into teaching for."

> "We have been able to be reflective together in the department about our own practice."

> "I have been allowed to take risks, to push myself out of my comfort zone and to try out new ideas – and the pupils are enjoying it too."

At a meeting with the adviser in April 2008, the head told the adviser that staff were beginning to use co-coaching to address other issues together. He gave an example of one teacher who was previously always judged as just 'satisfactory' and who was now always judged as 'good' and sometimes 'outstanding'; this has been confirmed by an observation carried out by the support and monitoring inspector.

In May 2008, the adviser interviewed staff about the impact of co-coaching on their use of AfL, and pupils filled in questionnaires, as they did twelve months ago, to give their views on the use of various aspects of AfL in their lessons. Results from both groups were very positive and it was clear that practice was more consistent than it was one year ago.

In August 2008, KS4 results demonstrated a 10 per cent improvement in 5+ A*–C grades. At an Awards evening, the headteacher publicly acknowledged the positive impact on results of peer mentoring and staff co-coaching.

What are we doing next?

The adviser has collated the results of the recent pupil questionnaires and has met with the head teacher to discuss both the teacher interviews and the questionnaire findings. She has written a summary of the findings and given some recommendations, which were discussed with the head teacher. The head will decide which of the recommendations to put into practice and is committed to sustaining the co-coaching programme. The adviser has agreed to lead training on co-coaching skills with staff new to the school next term (currently at 25 per cent of all staff).

In January 2009, the school hosted a 'showcase' open afternoon for other Warwickshire schools, with presentations from senior leaders and co-coaching teachers. Co-coaching remains an essential whole school CPD tool and has become a way of working for many of the staff here.

CASE STUDY 3

West Sussex Local Authority – Coaching across 40 schools
Case study by Lesley Smith, with Mark Wilson and Chris Behagg

This case study attempts to trace the development of coaching across 40 secondary schools in West Sussex. The work represents a fundamental shift towards working within a partnership approach with our schools, towards a 'rethinking' of how to develop a school's own capacity to improve and develop the curriculum needed by our students in the workplace of the twenty-first century.

Coaching places 'people and relationships' at the heart school improvement and recognizes that the most important resource we have is human creativity. It has been an exciting learning journey and this would not have taken place without the 'vision' of our Local Authority strategy managers, support from colleagues in schools, and the commitment and inspiration of Will Thomas who has acted as our coach and mentor over the past five years.

The context – starting with the strategy in 2004/5

Initial Local Authority interest in coaching began in 2003, following the publication of a number of Secondary Strategy publications, which heightened awareness of the potential of coaching as a mechanism for building capacity and leading school improvement. Coaching was highlighted as the most important factor in sustaining change, encouraging a trusting relationship that can be built between colleagues and allowing individuals to interrogate their practice at a deeper level. As a local authority West Sussex embarked upon a journey of exploration to assess how far coaching could enhance teaching and learning and so build capacity through a critical mass of emerging leaders within schools.

In September 2003 three consultants attended Will Thomas' 'Coaching for Performance' course. Inspired by this training, the LA wrote to all 40 secondary schools and invited them to receive what came to be known as 'The Three Day Coaching Package'. This involved the use of consultancy time and support for the equivalent of three days plus £1,000 to provide cover for teachers to develop in a peer-coaching capacity. All 40 of our schools accepted the proposal and schools began to recognize the potential of coaching as an extremely effective CPD tool designed to promote collaborative cross-curricular working, unusual in many of our secondary schools. As a result of this initiative and inspired by the published work of some pioneering schools like Brislington in Bristol, most schools had 'grown' two to four professional coaches by the end of 2004.

Responses to a progress evaluation sent to all 40 secondary schools at the end of the year were extremely positive and indicated a desire to be further involved in the next phase. At the same time 15 LA consultants undertook the TLO 'Coaching and the Learning School' training and two consultants returned to work with Will Thomas on his Advanced Coaching Training programme. Variation in approaches and indeed in the use of the terminology 'coaching' and 'mentoring' provided a necessary stimulus to clarify thinking and the LA's vision of how coaching could contribute to cultural change within West Sussex schools. Will Thomas' contribution to the team's thinking led to his being invited to take on the role of coach and mentor to the coaching team in its shaping and planning for the future.

2006/7: the creation of the Cohort One Schools Group

Nine schools were selected on the basis of individual action plans which clearly exemplified their vision for coaching and the way consultancy would be used to further develop their coaches. It was a condition of selection that they take a key role in working with other schools within their locality and working with the LA to promote the coaching ethos.

Recognizing the importance of involving Senior Leaders in the coaching initiative, the coaching team ran a conference to which head teachers and deputies from the selected schools were invited, in order to ensure that coaching was at the heart of school planning.

The Local Authority was keen to promote a diverse planning approach. A further conference enabled schools to report on their progress and to share their different coaching models. The variation and vision of coaching that emerged was impressive and challenging. Evaluations from the day acknowledged the benefits of sharing from each of the schools, and the time given to planning with the trainers.

A similar conference was also offered to the remaining 31 schools that had not been selected for intensive work. Fourteen of these schools attended the second day and their presentation of coaching models convinced us that the potential to impact upon school improvement at every level was convincing. Additional CPD training was also offered to 21 of the county's ASTs working in primary and secondary sectors.

At the end of the summer term a school in particularly challenging circumstances was invited to join the phase two group. This was a real opportunity to test the potential of coaching, the school having been assigned a 'notice to improve' category. Throughout the next two terms the work in evolving the coaching models with the ten schools was challenging and stimulating. Three consultants worked closely with Will, receiving telephone coaching conversations. These were vital in refining the coaching skills and moving the skills from a structured model into 'meta coaching' by which is meant a more intuitive and conversational style, which relaxed colleagues and allowed coaching to be more challenging.

Evaluating impact on classroom teaching remains the biggest challenge for the team, its position as pioneers meaning that there is little previous research against which to test hypotheses. In February 2007 two conferences attempted to tackle this issue. The ten Cohort One schools returned to update each other on their progress and to be the first to receive new materials commissioned from Will Thomas: 'Performance Indicators and Measures for Formative CPD in Education.' A further day offered an opportunity for the 14 schools plus any additional ones to receive the same training.

The coaching team had come to recognize ASTs as having a vital role in underpinning coaching in their schools and additional training was made available to the 21 who had already received training from Will, plus a second cohort who came to be trained for the first time.

The mentoring role has been a crucial factor in shaping and challenging the team's thinking.

2007/8

Intensive support by the LA across secondary schools continued in the third year. The intention was to build upon the work already achieved in 2006/7 with the ten Cohort One schools, while recognizing the excellent start made by other secondary schools and attempting to broaden the level of expertise across more schools.

Cohort Two schools

It was a primary aim of the Local Authority to extend the number of schools developing coaching as a means of building capacity and developing teaching and learning. All secondary schools were invited to bid for consultancy support and possible funding. By the summer of 2007 the number of secondary schools working with the Local Authority had grown to 24. At the same time other schools were working independently and indicating a desire to work with the Local Authority.

In the latter part of 2008 the Coaching Training Unit, as the group had come to be known, issued this statement summing up its purpose, progress and intentions. Its intended audience was senior members of the West Sussex Learning Service.

What follows is the West Sussex Coaching Training Unit's statement issued in 2008.

west sussex county council

Adults and Children | **Learning**

Coaching Training Unit Statement 2008

This statement details the group's tremendous achievements over the last year, its intentions for the coming year and the means by which they will be realised.

Why coaching?

Coaching is concerned with helping people to become the very best that they can be. Coaching offers a partnership approach to learning which helps the person being coached to identify and enhance their strengths and then to feel confident to tackle areas they wish to develop. It is about opening up possibilities by creating opportunities for reflective thought and problem solving. In essence coaching is a powerful agent for cultural change via collaborative enquiry.

The Coaching Training Unit team has succeeded in establishing the notion of coaching as a powerful agent for change. Our thinking is now focused upon the notion of 'the re-culturing of schools', nurturing collaborative learning groups or communities whose use of the coaching approach is key.

What has been achieved

The team has:

- worked fairly intensively with a significant number of secondary schools in addition to others where the touch has been lighter.
- delivered coaching training at introductory and advanced level
- delivered one-to-one coaching tutorials to facilitate deep learning
- facilitated two additional training sessions for ASTs to take them to higher levels of coaching and NLP, enabling them to work more effectively across schools
- developed and implemented coaching training for colleagues within the Learning Service and 19 teachers on the Leading Teachers Programme
- continued to develop our own expertise in both coaching and NLP, for example, regular attendance at out-of-hours NLP Practice Group sessions

The outcomes of the coaching in these schools:

Teachers are reporting a shift in the culture within schools as coaching continues to place high-quality professional relationships at the heart of teachers' practice with a clear focus on school improvement. Where coaching is most successful:

- Teachers are constantly reviewing and improving their practice.
- Teachers are taking risks in teaching and learning
- Teachers are ascribing improvements in their practice to coaching

west sussex county council

Adults and Children | Learning

- Teachers are working collaboratively
- Teachers are increasingly engaged in research

We are now observing steps towards:

- Better behaviour
- More independent learning
- Lessons which are well-planned with active learning opportunities

Schools are also beginning to recognise the opportunities to develop their own coaching model. There is evidence that some schools are making bold strides in school improvement, using coaching as a development tool linked to their specific whole school initiatives. For example:

- School A: coaching conversations taking place within the whole-school context to develop Assessment for Learning
- School B: using a specialist coaching approach to target attainment in specific curriculum areas
- School C: using TDA funding to support coaching of each member of a faculty in common strategies to enhance results in a compulsory subject at Key Stage 4
- School D: using coaching to develop peer-coaching amongst students
- A number of high-performing schools are using coaching to move from 'good' to 'outstanding'
- A number of schools in challenging circumstances are embracing coaching's unique blend of support and challenge to target under-achievement with a resultant positive impact on teacher retention
- The coaching team is leading training in enhanced practice at Middle Leadership level, having identified this group as a key driver of sustainable school improvement. Thirteen schools have participated in Middle Leader training this year, with five further schools currently planning their own in-house package with us.

The Way Forward

Within County
The team is committed to working with schools who are

- keen to commence their development of coaching
- embedding coaching at a more advanced level to deliver their school improvement plan

west sussex county council

Adults and Children|**Learning**

- developing strategies to measure the impact of coaching on classroom performance

Beyond County

The team is committed to raising the profile of West Sussex as a national leader in the field of coaching within education.

Priorities for the coming year have been identified as:

- the marketing, at both local and national level, of the team-produced interactive training DVD, filmed at two schools

- the planning, filming and production of a follow-up DVD / book, showing different models of coaching (both DVDs are produced in collaboration with Will Thomas at Vision for Learning

- continued liaison with external coach and mentor, Will Thomas

- the launch of a national coaching network of Local Authorities committed to the promotion of coaching within schools

- further investigation of accreditation of West Sussex coaching training at Masters level through currently fostered links with Brighton and Chichester Universities

The Coaching Training Unit are happy to receive enquiries from colleagues involved in this field. They can be contacted at the email addresses below.

Lesley Smith: lesley.smith@westsussex.gov.uk
Chris Behagg: chris.behagg@westsussex.gov.uk
Mark Wilson: mark.wilson@westsussex.gov.uk

External Coach and Mentor: willthomas@visionforlearning.co.uk

Networking and coaching

Networking now has its own educational three-letter acronym – NLCs. These are Network Learning Communities – a powerful idea if done with care. Networking is taken to mean the deliberate coming together of two or more individuals or their separate organizations in order to explore mutual benefit. By its very nature networking occurs around an event or scheduled experience, with individuals who do not yet know if they are able to help each other. Coaching could be a very useful glue to hold any possible networking arrangement together.

Linking with other schools and organizations provides a variety of benefits. Drawing talent from a wider pool allows a deliberate match of experience, need or attitude. It could also provide opportunity for a deliberate mismatch – there is something creative about the curmudgeon being coached by the cheerleader. Individuals who are sharing the coaching experience broaden their skills and help people deal with issues that, although similar, do not have that tired, close-to-home feel. There may also be issues of confidentiality that even the most open individual may feel guarded over when coached by a colleague.

Networking increases the likelihood of benefiting from what some behavioural psychologists call 'synchronicity' – coincidence. Described in Carolyn North's book *Synchronicity: The Anatomy of Coincidence* (1994), the essential premise is that 'when you know where you are going and are positive about the journey, you see all the route signs along the way'. When you are buying a house you see 'For Sale' signs. A clear idea of your goal sensitizes your change radar – you notice the phenomena that service your goal. The fascinating research of Dr Richard Wiseman has legitimized scientific discussions on the nature of luck. In his book *The Luck Factor* (2004) he characterizes luck as an attitude. He explains that people can be classified as lucky and unlucky based on how they think about themselves and their lives. He describes how lottery winners falling in to the two groups are interviewed about the way their wins have affected them. Those who regarded themselves as unlucky in life were just as unhappy a year after their win (in spite of their incredible luck in winning the lottery!) as they were before it. It is a question of perspective. In another experiment he asked lucky and unlucky volunteers to count pictures in a newspaper. Both groups did this. The lucky people (those who saw themselves as lucky in life) not only counted the pictures, but also noticed that in one picture there was an ad that explained that they could claim a £100 cash prize from the researcher. Unlucky volunteers did not respond to this. Dr Wiseman identified just four basic principles which lucky people consistently apply:

- maximize your chance opportunities
- listen to your lucky hunches

- expect good fortune
- turn your bad luck into good.

What if these principles could be applied to schools? Networkers who are sure of themselves and are sufficiently self-confident about their direction increase the likelihood of meeting the right person, falling into the right business arrangement or coming across an offer of help. Networking also tests the quality of your ideas in a marketplace. It is exposure to peer evaluation. Learning to be meaningful requires application and testing in a wide variety of contexts. Coaching builds morale. Coaching through a network can build morale and a sense of a wider community at the same time.

Networks of schools can fail miserably when they create pools of ignorance. Simply putting people of a similar role in a room with an empty agenda is a disservice. To assume that the profession is sitting on all the answers and they can be unlocked by putting like minds together is naïve. Avoid woolly propositions such as 'There's benefit in meeting colleagues' as any sort of basis for networking. There is a difference between understanding an issue and finding an answer.

Some poor starting points for networking include:

- There's money available for us to work together.
- It's always good to share with colleagues.
- If we get people together they will come up with the answers.
- Everyone knows how to work together in groups.
- Once we get started we'll agree a theme.
- Disagreement is a productive dynamic.
- At the end of the day we are all here for the same reasons.
- Let's have a conference.

To learn through networking, be clear about these sorts of challenges from the outset:

Outcomes:	What – specifically – do we want from networking? How will we know if we have achieved it?
Purpose:	Is our outcome best achieved in a networked group?
Facilitation:	What do we understand by networking? How will networking be facilitated and by whom?
Positive climate:	How should we maintain a solutions focus to our activities?
Open enrolment:	How do people get involved? What preparation, if any, is needed?
Exit points:	When will we have completed? What do we produce if anything?
Route to expertise:	How do we access support if it is needed? What do we do to avoid pooling ignorance?
Clear boundaries:	What is our remit?
Technology:	What technological support can we use to further our networking aims? Is it possible to share grassroots knowledge using shared technology?

Why not network with other organizations in related fields such arts groups, theatres, sports clubs or the local historical association? Coaching provides a tool for this to take place on equal terms. Why not borrow from other disciplines? Follow the maxim from Auguste Renoir, 'Allez voir les productions des autres, mais ne jamais copier que sur nature.' [Always observe the works of others but never steal except from nature.]

A whole-organization vision for coaching – some questions to support you

The following can help you to take the steps towards building and actualizing a vision for realizing the human potential in your school or college.

1 What does 'realizing human potential' mean to you and your organization?

2 From what you have learned today, how can coaching help your organization to succeed? What are the benefits for each group of stakeholders?

3 What will your 'coaching organization' look like, sound like and feel like five years from now?

4 In terms of helping people to overcome limitations to success, what is your organization like now?

5 What have you already tried to help overcome such limitations?

6 How successful were those interventions?

7 What would your organization be like if every member of the school community from governors through to leaders, teachers, pupils and parents all improved:

   - their listening skills?

   - their use of open questions?

   - their understanding of developing and maintaining high self-esteem?

   - their ability to maintain a positive and objective view of events?

8 How would your school be different if there were no 'put-downs' of staff or students?

9 What would the 'coaching organization' look like, sound like and feel like? What is your vision for coaching in your organization?

10 What are the steps to take in the next five years to achieving this vision?

Great organization-wide questions to ask

It is easier to stay in the comfort zone when faced by any sort of challenge. Change involves posing some uncomfortable questions. By asking questions – of yourself and others – that threaten to disturb the status quo you expose the real likelihood of change. Below are some questions that all schools should ask themselves.

1 Out of ten, score how high 'learning about learning' is on your day-to-day school agenda. What three things could you do to improve that score by one?

2 How do you know where excellent learning is taking place in your school?

3 What do you do where there are 'inappropriate' learning methods?

4 Do your colleagues know what good learning is like? How do they share their understanding of what excellent learning is like?

5 In what ways do you personally model excellent learning in your professional role?

6 How and when do your students get to discuss excellent learning?

7 In what ways do your students get to know how to become better learners?

8 How do you induct new staff into the learning methods used by the school?

9 Who makes the decisions relating to learning in your school?

10 As a teacher, why is your lesson worth behaving for?

Further training and coaching accreditation

Vision for Learning offers introductory and advanced coaching programmes to education professionals. These courses form part of an accredited coaching qualification in conjunction with the University of Worcester and Masters-level credits. At the time of going to press this accreditation was part-funded by the Teacher Development Agency.

For more information visit:
For training: www.visionforlearning.co.uk
For accreditation: www.instituteofeducationalcoaching.co.uk

Summary

Coaching can lead to significant positive changes in organizations towards 'learning cultures' and viral analogy is a helpful way to explain how change can be effected.

There are a number of models of coaching emerging in schools from modest uses of coaching skills to support people in schools these include co-coaching, specialist coaching, coaching cascades, 'Martini' coaching, student coaching and coaching for learning.

Coaching can be a planned activity or it can be ad hoc.

There seem to be a number of factors essential to embedding coaching in organizations: a clear **Purpose** for its use, explicit awareness of the **Values and Principles** upon which coaching sits, a **Vision** for the development of coaching, **Working Agreements** set up with those involved, giving it **Time and a Place** to happen, and developing the **Skills and Structures**.

▶ Using a model of team coaching helps the coach to understand the process by which teams develop.

▶ The quality and the impact of the coaching need to be borne in mind in developing wider models of organizational coaching. Network Learning Communities provide a virtual learning space and an opportunity to effect change. Coaching skills and models can help structure this change.

▶ Networking provides great scope for multiplying the benefits of a coaching approach.

Since the first edition of this book coaching has come a long way in education. There is still much scope for development in organizations currently using the approaches and those that have yet to explore them. This chapter serves both as a set of useful learning from current experience and as a vision for a future of highly intra- and inter-personally intelligent individuals who understand what motivates themselves and others.

Questions

1   Where is truly non-directive coaching operating in your school at the moment?

2   Where is pseudo-non-directive coaching operating?

3   How might an institutional perspective on coaching benefit your school?

4   What is your vision for non-directive coaching in your school?

5   What is your first step towards achieving this vision?

6   How might non-directive coaching be blended with other support processes?

1   Where is truly non-directive coaching currently operating in your organization?

2   Where is pseudo-non-directive coaching operating?

3   How might a wider practice of coaching benefit your team or institution?

4   What is your vision for coaching in your work-place?

5   What might your first steps be to achieving this vision?

6   How would you support people to develop the skills of coaching and blend it with their existing practice such as mentoring, counselling, guidance and teaching?

Masterclass

▶ *In your organization, what is not working at the moment through a telling, rather than coaching, approach? Consider how coaching might have more impact in the longer term on this issue.*

▶ *Promote discussion about the similarities between non-directive coaching and learning. In what ways is effective learning in classrooms about being coached rather than told?*

▶ *Use the metaphor of a hot-air balloon to float higher or lower over the school or a challenging issue within it to consider that issue. Begin by noticing how high your balloon is floating above the issue when you first approach it. Take the balloon to different altitudes and see what you learn.*

▶ *Consider the concept that 'we make our own luck' referred to in this chapter. Encourage thinking in school that asks the question: 'In this challenging situation how could we act to improve our learners' luck?'*

Since 2004, when the first edition of this book was published, there have been significant developments in the use of coaching across teams and whole schools and colleges. While maintaining the integrity of the original text , much of which still stands, we have added to this chapter with case studies from organizations using coaching to effect change. Such organizations have embraced the move towards building an organizational coaching culture which enshrines principles of coaching similar to those outlined in Chapter 2.

Bibliography

Coaching and mentoring

Carnegie, Dale (1994) *How to Win Friends and Influence People*, Pocket Books

Chandler, L. (2002) 'Professional development using non-directive coaching', *National School Improvement Network News*, no. 24

Clutterbuck, D. and Megginson, D. (2005) *Making Coaching Work – Creating a Coaching Culture*, CIPD

Coaching Academy, The (2002) *The Ultimate Coach Training Course,* The Coaching Academy

Copley, Anne (2006) *Challenging Behaviour*, Network Educational Press

Downey, M. (2003) *Effective Coaching*, Texere

Flaherty, J. (1999) *Coaching: Evoking Excellence in Others*, Butterworth-Heinemann

Herrrington, C. (2004) 'Change of direction or another junction on the road of life?', *Coaching Chronicle*, UK College of Life Coaching and The College of Executive Coaching, May, issue V

Hughes M. (2004) *Coaching in Schools*, Jigsaw Pieces

Institute of Education (2002) 'Professional development using non-directive coaching', *National School Improvement Network News*, no. 24, Autumn

Jackson, P.Z. and McKergow, M. (2002) *The Solutions Focus*, Nicholas Brealey

Landsberg, M. (1997) *The Tao of Coaching*, HarperCollins Business

Lawley, J. and Tompkins, P. (2000) *Metaphors in Mind Transformation through Symbolic Modelling*, The Developing Company Press

Martin, C. (2001) *The Life Coaching Handbook*, Crown House Publishing

McDermott, I. and Jago, W. (2003) *The NLP Coach*, Piatkus

McLeod, A. (2003) *Performance Coaching*, Crownhouse Publishing Ltd

McLeod, J. (1999) *An Introduction to Counselling*, Open University

Olivero, G., Bane, K. Denise and Kopelman, R.E. (1997) 'Executive coaching as a transfer tool: effects on productivity in a public agency', *Public Personnel Management*, Winter

Rock, H.M. (2002) 'Job-embedded professional development and reflective coaching', *Classroom Leadership*, 5, 8

Smith, Alistair (2001) *Bright Sparks*, Network Educational Press

Taylor, J. and Nguyen, A.N. (2006) *An Analysis of the Value-Added by Secondary Schools in England: Is the Value-Added Indicator of Any Value?*, Lancaster University

Thomas, W. (2005) *Coaching Solutions Resource Book*, Network Educational Press

Thomas, W. (2005) *The Managing Workload Pocketbook*, Teachers Pocketbooks

Whitworth, L., Kimsey-House, H. and Sandahl, P. (1998) *Co-Active Coaching*, Davies-Black

Zeus, P. and Skiffington, S. (2003) *The Coaching at Work Toolkit*, McGraw-Hill

Formative feedback

Black, P. and Wiliam, D. (1998) *Inside the Black Box: Raising Standards Through Classroom Assessment*, King's College London

Black, P. and Wiliam, D. (2002) *Working Inside the Black Box: Assessment for Learning in the Classroom*, King's College London

Clarke, Shirley (2001) *Unlocking Formative Assessment*, Hodder and Stoughton

Clarke, Shirley (2003) *Enriching Feedback in the Primary Classroom*, Hodder and Stoughton

Motivation

Bandura, A. (1997) *Self-Efficacy: The Exercise of Control*, Freeman

Brooks and Goldstein (2004) *The Power of Resilience*, McGraw-Hill

Brophy, J. (1998) *Motivating Students to Learn*, McGraw-Hill

Covington, M.V. (1998) *The Will to Learn: A Guide to Motivating Young People*, Cambridge University Press

Dilts, R. (1990) *Changing Beliefs with NLP*, Meta Publications

Dweck, C.S. (1999) *Self Theories: Their Role in Motivation, Personality and Development*, Taylor and Francis

Knight, Sue (1995) *NLP at Work*, Nicholas Brealey Publishing

Mihata, Kevin (1997) 'The Persistence of "Emergence"', in Raymond A. Eve, Sara Horsfall and Mary E. Lee (eds) *Chaos, Complexity and Sociology: Myths, Models and Theories*, pp. 30–8

North, Carolyn (1994) *Synchronicity: The Anatomy of Coincidence*, Regent Press

Owen, Nick (2001) *The Magic of Metaphor*, Crown House Publishing

Seligman, M. (1991) *Learned Optimism*, Knopf

Sperber, Daniel (1996) *Explaining Culture. A Naturalistic Approach*, Blackwell

Wiseman, R. (2004) *The Luck Factor*, Arrow Books

Leadership

Bambino, D. (2002) 'Critical friends', *Educational Leadership*, 59, 6

Best, B. and Thomas, W. (2003) *The Head of Department Pocketbook*, Teachers Pocketbooks

Blanchard, Ken (1981) *The One Minute Manager*, Berkley Books

Campaign for Learning (2002) *Coaching at Work Survey*, Chartered Management Institute

Collins, Jim (2001) *Good to Great*, Random House

Covey, S. R. (1998) *The Seven Habits of Highly Effective People*, London

Gladwell, M. (2000) *The Tipping Point: How Little Things Can Make a Big Difference*, Little, Brown and Company

Goleman, D., Boyatzis, R. and McKee, A. (2002) *Primal Leadership*, Harvard Business School Press

Novak, J. (2002) *Inviting Educational Leadership*, Pearson Education

Perkins, D. (1992) *Smart Schools*, Free Press

Taylor, David (2002) *The Naked Leader*, Capstone

General

Baron-Cohen (2003) *The Essential Difference*, Perseus

Best, B. and Thomas, W. (2007) *The Creative Teaching and Learning Toolkit*, Continuum

Best, B. and Thomas, W. (2008) *The Creative Teaching and Learning Resource Book*, Continuum

Best, B. and Thomas, W. (2008) *Everything You Need to Know About Teaching But Are Too Busy to Ask*, Continuum

Bizot, Francois (2003) *The Gate*, Vintage Books

Copley, Anne (2006) *Challenging Behaviour*, Network Continuum

Haddon, Mark (2004) *The Curious Incident of the Dog in the Night Time*, Vintage Books

Morris, Desmond (2002) *Peoplewatching*, Vintage Books

Stockdale, Jim and Stockdale, Sybil (1990) *In Love and War*, Naval Institute Press

Stover, Matthew Woodring (2002) *Traitor*, Arrow Books

Useful websites

Education coaching – training and professional coaching

www.visionforlearning.co.uk   Coach training/personal and professional coaching

www.instituteofeducationalcoaching.co.uk
                                     Coaching Accreditation

www.alite.co.uk   Training, coaching and personal insight

Other coach training

www.centreforcoaching.com   Coach training centre and consultancy

www.brookes.ac.uk/schools/education/macoachment.html
                                     Oxford Brookes University courses

www.the-coaching-academy.com   Life and corporate coach training

www.angusmcleod.com   Coaching resources website

Further coaching bodies networks and resources

www.coachfederation.org.uk   The International Coaching Federation site

www.emccouncil.org   UK best practice in coaching and mentoring

www.coachville.com   Coach training organization

www.busygirl.com   Corporate and Entrepreneurial Women's Network

www.haygroup.co.uk   Hay Group UK

www.ascd.org/readingroom/classlead/0205/rock.html
                                     Reflective coaching – article

www.ascd.org/publications/ed_lead/200203/bambino.html
                                     Critical friendship

www.catalyst-chicago.org/06-02/0602boston.htm
                                     Boston schools coaching – programme

Specialist coaching sites

www.in2uition.net   Coaching afloat – specialist coaching at sea

www.coachingpsychologyforum.org.uk
                                     Forum for coaching psychologists

www.cleanlanguage.co.uk   The Developing Company (UK)

Index

Note: Page ranges with the suffix c include case study; page references in italics refer to figures.

Training in coaching skills and personal and professional insight opportunities

Training courses in the practical aspects of coaching are available as a school INSET programme and as a public course programme. One-to-one personal and professional coaching is offered to assist you and your organization to move forward. For further details on training programmes and personal coaching run by the authors of this book visit www.visionforlearning.co.uk and alite.co.uk. For professional accreditation in coaching visit: www.instituteofeducationalcoaching.co.uk

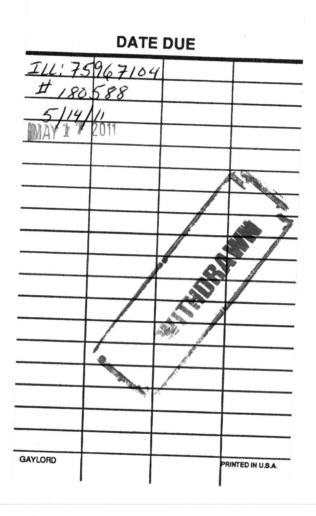